# SOURCES OF ANGLO-SAXON LITERARY CULTURE
## The Apocrypha

INSTRUMENTA ANGLISTICA MEDIAEVALIA 1

SOURCES OF
ANGLO-SAXON
LITERARY CULTURE

# THE
# APOCRYPHA

Edited by
Frederick M. Biggs

Medieval Institute Publications
Kalamazoo, Michigan

**Library of Congress Cataloging-in-Publication Data**

Sources of Anglo-Saxon literary culture. The apocrypha / edited by Frederick M. Biggs.
    p. cm.   (Instrumenta Anglistica mediaevalia ; 1)
  "This volume brings up to date the entries on apocrypha first published in Sources of
Anglo-Saxon literary culture: a trial version, ed. Frederick M. Biggs, Thomas D. Hill,
and Paul E. Szarmach with the assistance of Karen Hammond, Medieval &
Renaissance Texts & Studies 74 (Binghamton, N.Y., 1990), pp. 22–70" — Foreword.
  Includes bibliographical references and index.
  ISBN 978-1-58044-119-3 (pbk. : alk. paper)
  1. Apocryphal books—Criticism, interpretation, etc. 2. Christian literature, English
(Old)—History and criticism. 3. Christian literature, Latin (Medieval and
modern)—England—History and criticism. 4. English literature—Old English, ca.
450–1100—Sources. 5. England—Intellectual life—To 1066. I. Biggs, Frederick M.
II. Title: Apocrypha.
BS1700.S68 2007
229.00942'0902—dc22

                              2006101231


ISBN 978-1-58044-119-3

Printed in the United States of America

# CONTENTS

FOREWORD                                                     ix

GUIDE FOR READERS                                            xiii

APOCRYPHA                                                    1

OLD TESTAMENT APOCRYPHA                                      3
    Life of Adam and Eve                 3
    De plasmatione Adam                  4
    Cave of Treasures                    6
    Jubilees                             6
    Pseudo-Philo Biblical Antiquities    7
    1 Enoch                              8
    1 Enoch [fragment]                   9
    2 Enoch                              10
    [Prayer of Moses]                    10
    Jannes and Jambres                   10
    Assumption of Moses                  12
    [Lamentation of Seila]               12
    [Vision of Kenaz]                    12
    Solomon and Saturn                   12
    Prayer of Manasse                    13
    4 Ezra                               14
    Revelation of Ezra                   15
    Psalm 151                            16
    [Song of David]                      17
    Apocryphon of Ezechiel               17
    Sibylline Oracles                    17
    Versus sibyllae de iudicio           18
    Pseudo-Methodius Revelations [Recension 1]   19
    Pseudo-Methodius Revelations [Recension 2]   20

APOCRYPHA ABOUT CHRIST AND MARY 21
    Protevangelium of James 21
    Protevangelium of James [Sermon] 23
    Gospel of Pseudo-Matthew 23
    Gospel of Pseudo-Matthew [Sermon] 25
    De Nativitate Mariae 25
    Questions of Bartholomew 26
    Book of the Resurrection of Christ by Bartholomew 28
    Gospel of Nicodemus 29
    Vindicta Salvatoris 31
    Transitus of Pseudo-Melito (B$^2$) 33
    Transitus W 35

APOCRYPHAL ACTS 37
    Pseudo-Abdias Apostolic Histories 38
    Acts of Andrew 40
    Acts of Andrew and Matthias 40
    Martyrdom of Andrew 42
    Martyrdom of Bartholomew 43
    Pseudo-Clement Recognitions 43
    Pseudo-Clement Letter to James 45
    Martyrdom of James the Great 45
    Martyrdom of James the Less 46
    Pseudo-Melito Martyrdom of John 47
    Martyrdom of Mark 48
    Martyrdom of Matthew 49
    Matthias 50
    Pseudo-Linus Martyrdom of Paul 50
    Actus Vercellenses 51
    Pseudo-Linus Martyrdom of Peter 51
    Pseudo-Marcellus Martyrdom of Peter and Paul 52
    [Conflictio apostolorum Petri et Pauli cum Simone Mago
       et Passiones eorundem] 53
    Martyrdom of Peter 53
    [Pseudo-Marcellus Epistolae I et II ad fratres Nerei et
       Achillem] 53
    Martyrdom of Philip 53
    Martyrdom of Simon and Jude 54
    Martyrdom of Thomas 55

APOCRYPHAL EPISTLES 57
    Letters of Christ and Abgar 57
    Epistle of Paul to the Laodiceans 58
    Sunday Letter 58
    Sunday Letter [clm 9550] 59

Sunday Letter [lost]                                                  60
Sunday Letter [Tarragona]                                             60

APOCRYPHAL APOCALYPSES                                                63
    Shepherd of Hermas [Vulgata]                                     63
    Sheperd of Hermas [Palatina]                                     65
    Apocalypse of John                                               66
    Apocalypse of the Virgin                                         66
    Apocalypse of Paul                                               67
    Apocalypse of Paul [Redaction XI]                                70
    Apocalypse of Peter                                              71
    Apocalypse of Thomas                                             71

MISCELLANEOUS                                                         73
    Apocrypha Priscillianistica                                      73
    Breviarium apostolorum                                           75
    [Delivering the Damned]                                          75
    Epistle of Barnabas                                              75
    Fifteen Signs before Judgment                                    76
    History of the Holy-Rood Tree                                    77
    Nomina locorum in quo apostoli requiescunt                       77
    Notitia de locis apostolorum                                     78
    Seven Heavens Apocryphon                                         78
    Sunday Lists                                                     79
    Three Utterances Apocryphon                                      80
    Three Utterances Apocryphon [Pal.lat. 220]                       81
    Three Utterances Apocryphon [clm 6433]                           82
    Three Utterances Apocryphon [clm 28135]                          82
    Trinubium Annae                                                  83

BIBLIOGRAPHY                                                          85

GENERAL INDEX                                                        111

INDEX OF MANUSCRIPTS                                                115

# FOREWORD

This volume brings up to date the entries on apocrypha first published in *Sources of Anglo-Saxon Literary Culture: A Trial Version*, ed. Frederick M. Biggs, Thomas D. Hill, and Paul E. Szarmach with the assistance of Karen Hammond, Medieval & Renaissance Texts & Studies 74 (Binghamton, N.Y., 1990), pp 22–70, which were themselves intended to correct and amplify the entries on apocrypha first assembled by J. D. A. Ogilvy in his *Books Known to the English, 597–1066*, Mediaeval Academy of America Publication 76 (Cambridge, Mass., 1967), pp 66–74. Ogilvy's objective in *Books Known to the English*, although never stated outright, was to produce an annotated catalogue of every book and author known in Anglo-Saxon England, and the 1990 *Trial Version* was the initial step in a more ambitious effort to achieve the same goal by employing the talents of a team of scholars equipped with better information and more advanced resources. The apocrypha entries in the 1990 *Trial Version* were a useful test case for the fledgling SASLC project because they involved several different types of texts in Latin, Greek, Coptic, Hebrew, Syriac, Ethiopic, Old English, and Irish with complex transmission histories that in some cases had never been carefully explored, even by apocrypha scholars. To mention just one example, the sixth-century collection of apostolic legends known as the Pseudo-Abdias *Apostolic Histories* or *Virtutes apostolorum* was last edited in 1719 by J. A. Fabricius (who merely reprinted an earlier edition from 1551) and was the subject of only one substantive scholarly essay during the whole of the twentieth century, yet students of Anglo-Saxon literature need to know about it since details from this collection that are unparalleled elsewhere in early Latin literature appear to lie behind the *Old English Martyrology* and the Old English poem *Fates of the Apostles*, and a sermon in the eleventh-century Pembroke 25 Homiliary is based on it as well (for details see the updated entry on the Pseudo-Abdias *Apostolic Histories* at pp 40–42 herein). Ogilvy did include an entry on the Pseudo-Abdias collection in his *Books Known to the English*, but his comments on it are frustratingly imprecise and inconclusive and in the end tell us very little about when or where or to whom the *Apostolic Histories* were known in pre-Conquest England. It was the task of the 1990 *Trial Version* to go beyond Ogilvy and document some ascertainable facts and probabilities concerning the transmission, use, and influence of this and other texts that circulated in Anglo-Saxon England. The task of the present volume is to refine the apocrypha entries even further by taking into account the sizeable body of scholarship on apocryphal literature that has appeared in the past sixteen years.

It is no doubt all too easy to point out the shortcomings and limitations of one's predecessors, but in this case it is essential to recognize that the overlapping disciplines of apocrypha scholarship and Anglo-Saxon studies as they existed back in the 1960s when Ogilvy was writing were very different from what they are now. In compiling his notes on apocrypha known to the Anglo-Saxons, Ogilvy took information from the best resources then available, citing from manuscript catalogues, from the source notes in editions of Old English and Anglo-Latin texts, from the eighteenth- and nineteenth-century editions of Greek and Latin apocrypha by Fabricius, Lipsius, and Tischendorf, from essays on Old English literature and Anglo-Saxon art by Förster, Priebsch, Saxl, and Willard, and from several of the pioneering studies of apocryphal literature by M. R. James, including his first series of *Apocrypha Anecdota* (1893), his 1910 essay on "Syriac Apocrypha in Ireland," his *Apocryphal New Testament* (1924), and his *Latin Infancy Gospels* (1927). The two latest works of scholarship Ogilvy consulted for these entries appear to have been Grattan and Singer's *Anglo-Saxon Magic and Medicine* (1952) and an article by Bertram Colgrave and Ann Hyde on "Two Recently Discovered Leaves from Old English Manuscripts" published in *Speculum* in 1962. We have to remember that at the time Ogilvy was writing, there were no standard reference tools for apocryphal literature such as we now have in Geerard's *Clavis Apocryphorum Novi Testamenti* (1992), Haelewyck's *Clavis Apocryphorum Veteris Testamenti* (1998), and DiTommaso's *Bibliography of Pseudepigrapha Research* (2001). Ogilvy had no recourse to the collected English translations of H. F. D. Sparks (1984), Schneemelcher and Wilson (1991), or J. K. Elliott (1993). He was unable to refer to the editions of apocryphal texts published in the Brepols series Corpus Christianorum, Series Apocryphorum, which began in 1983, nor to the Brepols journal *Apocrypha*, which was first issued in 1990. There was no Gneuss *Handlist* in Ogilvy's day, and of course the searchable electronic databases of Old English and medieval Latin texts that are now basic tools in the field were not yet in existence either. Ogilvy wrote long before all the books and articles on apocryphal literature in Anglo-Saxon England that have emerged in the past couple of decades, including the 1996 Cross volume on *Two Old English Apocrypha and Their Manuscript Source*, Mary Clayton's 1998 book on *The Apocryphal Gospels of Mary in Anglo-Saxon England*, and the collection of essays on *Apocryphal Texts and Traditions in Anglo-Saxon England* edited by Powell and Scragg in 2003. Since the time Ogilvy finished compiling his notes on apocrypha in the mid-1960s, in other words, the scholarly resources for investigating the history and transmission of apocryphal literature have undergone a revolutionary advance on several fronts, and we are consequently in a position today to survey the same territory with markedly different results.

In *Books Known to the English*, Ogilvy devoted not quite eight pages to a survey of works classed as "apocrypha," presenting notes on about thirty-five separate texts that he had found evidence to show were either possibly or certainly known in Anglo-Saxon England. The entries in the following pages, which have been masterfully compiled and edited (and for the most part written) by Frederick M. Biggs, address almost eighty separate apocryphal texts and are supported by a bibliography of over 500 titles. New to these revised and updated entries are discussions of *2 Enoch*, the *Assumption of Moses*, the *Versus sibyllae de iudicio*, the *Apocalypse of Peter*, and the *Apocalypse of the Virgin*, as well as a concluding Miscellaneous section that features several texts and collections of texts that are customarily referred to by medievalists as "apocrypha," including the *Apocrypha Priscillianistica*, the *Epistle of Barnabas*, the *Seven Heavens Apocryphon*, and the *Three Utterances Apocryphon*. The result is a significantly enlarged survey of apocryphal texts that in one way or another found their way to early medieval Britain and left their mark on Anglo-Saxon literary culture. Of particular interest to some readers will be the light which these entries shed collectively on the apocryphal reading of the Venerable Bede, who quotes directly from the Pseudo-Clement *Recognitions*, the *Martyrdom of Mark*, and the Marian Assumption apocryphon known as the *Transitus of Pseudo-Melito*, and who demonstrates indirect knowledge of the existence of the *Gospel of Matthias* and the *Shepherd of Hermas* (in both cases known to him only through the writings of patristic authors who knew these works first-hand). Bede was also evidently familiar with a version of the apocryphal motif known as *De plasmatione Adam*, which associates the four letters in Adam's name with the four corners of the earth, and there is just enough of a verbal echo in his account of the deathbed vision of the thegn of King Coenred in Book V of the *Ecclesiastical History* to suggest that he may have been modeling a portion of that story on the *Three Utterances Apocryphon*. (See also the entries for *4 Ezra*, the Pseudo-Abdias *Apostolic Histories*, and the *Apocalypse of Paul* for other, more tenuous links between Bede and apocryphal literature.)

These entries thus bring together much new information and take us considerably farther in our understanding of the transmission and reception of apocryphal literature in Anglo-Saxon England, but they are still only an interim report since a final set of entries on apocrypha will eventually be incorporated into *Sources of Anglo-Saxon Literary Culture. Volume Two: Adalbero of Laon to Audax*, now in preparation by Frederick M. Biggs. A third *A* volume, covering Augustine of Hippo to Avitus of Vienne, is also in the works, and additional volumes devoted to the rest of the alphabet are either planned or in active preparation as well. As individual entries or sets of entries of a significance and magnitude comparable to that of the apocrypha entries are completed before the rest of the volume in which they are scheduled to appear, they will occasionally be issued as separate publications in the newly inaugurated series Instrumenta Anglistica Mediaevalia, which is intended to serve as a forum for interim and subsidiary publications related to the Sources of Anglo-Saxon Literary Culture project.

Thomas N. Hall
SASLC Project Director
October 2006

# GUIDE FOR READERS

As a contribution to the *Sources of Anglo-Saxon Literary Culture*, the following set of entries conforms to the structure of this reference work as a whole; yet since they represent only one kind of work, fewer issues need to be addressed here. The minimal unit of *SASLC* is, indeed, the entry, each of which discusses a particular text known in Anglo-Saxon England. Individual entries may then be placed together under their author or grouped, as they are here, into a larger generic unit. While the structure of *SASLC* as a whole is alphabetical, individual entries within a major-author or generic unit may be organized in different ways, which will be explained at the beginnings of these units.

Of course, identifying a "particular text" can be complicated both by the text itself and by the evidence of its use. Many apocryphal works circulated in various forms, often in different languages, and so establishing when a "version" becomes a new work can be a matter of judgment. Yet thanks to the efforts of editors and other scholars there is usually a consensus of opinion on these matters, which in turn has found expression in other reference works. Each entry, then, begins with a title and an abbreviation, which are followed by references to standard scholarship on the work. The next line designates the edition that best represents the version known in Anglo-Saxon England, but this does not necessarily mean that the version cited was known then. On occasions when a work circulated in more than one version (for example, the APOCALYPSE OF PAUL) each is given its own entry.

The previous example, the *Apocalypse of Paul* (on the use of typeface to signal cross-references, see below), may serve as a reminder that differing titles have been used for many apocryphal works since it has often been referred to as the *Visio Pauli*. Yet, in general, English titles have become more common in scholarship in this language as the works themselves have become better known. With this in mind, they have been used here when available; other titles are often mentioned in the entries. The abbreviations, however, which follow the system designed to be shared with *Fontes Anglo-Saxonici*, usually assume Latin titles for the works.

## HEADNOTE

Some of the evidence for the knowledge of a work in Anglo-Saxon England is summarized in an entry's headnote that covers manuscripts, booklists, Anglo-Saxon versions, quotations or citations, and references. Each category of evidence requires some comment.

MSS        *Manuscripts.* The inclusion of a work in a relevant manuscript provides firm physical evidence for its presence in Anglo-Saxon England. Helmut Gneuss's *Handlist of Anglo-Saxon Manuscripts* [HG] provides the basis for this category of evidence. Contributors have, of course, consulted other sources as needed, and have also been encouraged to include continental manuscripts, by definition outside of Gneuss's concern, which provide evidence (such as the use of an Anglo-Saxon script or the presence of Old English glosses) that a work was known in Anglo-Saxon circles. Manuscripts not in Gneuss's list are preceded by a question mark in the headnote, and are discussed in the body of the entry.

Lists        *Booklists.* Although less informative than a surviving manuscript, the mention of a work in wills, lists of donations, or inventories of libraries from our period provides a good indication that it was known. In "Surviving Booklists from Anglo-Saxon England" Michael Lapidge [ML] edits the remaining catalogues of manuscripts from our period, and identifies, whenever possible, the work in question. Here, however, only three items in one list, the Exeter list, concern us. Two refer to the GOSPEL OF NICODEMUS; in both cases scholars have identified the exact manuscripts in question. The third mentions "passiones apostolorum"; in this case we cannot be sure what work was meant.

A-S Vers        *Anglo-Saxon Versions.* Like the manuscript evidence, an Anglo-Saxon translation into Old English, or adaptation into Anglo-Latin, indicates that the source was known to the English at some time during the Anglo-Saxon period. The abbreviations for Old English texts are from the *Microfiche Concordance to Old English* [*MCOE*], and those for Anglo-Latin from Michael Lapidge's *Abbreviations for Sources and Specification of Standard Editions for Sources* (1988). In order to make our work self-contained, these abbreviations are expanded later in the bodies of the entries where they occur and the designated editions specified. Writers of individual entries have, of course, exercised judgment on how to represent the information when a translation or adaptation is quite loose, or when the use of a source is so limited that it is better considered a quotation.

Quots/Cits   *Quotations or Citations.* The source-notes of modern critical editions or other secondary scholarship often establish that Anglo-Saxon writers knew a work in full or in some shortened form. A citation, including both the name and the words of an author, is sometimes significant since it shows the knowledge of the origin of an idea or phrase. In itemizing these relationships, contributors first establish where in the edition specified at the start of each entry the passage occurs and then where it can be found in the Anglo-Saxon work. These references may take three forms, depending on the lineation of the edition cited: when a text is line numbered as a unit, only line numbers are used; when its sections (such as books or chapters) are line numbered separately, sectional divisions are in roman (upper case for larger divisions such as books, lower case for smaller ones such as chapters) followed by line numbers (for example, II.xx.3–4); and when it is line numbered by page (or column) or not provided with line numbers, page (or column) and line numbers are used (for example, 26.1–15 or 37.6–42.4). Anglo-Saxon texts are identified by abbreviations drawn from Lapidge (1988) and the *MCOE*, and usually refer to the editions designated in them; however, in order to keep our volume self-contained, these abbreviations are expanded in the bodies of the entries in which they occur and the designated editions identified. Finally, if the quotation or citation is noted in the specified edition of the Anglo-Saxon work, no further reference need be provided. If not, the source of the identification is mentioned in the body of the entry.

Refs          *References*. Although always open to interpretation, a specific reference to a work by an Anglo-Saxon writer may indicate its presence in England during our period. Line numbers are referred to in the same way as specified above under Quotations or Citations.

## BODY

The body of the entry discusses any information in the headnote that requires clarification or amplification, and then introduces other kinds of evidence for the knowledge of a work in Anglo-Saxon England, such as allusions in literary texts or distinctive iconographic motifs from the visual arts. It may also consider other questions, such as the temporal and geographical extent of the use of a work, and often concludes with a discussion of bibliography and work in progress.

## CROSS-REFERENCES

Readers are directed to other entries (written or projected) in *SASLC* by names in bold: large capitals are used for names that figure into the alphabetical scheme of the project as a whole (that is, known authors and the names of generic units, as well as the titles of anonymous works not gathered into generic units); small capitals are used for any division within a major-author or generic unit. Thus **AMBROSE** and **DE FIDE**. Names in small bold capitals need not, however, always refer to individual texts since some major-author and generic units are further divided into sections (for example, **OLD TESTAMENT APOCRYPHA** within **APOCRYPHA**. A name is placed in bold the first time (and only the first time) it appears in an individual entry or in a section of a major-author or generic unit.

## STANDARD RESEARCH TOOLS,

## STANDARD EDITIONS, AND BIBLIOGRAPHY

Some research tools and editions (listed below) are referred to by abbreviations without further bibliographical elaboration. When items in a research tool are numbered individually, references are to items (or to volume and item; for example, *CLA* 2.139); otherwise, references are to pages (or to volume and page; for example, *OTP* 2.249–95). When necessary, particular passages are identified by the system explained above under Quots/Cits. Other bibliographical references are by author and date; full information appears in the bibliography at the end of the volume.

References to the Bible are to the *Biblia sacra iuxta Vulgatam versionem*, ed. Robert Weber, 2nd ed. (Stuttgart, 1975).

ABBREVIATIONS

*AG*          Hans-Josef Klauck, *Apocryphal Gospels: An Introduction*, trans. Brian McNeil (London, 2003)

*ANRW*        *Aufstieg und Niedergang der römischen Welt: Geschichte und Kultur Roms im Spiegel der neueren Forschung*, ed. Joseph Vogt, Hildegard Temporini, and Wolfgang Haase (Berlin, 1972– )

*ANT*         J. K. Elliott, *The Apocryphal New Testament: A Collection of Apocryphal Christian Literature in an English Translation* (Oxford, 1993)

*AOT*         H. F. D. Sparks, *The Apocryphal Old Testament* (Oxford, 1984)

*AS*          *Acta Sanctorum*, ed. Socii Bollandiani, 1st ed., 71 vols (Antwerp and Brussels, 1643–1940); reprinted in 65 vols (Brussels, 1965–70)

*ASPR*        *The Anglo-Saxon Poetic Records*, ed. G. P. Krapp and E. V. K. Dobbie, 6 vols (New York, 1931–53)

*BaP*         *Bibliothek der angelsächsischen Prosa*, ed. Christian W. M. Grein, Richard P. Wülker, and Hans Hecht, 13 vols (Kassel, 1872–1933)

| | |
|---|---|
| *BCLL* | Michael Lapidge and Richard Sharpe, *A Bibliography of Celtic-Latin Literature 400–1200* (Dublin, 1985) [cited by no.] |
| *BEASE* | *The Blackwell Encyclopaedia of Anglo-Saxon England*, ed. Michael Lapidge, John Blair, Simon Keynes, and Donald Scragg (Oxford, 1999) |
| *BEH* | *A Bibliography of English History to 1485*, ed. Edgar B. Graves (Oxford, 1975) |
| *BHG* | François Halkin, *Bibliotheca Hagiographica Graeca*, 3rd ed., Subsidia Hagiographica 8a (Brussels, 1951); *Auctarium*, Subsidia Hagiographica 47 (Brussels, 1969); *Novum Auctarium*, Subsidia Hagiographica 65 (Brussels, 1984) [cited by no.] |
| *BHL* | *Bibliotheca Hagiographica Latina*, 2 vols, Subsidia Hagiographica 6 (Brussels 1898–1901); *Novum Supplementum*, ed. Henrik Fros, Subsidia Hagiographica 70 (Brussels, 1986) [cited by no.] |
| *BHM* | Bernard Lambert, *Bibliotheca Hieronymiana Manuscripta: La tradition manuscrite des œuvres de Saint Jérôme*, 4 vols in 7 parts, Instrumenta Patristica 4 (Steenbrugge, 1969–72) [cited by no.] |
| *BKE* | J. D. A. Ogilvy, *Books Known to the English, 597–1066*, Medieval Academy of America Publications 76 (Cambridge, Mass., 1967) |
| *BKE Add.* | J. D. A. Ogilvy, "Books Known to the English: Addenda and Corrigenda," *Mediaevalia* 7 (1984 for 1981): 281–325; reprinted in *Old English Newsletter* Subsidia 11 (Binghamton, N.Y., 1985) |
| *BPR* | Lorenzo DiTommaso, *A Bibliography of Pseudepigrapha Research 1850–1999*, Journal for the Study of the Pseudepigrapha, Supplement Series 39 (Sheffield, 2001) |
| *CANT* | Maurits Geerard, *Clavis Apocryphorum Novi Testamenti* (Turnhout, 1992) [cited by no.] |
| *CAVT* | Jean-Claude Haelewyck, *Clavis Apocryphorum Veteris Testamenti* (Turnhout, 1998) [cited by no.] |
| *CCSA* | *Corpus Christianorum, Series Apocryphorum* (Turnhout, 1983– ) |
| *CCSL* | *Corpus Christianorum, Series Latina* (Turnhout, 1953– ) |

| | |
|---|---|
| *CLA* | E. A. Lowe, *Codices Latini Antiquiores,* 11 vols (Oxford, 1934–66); Supplement (1971); 2nd ed. of vol 2 (1972) [cited by vol and no.] |
| *CPG* | Maurits Geerard, *Clavis Patrum Graecorum,* 5 vols (Turnhout, 1974–87); vol 6 *Supplementum* (Turnhout, 1998) |
| *CPL* | Eligius Dekkers, *Clavis Patrum Latinorum,* 3rd ed. (Turnhout, 1995) [cited by no.] |
| *CSEL* | *Corpus Scriptorum Ecclesiasticorum Latinorum* (Vienna, 1866– ) |
| *DACL* | *Dictionnaire d'archéologie chrétienne et de liturgie,* ed. Fernand Cabrol, 15 vols in 30 (Paris, 1907–53) |
| *DB* | *Dictionary of the Bible,* ed. James Hastings, 4 vols and an extra vol (New York, 1900–05) |
| *DS* | *Dictionnaire de spiritualité ascétique et mystique, doctrine et histoire,* ed. Marcel Viller, Charles Baumgartner, and André Rayez, 16 vols in 22 and *Tables générales* (Paris, 1937–95) |
| *EEMF* | *Early English Manuscripts in Facsimile,* 29 vols (Copenhagen, 1951–2002) |
| *EETS*<br>ES<br>OS<br>SS | *Early English Text Society*<br>Extra Series<br>Original Series<br>Supplementary Series |
| *GCS* | *Die griechischen christlichen Schriftsteller der ersten* [*drei*] *Jahrhunderte* (Leipzig, 1897– ) |
| *HBS* | *Henry Bradshaw Society* (London, 1891– ) |
| HG | Helmut Gneuss, *Handlist of Anglo-Saxon Manuscripts: A List of Manuscripts and Manuscript Fragments Written or Owned in England up to 1100,* Medieval and Renaissance Texts and Studies 241 (Tempe, Ariz., 2001) [cited by no.] |
| *IASIM* | Thomas H. Ohlgren, *Insular and Anglo-Saxon Illuminated Manuscripts: An Iconographic Catalogue* (New York, 1986) |
| *ICL* | Dieter Schaller and Ewald Könsgen, *Initia Carminum Latinorum Saeculo Undecimo Antiquiorum* (Göttingen, 1977) [cited by no.] |

ILRJH        Albert-Marie Denis et al., with Jean-Claude Haelewyck, *Introduction
             à la littérature religieuse judéo-hellénistique: Pseudépigraphes de l'Ancien
             Testament,* 2 vols (Turnhout, 2000) [cited by no.]

KVS          Hermann Josef Frede, *Kirchenschriftsteller: Verzeichnis und Sigel,* 4th
             ed., Vetus Latina: Die Reste der altlateinische Bibel 1/1 (Freiburg im
             Breisgau, 1996), with an *Aktualisierungsheft 2004* by Roger Gryson

MCOE         *A Microfiche Concordance to Old English: The List of Texts and Index of
             Editions,* compiled by Antonette diPaolo Healey and Richard L.
             Venezky (Toronto, 1980)

MGH          *Monumenta Germaniae Historica*
  AA             Auctores antiquissimi
  ES             Epistolae selectae
  SRM            Scriptores rerum merovingicarum

ML           Michael Lapidge, "Surviving Booklists from Anglo-Saxon England,"
             in *Learning and Literature in Anglo-Saxon England: Studies Presented
             to Peter Clemoes on the Occasion of His Sixty-Fifth Birthday,* ed.
             Michael Lapidge and Helmut Gneuss (Cambridge, 1985), pp 33–89

NCE          *New Catholic Encyclopedia,* ed. Thomas Carson, Joann Cerrito, et al.,
             2nd ed., 15 vols (Detroit, Mich., 2003)

NRK          N. R. Ker, *Catalogue of Manuscripts Containing Anglo-Saxon* (1957;
             reprinted with a supplement, Oxford, 1990)

NTA          *New Testament Apocrypha,* ed. Wilhelm Schneemelcher, trans. R.
             McL. Wilson, rev. ed., 2 vols (Louisville, Ky., 1991)

NTAP         James H. Charlesworth with James R. Mueller, *The New Testament
             Apocrypha and Pseudepigrapha: A Guide to Publications, with
             Excursuses on Apocalypses,* ATLA Bibliography Series 17 (Metuchen,
             N.J., 1987)

ODCC         *The Oxford Dictionary of the Christian Church,* ed. E. A. Livingstone,
             rev. 3rd ed. (London, 2005)

OTP          *The Old Testament Pseudepigrapha,* ed. James H. Charlesworth, 2 vols
             (London, 1983–85)

PG           *Patrologia Graeca,* ed. J.-P. Migne, 161 vols (Paris, 1857–66)

PL           *Patrologia Latina,* ed. J.-P. Migne, 221 vols (Paris, 1844–64)

PLS             *Patrologiae Latinae Supplementum*, ed. Adalbert Hamman, 5 vols
                (Paris, 1958–74)

RBMA            Friedrich Stegmüller, *Repertorium Biblicum Medii Aevi*, 11 vols
                (Madrid, 1950–80) [cited by no.]

RS              "Rolls Series": *Rerum Britannicarum Medii Aevi Scriptores* (London,
                1858–96)

SChr            *Sources chrétiennes* (Paris, 1940– )

SEHI            James F. Kenney, *The Sources for the Early History of Ireland. Vol. I:
                Ecclesiastical* (1929; reprinted with addenda by Ludwig Bieler, New
                York, 1966)

SS              *The Publications of the Surtees Society* (London, 1835– )

TU              *Texte und Untersuchungen zur Geschichte der altchristlichen Literatur:
                Archiv für die griechisch-christlichen Schriftsteller der ersten [drei]
                Jahrhunderte* (Leipzig and Berlin, 1882– )

                                                             Frederick M. Biggs

SOURCES OF ANGLO-SAXON LITERARY CULTURE

The Apocrypha

# APOCRYPHA

The term "apocrypha" is used here instead of "pseudepigrapha" because the perspective of this volume is not the same as that of modern scholars who customarily distinguish three kinds of biblical material: books from the Hebrew canon accepted as canonical by Catholics and Protestants, additional books from the Septuagint canon accepted by Catholics but not by Protestants, and books excluded by both groups. For Anglo-Saxon England, where the **BIBLE** was essentially the Vulgate, it is more appropriate to distinguish between the Bible as the canon and apocrypha as non-canonical books, a distinction suggested by contemporary writers such as **ALDHELM, BEDE,** and **ÆLFRIC** (see Biggs 2003 pp 11–21).

Yet defining the term remains difficult. While useful, the definitions employed by modern scholars — in particular Charlesworth (*OTP* 1.xxv and *NTAP* pp 1–17) and Schneemelcher (*NTA* 1.50–61); see also the introduction to *CAVT*, Charlesworth (1988), and the bibliography in *BPR* pp 113–15 — are perhaps too strict for our purposes because they exclude works that might have been considered "apocrypha" by the Anglo-Saxons. For example, the **PSEUDO-METHODIUS REVELATIONS**, now dated to the mid-seventh century and so too late for Charlesworth's criteria, is in some ways similar to Daniel. Thus this section attempts to be inclusive, drawing on the lists of texts included in the major studies. Following the divisions of the Bible, it groups the works into **OLD TESTAMENT APOCRYPHA, APOCRYPHA ABOUT CHRIST AND MARY, APOCRYPHAL ACTS, APOCRYPHAL EPISTLES,** and **APOCRYPHAL APOCALYPSES.** Gathered in a final section, **MISCELLANEOUS,** are works similar to other apocrypha and indeed often titled "apocrypha."

Identifying the particular works known or possibly known in Anglo-Saxon England is often complicated by the complex textual histories of many apocrypha. In some cases, it is possible to distinguish different versions of an apocryphon, which are treated in successive entries. In others, overlapping within apocryphal books makes it impossible to establish which were known. For example, as Cross (1979b p 17) notes, the **PSEUDO-ABDIAS APOSTOLIC HISTORIES** (also known as the *Virtutes Apostolorum*), which has been cited as a source for works such as the **OLD ENGLISH MARTYROLOGY** (*Mart*, B19, ed. Kotzor 1981; Rauer 2000; Rauer 2003; and Lapidge 2005), draws on earlier lives, and so is often indistinguishable from them. Finally, the presence of a single apocryphal motif need not prove that an entire work was known since recent studies, particularly of **HIBERNO-LATIN BIBLICAL COMMENTARIES** (see Wright 1990a and 2000) indicate that many circulated independently.

1

Contributors have signed their individual entries; the unsigned entries are my own. Thomas N. Hall and Charles D. Wright have both done much to improve the entire section. For further bibliography on individual texts, see the *ATLA Religion Database* (1949–current). Wright maintains an online *Apocrypha Bibliography* (http://netfiles.uiuc.edu/cdwright/www/apocrypha.html), as does the *Association pour l'étude de la littérature apocryphe chrétienne* (http://www2.unil.ch/aelac/).

Frederick M. Biggs

**Life of Adam and Eve** [ANON.Vit.Ad.Ev.]: *AOT* pp 141–67; *BPR* pp 164–65; *CAVT* 1.ii; *ILRJH* 1; *OTP* 2.249–95; *RBMA* 74; Verheyden 1995 pp 390–92.
    ed.: Meyer 1878 pp 221–43.

*MSS – Refs*        none.

The *Life of Adam and Eve*, also known as the *Vita Adae et Evae,* expands on the story in Genesis 3–5. Following their expulsion from the Garden, Adam and Eve seek forgiveness, planning for one to stand for forty days in the Jordan and the other for thirty-seven days in the Tigris, but Eve is again deceived by Satan, who then describes his expulsion from heaven. Cain and Abel are born, and Cain slays Abel. Seth is born, and Adam recounts to him his journey to "the Paradise of righteousness" (*OTP* 2.266; 25.3). After many years, Seth and Eve return to paradise but fail to obtain "the oil of mercy" (40.1) for Adam, who dies amid "great wonders in heaven and on earth" (43.2). Before she dies, Eve instructs her children to record all they have learned from her and from Adam on tablets of stone and of clay, since one could survive a judgment of water, the other a judgment of fire.

Related to the *Life* are versions of these events in Greek, Slavonic, Armenian, and Georgian, with additional fragments surviving in Coptic. Anderson and Stone (1999) publish the five main versions (the Greek and Latin in the original languages; the others in translation) in parallel columns. The relationships between them remain unresolved, hindering firm conclusions about the origin of the apocryphon, although Tromp (2002 p 36) notes that "it is generally agreed that the Armenian, Georgian, Slavonic and Latin versions were translated from Greek originals." According to Sparks (*AOT* p 142), "all that can be safely said about it is that the author, whether Jew or Christian, constructed his narrative making use of Jewish traditions or written sources as were known to him; that he almost certainly wrote in Greek; and that in all probability he is to be dated within the first three Christian centuries" (see further Stone 1992; Anderson 1998 pp 10–11; Anderson, Stone, and Tromp 2000; Pettorelli 2002; and *ILRJH* pp 25–28).

The Latin material, now known in 106 manuscripts, is currently divided into five groups (Pettorelli 1999a; see also Stone's assessment, 1992 pp 19–25, of Murdoch 1976, who argues for a more fluid understanding of the tradition; Murdoch 2003 p 43; and *ILRJH* pp 13–16). Meyer's 1878 edition represents the version most likely to have been known in Anglo-Saxon England. Working from later English manuscripts, Mozley (1929) presents a text that includes additional material (such as the two motifs discussed in the following entry) and connects the apocryphon to the legends concerning the wood of the Cross.

Pächt (1961 p 169) suggests that the illumination in the illustrated Old English *Hexateuch* (B8.1.4.1–6; London, BL Cotton Claudius B.iv; *IASIM* 191.17) of an angel instructing Adam and Eve in tilling the earth after the Fall is related to this apocryphon. The other possibility, JUBILEES 3.15, is less likely since here Adam and Eve are instructed before the Fall. The illumination is reproduced in *EEMF* 18 and is discussed on pp 19 and 65.

Groos (1983) cites Satan's account of his expulsion from heaven as a possible source for the question of angelic seniority in line 4b of *Guthlac A* (*GuthA*, A3.2; ed. Roberts 1979; see further Wright 1987 pp 130–33). J. M. Evans (1968 p 146 note 4) suggests that this account may underlie Lucifer's explanation of his rebellion in lines 84–86 of *Christ and Satan* (*Sat*, A1.4; ed. Finnegan 1977). In their commentary on question 24 in the Old English prose *Solomon and Saturn* (*Sol I*, B5.1; SOLOMON AND SATURN), Cross and Hill (1982 p 89) cite the *Life of Adam and Eve* 24 as a possible ultimate source for the claim that Adam had thirty sons and thirty daughters; see also C. D. Wright and R. Wright (2004 p 112). The *Life* and other apocryphal texts, in particular *Jubilees* and 2 ENOCH, have also been cited as a possible ultimate sources for themes in *Genesis B* (*GenB*, A1.1; ed. *ASPR* 1): see in particular Doane (1991 pp 96–97). As a translation of an Old Saxon poem, it would be removed one step further from any direct Anglo-Saxon use of apocryphal material; see Cole (2001 p 160 note 11), who also proposes GREGORY THE GREAT's DIALOGI as a possible intermediate source.

Another Latin text, based on two manuscripts of an Austrian legendary, is published by Eis (1935 pp 241–55). Pettorelli (1998) has edited the South-German redaction, and (1999b) a version preserved in Paris that appears to represent a stage of the Latin tradition closer to the original Greek than that in Meyer. On the Irish and Hiberno-Latin material, see McNamara (1975 pp 23–24) and Wright (1987 pp 130–33). Revard (2005) reviews recent scholarship in considering the work's relationship to Milton's *Paradise Lost*.

**De plasmatione Adam** [ANON.Plasmat.Adam]: *BPR* p 448; *CAVT* 10; *CPL* 1155f viii; *ILRJH* pp 47 and 150; *RBMA* 75,22.
    ed.: Förster 1907–08 pp 479–81.

*MSS*    1. Cambridge, Corpus Christi College 326: HG 93.
         2. Durham, Cathedral Library A.IV.19: HG 223.
*Lists*    none.
*A-S Vers*    *Sol I* (B5.1).
*Quots/Cits – Refs*    none.

Although listed as a single item in *CAVT*, the two brief texts referred to as "Adam Octipartite" and "Adam's Name" do not always appear together in Anglo-Saxon sources. *CAVT* does not refer to the Durham manuscript. In *BPR*, DiTommaso (following a private communication from C. Böttrich) writes, "the text is not a fragment of 2 Enoch 30; rather, it is part of [a] tradition found throughout medieval literature and that has 2 Enoch 30 as it[s] most important parallel"; see further Böttrich (1995) and Verheyden (1995 pp 410–11) and **2 ENOCH** below.

The motif that describes Adam's creation from eight substances may rest ultimately on 2 Enoch 30.8J (*OTP* 1.150). It is widespread in Insular circles, appearing in the eighth-century **LIBER DE NUMERIS** (**HIBERNO-LATIN BIBLICAL COMMENTARIES**, no. 39; see Wright 1990a pp 113–14; see also the **QUESTIONS OF BARTHOLOMEW**) and later texts; see also C. D. Wright and R. Wright (2004 p 86) for continental manuscripts. It occurs in an Anglo-Saxon context in the additions to the *Durham Collectar* (see **LITURGY, DAILY OFFICE BOOKS**) — and so is included in *SS* 140 p 192 but not in *HBS* 107 — made at Chester-le-Street by Aldred the Provost around 970 (see *EEMF* 16 p 15); Aldred also glossed the text (*DurRitGlCom*, C13.1; ed. *SS* 140). This motif occurs in questions 8 and 9 of the prose *Solomon and Saturn* (*Sol I*; ed. Cross and Hill 1982 p 26 lines 8–18; see also their discussion of sources and analogues, pp 68–70, and **SOLOMON AND SATURN**). In a forthcoming paper, Charles D. Wright focuses on a detail, Adam's eyes, which are usually said to have been created from the sun. He identifies one group of texts, including both the additions to the *Durham Collectar* and the prose *Solomon and Saturn*, in which they are said to have been made "from a pound of flowers"; he connects this tradition to the Alfred Jewel and Fuller Brooch to explain why "Sight" holds flowers.

Along with the description of Adam's material creation in the Cambridge manuscript (but not in the Durham manuscript) is another motif also perhaps derived from 2 Enoch 30.13–14J (*OTP* 1.152; also mentioned in the **SIBYLLENE ORACLES** 3.24–26: *OTP* 1.362; see also Turdeanu 1974 pp 184–88), the derivation of his name from four stars. This motif underlies questions 6 and 7 of the Old English prose *Solomon and Saturn* (see Cross and Hill 1982 pp 66–67). A version of the motif that links Adam's name to the four corners of the world but does not mention stars occurs in **BEDE's COMMENTARIUS IN GENESIM** (*CCSL* 118A.II.729–33) and in **ALCUIN's IN IOHANNIS EVANGELIUM** (*PL* 100.777); both apparently follow **AUGUSTINE's ENARRATIONES IN PSALMOS** (*CCSL* 38.XCV.15.6–12) or his **TRACTATUS IN EVANGELIUM IOANNIS** (*CCSL* 36.IX.14.9–14 and X.12.2–12). D'Alverny (1976 p 169) finds a trace of this motif in one of the illuminations in **BYRHTFERTH's ENCHIRIDION** (*ByrM* 1, Crawford, B20.20.1), printed as the frontispiece in *EETS* OS 177 (see also *EETS* SS 15.14 and 256; and Böttrich 1995 pp 84–85): the cardinal points are also given the names that spell out Adam and are reinforced with separate capitals.

Förster (1910; reprinted in *PLS* 4.938–41) prints another version from Sélestat, Bibliothèque Humaniste 1, also edited by Munier (1994 p 11). For further references to Hiberno-Latin and Irish texts, see McNally (1957 p 72), McNamara (1975 pp 21–23), Tristram (1975), and Wright (1987 pp 140–43). Hill (1977a) cites the theme as relevant to the "Æcerbot Charm" (*MCharm* 1, A43.1; ed. *ASPR* 6). See also Cerbelaud (1984) for a general discussion of the theme.

**Cave of Treasures** [ANON.Cav.Thes.]: *BPR* pp 211–17; *CAVT* 11; *ILRJH* pp 30–36; *RBMA* 76.1–8.
    ed.: Ri 1987.

*MSS – Refs*        none.

    Also known as the *History of the Patriarchs and the Kings Their Successors from the Creation to the Crucifixion of Christ* and attributed to **EPHREM THE SYRIAN**, this work was written in Syriac probably during the fourth or fifth century. It expands on biblical history, concentrating on the major figures from Creation to Pentecost. Its early sections are closely related to the **LIFE OF ADAM AND EVE** (Anderson 2000 p 74) and it influenced the **PSEUDO-METHODIUS REVELATIONS**. Translations exist in Arabic, Ethiopian, and Georgian, but have not been found in Greek or Latin.
    In discussing the sources of the first commentary on the Pentateuch 44 from the Canterbury School of **THEODORE OF CANTERBURY** and **HADRIAN**, Lapidge (in Bischoff and Lapidge 1994 pp 236–37, 310, and 445) cites the *Cave* (in the translation of Budge 1927 pp 66–67) as "an exact parallel to the Commentator's statement, whereby 'at the third hour of the day Adam and Eve ascended into Paradise, and for three hours they were in shame and disgrace, and at the ninth hour their expulsion from Paradise took place.'" The Commentator attributes this remark to **JOHN CHRYSOSTOM**, but Lapidge asserts that "no such statement" appears in his work, and that "it is difficult to parallel so rigid a numerical scheme in any Greek source" (p 236). Lapidge also finds a parallel in the *Cave* for the remark in the second commentary on the Gospels 3 that "the wise men were on the road for two years, since the star appeared to them two years before Christ's birth" (p 397); this claim is again attributed to Chrysostom. As Lapidge explains (pp 503–04), this claim could derive from the works of Chrysostom or, more likely, **PSEUDO-CHRYSOSTOM**; yet it might also derive from the *Cave*, which declares: "Now it was two years before Christ was born that the star appeared to the Magi" (Budge 1927 p 203). Wright (1987 p 132 note 41) refers to the *Cave* in discussing apocryphal traditions attributing Satan's fall to envy of Adam's exalted rank. Finally, Anlezark (2002 pp 29–32) proposes the *Cave* as the source for the motif of an "ark-born" son of Noah found in Anglo-Saxon genealogies; Hill (1987) had previously suggested the *Pseudo-Methodius Revelations* as the source. Citing Bischoff and Lapidge (1994), Anlezark identifies Theodore as a likelier conduit of this idea.
    Budge (1927) provides an English translation based on one manuscript. Ri (1987) edits the text from nineteen manuscripts and gives a French translation.

**Jubilees** [ANON.Jub.]: *AOT* pp 1–139; *BPR* pp 617–72; *CAVT* 132; *ILRJH* 9; *OTP* 2.35–142; *RBMA* 77; Verheyden 1995 pp 387–88. See the **LIFE OF ADAM AND EVE** and **1 ENOCH**.
    ed.: *AOT* pp 10–139.

*MSS – A-S Vers*    none.
*Quots/Cits*    see below.
*Refs*    none.

The earliest surviving fragment dates the *Book of Jubilees* (also known as the *Little Genesis* and the *Testament* or *Apocalypse of Moses*) to before around 150 B.C.; on what can be determined about its author, see VanderKam (1997 pp 19–20) and *ILRJH* pp 394–98. It recounts stories from Genesis and the beginning of Exodus. A Greek translation, of which only extracts survive, was itself translated into Ethiopic and Latin. The Ethiopic preserves the full text. The Latin, from a single fragmentary manuscript (Milan, Biblioteca Ambrosiana C 73 inf.; *CLA* 3.316), contains about a fourth of the work. (Fragments have also been found in Hebrew and Syriac.) It is mentioned by **JEROME** (**EPISTOLA AD FABIOLAM** 78, *CSEL* 55.68 lines 14–17) and is condemned in the **GELASIAN DECREE** (ed. Dobschütz, *TU* 38/4 line 286).

According to Lapidge (in Bischoff and Lapidge 1994 pp 199–200), the author of the *Biblical Commentaries* from the School of **THEODORE OF CANTERBURY** and **HADRIAN** knew this work "in some form," since he cites it by name twice, first for the claim that Adam spent seven years less forty days in paradise (pp 310–11 and 445), and later in connection with Lamech's slaying of Cain (pp 314–15 and 446). Lapidge notes that while the first detail does appear in the apocryphon as it has survived (but only in the Ethiopic), the second does not: "possibly the Commentator had misremembered the text" (p 200). He also suggests that *Jubilees* "may have been the source of the Commentator's report that Enoch was transported to Paradise located on a mountain . . . as well as of the report that Abel was stoned by Cain" (p 200); see also McNamara (2003b pp 79–80). For *Genesis B*, see the **LIFE OF ADAM AND EVE**.

The translation in *AOT* relies on Charles (1895) and his English translation (1902); see also *OTP* 2.52–142. VanderKam (1989), whose edition replaces that of Charles, follows Ceriani (1861 pp 15–54) for the Latin text.

**Pseudo-Philo Biblical Antiquities** [ANON.Ant.Bibl./PS.PHIL.]: *BPR* pp 765–84; *CAVT* 131; *ILRJH* 10; *OTP* 2.297–377; *RBMA* 6980,2; Verheyden 1995 pp 386–87. ed.: *SChr* 229.

Ogilvy (*BKE* pp 69, 71, 73) indirectly refers to this work, composed in Hebrew in the first century B.C., when he discusses four fragments, the "Prayer of Moses," the "Vision of Kenaz," the "Lamentation of Seila," and the "Song of David," all printed by James (1893 pp 166–85) from Phillipps MS 391 (now Berkeley, University of California, Bancroft Library UCB 17; contents described by Schenkl 1891–1908 no. 1002). Cohn (1898) recognized the fragments to be from the Pseudo-Philo *Biblical Antiquities*. The manuscript is listed in the 30 November 1965 sale catalogue of Sotheby & Co. (*Bibliotheca Phillippica* 1965), where it is dated to the second half of the eleventh century (early twelfth century in Kisch 1949 p 27) and is said to come from the Abbey of St. Matthias, Trier. Thus there is currently no evidence for the knowledge of this work in Anglo-Saxon England.

**1 Enoch** [ANON.Hen.]: *AOT* pp 169–319; *BPR* pp 355–430; *CAVT* 61; *ILRJH* 2; *OTP* 1.5–89; *RBMA* 78,16; Verheyden 1995 pp 403–06.
    ed.: Black 1985 pp 25–102.

*MSS*    see below.
*Lists – A-S Vers*    none.
*Quots/Cits*    ? Hen. 6–7: BEDA.Comm.epist.cath. 340.226–27.
*Refs*    BEDA.Comm.epist.cath. 340.220.

    *1 Enoch* (or *Henoch*; also known as *Enoch aethiopicus* and the *Ethiopic Apocalypse of Enoch*), a composite work attributed to Enoch (Genesis 5.24) but composed in Hebrew or Aramaic between 200 B.C. and A.D. 100, presents eschatological themes, a discussion of the fallen angels, and astronomical lore. A Latin fragment in an Anglo-Saxon manuscript is discussed in the next entry.

    According to Kaske (1971), **BEDE**'s discussion of this work in his **COMMEN-TARIUS IN EPISTOLAS SEPTEM CATHOLICAS** (ed. *CCSL* 121) "is clearly based on a similar discussion by Augustine in *De civitate Dei*" (*CCSL* 48.XV. xxiii.104–24), but "it does at least raise the question of whether Bede may not have known of the *Book of Enoch* directly" (p 422; see also Acerbi 1996 p 132 and Biggs 2003 pp 12–13). The passage Kaske cites as suggesting independent knowledge by Bede is referred to as *1 Enoch* 6–7 in the *CCSL* edition of Bede's commentary, although **AUGUSTINE** may be Bede's only source.

    As evidence for the circulation of *1 Enoch*, James (1909–10) identified a number of early Insular works that include the motif of the seven archangels: Cuthbert's coffin (see Kitzinger 1956 pp 273–77); the additions to the *Durham Collectar* (printed in *SS* 140.145, 146, and 198, but not in *HBS* 107; see *EEMF* 16 and **LITURGY, DAILY OFFICE BOOKS**); the *Book of Cerne* (ed. Kuypers 1902 p 153; see Brown 1996 and **PRAYERBOOKS**); a fragmentary Anglo-Saxon prayerbook, London, BL Harley 7653 (fol 4r; *CLA* 2.204; *HBS* 10.85; NRK 244; and *Prayerbooks*); Cambridge, Corpus Christi College 41, p 326 (see Storms 1948 p 315, who prints from Cambridge, Gonville and Caius College 379); and the *Textus Roffensis* (*EEMF* 7 fol 116v); as well as several other Irish and continental examples. Hill (1974) adds that the names from the list occur in the prose *Pater Noster Dialogue* (*Sol II*, B5.3; ed. Menner 1941 p 169 lines 3 and 9) and that **BONIFACE** condemns a prayer containing the names of eight angels (*MGH* ES 1.117; see Russell 1964 pp 236–38). Cross (1986) discusses the possibility of Irish biblical commentaries as intermediaries for such material (see McNally 1957 p 28 for a further Irish example).

    Menner (1941) cites this work three times for parallels to the poetic **SOLOMON AND SATURN** (*MSol*, A13; lines 247a–48b, 253b, and 263–64). Anlezark (2003) considers it a possible source for lines 441–66, the account of the fall of the angels. The

possibility that it may underlie the depiction of Grendel and Grendel's mother in
BEOWULF (*Beo*, A4.1; ed. Klaeber 1950) has long intrigued critics, with three details
commanding the most attention: the monsters' cannibalism, their home in the waste-
land, and the "el" ending of Grendel's name; see in particular Bouterwek (1856 p 401),
Emerson (1906 p 878 note 1), Kaske (1971), Peltola (1972), Mellinkoff (1979 and
1981), Cross (1986 pp 82–83), and Orchard (1995 pp 64–66 and 76).

Two of the illuminations of Enoch, one in the Old English *Hexateuch* (B8.1.4.1–
6; London, BL Cotton Claudius B.iv.; *IASIM* 191.35) and another in the *Junius
Manuscript* (Oxford, Bodleian Library, Junius 11; *IASIM* 163.35), illustrate Genesis
5.24, the translation of Enoch, and show no apparent influence of the apocryphal
tradition; see, in contrast, Coatsworth (2003). A second illustration in the *Junius
Manuscript*, however, is less straightforward, showing "Enoch, nimbed and holding an
open book, trampl[ing] a dragon, while an angel addresses him" (*IASIM* 163.34; see
Karkov 2001 pp 9 and 87). Neither the Vulgate nor *Genesis A* (*GenA*, A1.1; ed. Doane
1978 lines 1195–1217a) accounts for this depiction; Gollancz (1927 p xliv) suggests
that it may represent Enoch as the inventor of writing (JUBILEES 4.18) or as the author
of an apocryphal book (see *1 Enoch* 13.6, 14.7, etc.). Similarly, Gollancz suggests that
the sign above the family inhabiting the first city earlier in the *Hexateuch* (*IASIM*
191.22) is the sign of Aries, and can be explained by assuming a confusion of Cain's
son Enoch (Genesis 4.17) and Jared's son Enoch (Genesis 5.19): the latter, according to
*Jubilees* 4.17, composed an astronomical text. According to Milik (1976 p 11) this
passage from *Jubilees* refers to *1 Enoch* 72–82.

The English translation by Black (1985) relies on Charles (1912) but seeks to
incorporate new textual evidence, including the editions of Milik (1976) and Knibb
(1978). See also the translations in *AOT* pp 184–319 and *OTP* 1.13–89. VanderKam
(1984) provides useful background.


**1 Enoch** [ANON.Hen.lat.]: *BPR* p 360; and see previous entry.
    ed: James 1893 p 148.

*MSS*     London, BL Royal 5.E.XIII: HG 459.
*Lists – Refs*     none.


A Latin fragment of chapter 106, which describes Moses's miraculous form at
birth and foretells the Flood, survives in BL Royal 5.E.XIII, fols 79v–80r. James's
conclusion, that it proves there was a complete Latin version (1893 p 150), is no
longer accepted; see McNamara (2003b pp 78–79). Chapters 106–07 are thought by
some to come from an independent *Book* (or *Apocalypse*) *of Noah* (*OTP* p 5; Black
1985 p 23). Milik (1976 pp 78–81), who argues that "there is no irrefutable evidence
for the existence of a Latin version of the Enochic writings," proposes that the fragment and its surrounding passages are "probably some extracts from a chronicle or
from a collection of Exempla or of Testimonia." Two other possible extracts in Latin
from chapters 1.9 and 99.6–7 are discussed by Verheyden (1995 pp 404–06).

Dumville (1973 p 331) identifies Royal 5.E.XIII as a manuscript produced in Brittany in the ninth century but states that it "was in England (perhaps Worcester) during the next century." A tenth-century Worcester provenance is accepted by Reynolds (1983 p 107), Petitmengin (1993 pp 622–26), Hall (1996 pp 48–49), and Ambrose (2005 pp 208–14).

**2 Enoch** [ANON.Hen.sl.]: *AOT* pp 321–62; *BPR* pp 431–49; *CAVT* 66; *ILRJH* 3; *OTP* 1.91–213; *RBMA* 79; Verheyden 1995 pp 407–12.
    ed.: *OTP* pp 102–213.

*MSS – Refs*        none.

This work, also called the *Slavonic Apocalypse of Enoch* and the *Book of the Secrets of Enoch*, is known from two main recensions, both preserved in Slavonic and translated in the edition specified above. It expands on Genesis 5.21–32, describing Enoch's journey through the seven heavens, his report of this experience to his sons, and the deeds of his successors, Methuselah, Nir, and Melchizedek. Andersen (*OTP* 1.95) notes that "dates ranging all the way from pre-Christian times to the late Middle Ages have been proposed" for its production; Böttrich (2001 p 451) and Orlov (2003 p 302), while disagreeing on much else, both place the work near the end of the first century A.D.

In discussing question 54 in the Old English prose SOLOMON AND SATURN (*Sol I*, B5.1), Cross and Hill (1982 p 54) note *2 Enoch* 8 as a possible ultimate source for the identification of the four rivers of paradise with milk, honey, oil, and wine; they also suggest the APOCALYPSE OF PAUL. For other possible influences of *2 Enoch*, see DE PLASMATIONE ADAM and the SEVEN HEAVENS APOCRYPHON; for *Genesis B*, see the LIFE OF ADAM AND EVE.

**Prayer of Moses:** *CAVT* 138; *RBMA* 89,7: see PSEUDO-PHILO BIBLICAL ANTIQUITIES.

**Jannes and Jambres** [ANON.Jann.J.]: *BPR* pp 559–63; *CAVT* 129; *ILRJH* 13; *OTP* 2.427–42; *RBMA* 89,13; Verheyden 1995 pp 412–13.
    ed.: Pietersma 1994 pp 97–280.

*MSS*        London, BL Cotton Tiberius B.v: HG 373.
*Lists*        none.
*A-S Vers*        *Mambres* (B8.5.7).
*Quots/Cits – Refs*        none.

Although not named in the Old Testament, Jannes and Jambres (Jamnes and Mambres in the Vulgate) are said in 2 Timothy 3.8 to have "resisted Moses," suggesting that a tradition identifying them with the two magicians in Pharaoh's court who opposed the Israelites' departure from Egypt (Exodus 8) was already established. On a possible reference to them in the *Damascus Document*, from ca. 100 B.C., see *OTP* 2.427 and Pietersma (1994 pp 12–23). Two fragmentary Greek papyri, one in the Nationalbibliothek in Vienna and the other in the Chester Beatty Library in Dublin, dated to the third and fourth centuries A.D. respectively, confirm the existence of an early apocryphon about them. There are also references to such a book in **ORIGEN** and **AMBROSIASTER** (see Pietersma 1994 pp 43–47, and Biggs and Hall 1996), and a "Paenitentia Jamne et Mambre" is condemned in the **GELASIAN DECREE** (ed. Dobschütz, *TU* 38/4 lines 303–04).

Appended to the end of the **MARVELS OF THE EAST** in the London manuscript are two passages in Latin, with Old English translations followed by a full-page illustration, relating how Mambres uses his brother's magical books to summon his shade from the underworld and how Jannes then warns Mambres of hell's torments and adjures him to lead a better life. The relationship between these passages and the Greek text is problematic: they may correspond to passages near the end of the apocryphon (see *OTP* 2.440–41 and Pietersma 1994 pp 218–19), but Biggs and Hall (1996 pp 70–74) note their self-contained nature (see also Verheyden 1995 p 413). These passages were first printed by Cockayne (1861) and James (1901), and then more carefully edited and discussed by Förster (1902). Pietersma (1994 pp 280–81) edits and translates the Latin with two plates of the manuscript (pp 302–03).

The magicians are mentioned by name in three other Old English texts: *Orosius* (*Or*, B9.2; ed. Bately, *EETS* SS 6.26 lines 19–22); ÆLFRIC's "On Auguries" (*ÆLS*, Auguries, B1.3.18; ed. Skeat, *EETS* OS 76 and 82.372 line 114); and the anonymous *Life of St. Margaret* (*LS* 14 [MargaretAss 15], B3.3.14; ed. Clayton and Magennis 1994 p 167). They have also been identified in two illustrations in the Old English *Hexateuch* (B8.1.4.1–6; London, BL Cotton Claudius B.iv; *IASIM* 191.252 and 258), in the miracle of the rods (Exodus 7.12) and in the plague of lice (Exodus 8.18). None of these literary references or illustrations, however, is manifestly dependent upon the apocryphon, and one, Ælfric's "On Auguries," relies on the **MARTYRDOM OF PETER AND PAUL** (see Biggs and Hall 1996). Lionarons (1998) notes that a line in a version of the *Martyrdom of Peter and Paul* interpolated into **WULFSTAN OF YORK**'s *De temporibus Antichristi* (*HomU* 58; Nap. 16; B3.4.58; ed. Napier 1883 p 98 lines 8–11) must refer to the two even though they are not named.

The order of material in Pietersma's edition (1994) differs from that in the translation by R. T. Lutz (*OTP* 2.437–42).

Thomas N. Hall

**Assumption of Moses** [ANON.Ass.Mos.]: *AOT* pp 601–16; *BPR* pp 731–53; *CAVT* 134; *ILRJH* 11; *RBMA* 89,1–5.
  ed.: Tromp 1993 pp 6–24.

*MSS – Refs*        none.

This work (also called the *Testament of Moses*), in which Moses reveals Israel's future to Joshua, survives only as a Latin fragment in the Milan, Ambrosian Library manuscript (C 73 inf.; *CLA* 3.316) that also contains part of the Latin translation of JUBILEES. It was probably written in Greek in the early first century A.D. in Palestine (Tromp 1993 pp 115–23).

The end of the work has been lost but probably contained a description of a struggle between Michael and the devil over Moses's body (Tromp 1993 pp 270–81). According to Lapidge (in Bischoff and Lapidge 1994 p 200), it is "very possibly" to this lost section that the author of the *Biblical Commentaries* from the Canterbury School of **THEODORE OF CANTERBURY** and **HADRIAN** refers twice with the phrase "sunt qui dicunt" (see also pp 404–05, 410–11, 517, and 522).

Tromp (1993) replaces the edition by Charles (1897) and offers a review of previous scholarship; see more recently Hofmann (2000). The work is translated in *AOT* pp 606–16.

**Lamentation of Seila:** *CAVT* 148; *RBMA* 89,16. See PSEUDO-PHILO BIBLICAL ANTIQUITIES.

**Vision of Kenaz:** *CAVT* 147; *RBMA* 91,4. See PSEUDO-PHILO BIBLICAL ANTIQUITIES.

**Solomon and Saturn:** *BEASE* pp 424–25; *CAVT* 159; see *CAVT* 160 and *RBMA* 108,15.

The relationships of what are considered four separate texts in Old English — two poems called *Solomon and Saturn I* and *Solomon and Saturn II* (*MSol*, A13; ed. Menner 1941 pp 80–104) and two prose dialogues also called *Solomon and Saturn I* (*Sol I*, B5.1; ed. Cross and Hill 1982 pp 25–34) and *Solomon and Saturn II* (*Sol II*, B5.3; ed. Menner 1941, pp 168–71) — to each other, much less to the larger tradition of apocrypha, are far from clear. The more important manuscript for the two poems and for the second prose text is Cambridge, Corpus Christi College 422 (NRK 70; *EEMF* 23 nos. 12.2.1–12.25; the opening of the first poem also appears in Cambridge, Corpus Christi College 41: see NRK 32; *EEMF* 23 nos. 12.1.1–3). In it the first poem and the prose text are presented as a single unit; Wright (1993 p 234) suggests they may translate "two parts of the same Latin source, and if so, are probably by the same author." The prose text breaks off in mid-sentence due to the loss of a leaf, creating uncertainty about the status of nine lines of poetry on the following leaf that precede the beginning of the second poem (Menner prints them as the conclusion to the second poem). In contrast to Menner (1941), who suggests that the first poem draws on the second and influenced the second prose text, O'Neill (1997 p 164) argues that they all "are the products of the same school, though not necessarily the same author," which he would associate with King **ALFRED**. He considers the first prose dialogue "unrelated" (p 139 note 1). Unlike the other texts, which contrast representatives of Christian and pagan learning, this work, aside from the naming of the two participants, is similar to the **IOCA MONACHORUM** question-and-answer dialogues; see Cross and Hill (1982 pp 3–13).

These texts might well be classed as apocrypha because of their association with Solomon and because of their use of other apocrypha. The **GELASIAN DECREE** (ed. Dobschütz, *TU* 38/4 line 332; see also p 319) lists an "Interdictio Salomonis" (in some manuscripts "Contradictio Salomonis"), which James (1906 pp 563–64) believed to be the "foundation" of the Old English texts. This work has not been identified, and so its relationship to other Solomon literature, particularly the *Testament of Solomon* — in which the Old Testament ruler interrogates various demons (*RBMA* 108,3 and *OTP* 1.935–87) — remains uncertain. Menner (1941 p 24) concedes that it "could not be the immediate and sole source of a poem that contrasted Germanic and Christian wisdom." He does discuss the traditions about Solomon (pp 21–26) and "oriental" elements in each poem (especially pp 45–49 and 59–62), but the connections remain general; see further O'Brien O'Keeffe (1991) and O'Neill (1997). The first prose dialogue contains some apocryphal motifs, most notably "Adam Octipartite" and "Adam's Name" (**DE PLASMATIONE ADAM**) but apparently derives these from similar lists of questions or from Irish biblical commentaries (see **HIBERNO-LATIN BIBLICAL COMMENTARIES**; Wright 1990a and 1993).

**Prayer of Manasse** [ANON.Or.Man.]: *BPR* pp 717–26; *CAVT* 178; *ILRJH* 20; *ODCC* p 1032; *RBMA* 93.
ed.: Weber 1975 p 1909.

*MSS – Refs*          none.

This short penitential prayer ascribed to Manasse, king of Juda (4 Kings 21.1–18) is included in some early Greek Bibles and is printed in Clementine editions of the Vulgate. Weber's edition (1975) represents three thirteenth-century manuscripts; see also Schneider (1960).

Verse 9 is echoed in a prayer on fol 28v of London, BL Royal 2.A.XX (HG 450), which declares: "multiplicata sunt delicta mea uelut harena quae est in litore maris" ("my sins are multiplied like the sand on the sea shore"; Sims-Williams 1990 p 319).

Sims-Williams suggests that it "may have been transmitted to England in the Roman Antiphonary, in which it occurs as a respond."

**4 Ezra** [ANON.4Ezra]: *BPR* pp 469–524; *CANT* 318; *CAVT* 180–83; *OTP* 1.516–59; *RBMA* 95; Verheyden 1995 pp 395–97.
    ed.: Weber 1975 pp 1931–74.

*MSS – Refs*       none.

A number of manuscripts of the Vulgate contain, following the title in Weber's edition, a "Liber Ezrae Quartus" (IV Esr; Esdras is the Greek form of the Hebrew name Ezra), which modern scholars would recognize as made up of three parts: an original work containing seven visions granted to Salathiel or Ezra (chapters 3–14; also called *4 Ezra* and the *Apocalypse of Ezra*; *CAVT* 180 and *ILRJH* pp 815–53); two introductory chapters (1–2; also called *5 Ezra*; *CAVT* 182) recounting God's command to Ezra to chastise Israel, their rejection of him, his turning to the gentiles, and his vision of a great multitude on Mount Sion; and two concluding chapters (15–16; *6 Ezra*; *CAVT* 183) denouncing God's enemies and calling on his chosen people to put their trust in him. The original core of the work was composed in the late-first century A.D. and also survives in various Oriental versions. The additions were probably composed between the late-second and the fourth centuries and were associated with *4 Ezra* by the mid-fifth century (see Bergren 1998 pp 5–9). If any Anglo-Saxon readers knew this work, it was probably as combined in the **BIBLE**, and so the three parts are considered here in a single entry.

Ogilvy concludes too readily from a passage quoted in James's introduction to Bensly's edition (Bensly and James 1895) that "the French family of manuscripts" is "thought to rest on an English archetype" (*BKE* p 69). According to Bischoff (1965–68 p 24), the manuscript in question (now Paris, Bibliothèque Nationale lat. 11505) is from Saint-Germain-des-Prés in Paris, although the illuminated initials may show the influence of Insular practice. The Romano-British author **GILDAS** (**DE EXCIDIO BRITANNIAE** 60; ed. *MGH* AA 13.59; see also Winterbottom 1978 pp 115–16 and 157; *BEASE* p 204) quotes 15.21–27 and 16.3–12. All three parts were apparently known in Irish circles (see McNamara 1975 p 27).

A number of motifs perhaps derived ultimately from the three parts have been noted in Old English texts, particularly *Christ III* (*ChristC*, A3.1; ed. Cook 1909; see Grau 1908, Hill 1986, Biggs 1986, and Biggs 1989–90), yet here the intermediate sources are probably **HIBERNO-LATIN BIBLICAL COMMENTARIES** (see Wright 1990a and 2000). Love (2000b) lists 15.4 as an "antecedent source" for a phrase in **BEDE**'s **COMMENTARIUS IN APOCALYPSIM** (*PL* 93.160) and 8.44 as the probable source for a phrase in a spurious charter from the end of the Anglo-Saxon period; see, however, Biggs (2003 pp 4–5). Wright (1993 pp 185–87) explains that 6.42 is the antecedent source for the claim in the "Devil's Account of the Next World," an exemplum found in *Vercelli Homily* 9 (*HomS* 4, B3.2.4; ed. Scragg, *EETS*

OS 300.158–84) and other homilies (see Robinson 1972 p 369 note to lines 30–32), that "this earth is not but as the seventh part over the great Ocean" (trans. Wright 1993 p 285); he details possible intermediary sources in Irish exegesis. In discussing four questions in the Old English prose SOLOMON AND SATURN (*Sol I*, B5.1), Cross and Hill (1982 pp 93–96) cite 5.23–27 as a possible ultimate source for the identification of a best plant, best bird, best water, and best tree.

For an English translation, see *OTP* 1.525–59. Weber's *Biblia sacra iuxta Vulgatam versionem* collates only five manuscripts. Klijn (*TU* 131) draws on the known Latin manuscripts for his edition of chapters 3–14; see Stone (1990) for a commentary on these chapters. Patristic citations mainly from **AMBROSE** can be found in Violet (*GCS* 18.433–38, but see Stone 1990 p 4 note 35, who states that those of **TERTULLIAN** and **CYPRIAN** have been challenged). Useful overviews are Stone (1982) and Longenecker (1995).

**Revelation of Ezra** [ANON.Rev.Ezra]: *BPR* pp 523–24; *CAVT* 185; *RBMA* 99.
    ed.: Mercati 1901 pp 77–79.

*MSS*    1. London, BL Cotton Tiberius A.iii: HG 363.
    2. London, BL Cotton Titus D.xxvi: HG 380.
*Lists*    none.
*A-S Vers*    1. *Prog* 3.9 (Först; B23.3.3.9).
    2. *Prog* 5.1 (Warner; B23.3.5.1).
    3. *Prog* 6.4 (Cockayne; B23.3.6.4).
*Quots/Cits – Refs*    none.

The *Revelation of Ezra*, which predicts the weather for the coming year on the basis of the week day on which the new year falls, is closer in genre to the **PROGNOSTICA** than to the apocrypha; it is, however, associated with Ezra in the seventh-century *Chronicle* of John of Nikion and in Latin manuscripts such as Rome, Vatican City, Biblioteca Apostolica Vaticana Pal.lat. 1449 (Mercati 1901). The two eleventh-century manuscripts in the BL (printed in Birch 1892 pp 257–58 and Förster 1908 pp 296–97) do not associate the work with Ezra. The work also occurs in Rome, Vatican City, Biblioteca Apostolica Vaticana Pal.lat. 235, but beyond the portion of this manuscript accepted in HG 910.

In addition to the glossed Latin text, Cotton Tiberius A.iii also includes a version only in Old English (*Prog* 3.9; ed. Förster 1908). The other two Old English versions, *Prog* 5.1 (ed. Warner, *EETS* OS 152) and *Prog* 6.4 (ed. Cockayne 1864–66 3.162–64), are from the twelfth century. *Prog* 6.4, unlike the other versions known in Anglo-Saxon England, associates the predictions with Christmas rather than with the new year; this tradition is also found in London, BL Sloane 475, a manuscript not included in HG but dated by Matter (1982 p 389) to the eleventh century.

Matter (1982) pays special attention to the English transmission of the work and also provides a translation of the Latin. In addition to the Latin texts printed by Mercati (1901), a version appears in *PL* 90.951 among the doubtful works of **BEDE**.

**Psalm 151** [ANON.Ps.Sal.151]: *CAVT* 202; *ILRJH* 14; *OTP* 2.610–12; *RBMA* 105,2; Verheyden 1995 pp 393–94.
    ed.: Weber 1975 p 1975.

*MSS*    1. Cambridge, Corpus Christi College 272: HG 77.
    2. Cambridge, Corpus Christi College 391: HG 104.
    3. Cambridge, Corpus Christi College 411: HG 106.
    4. London, BL Additional 37517: HG 291.
    5. London, BL Arundel 60: HG 304.
    6. London, BL Cotton Galba A.xviii: HG 334.
    7. London, BL Cotton Vespasian A.i: HG 381.
    8. London, BL Cotton Vitellius E.xviii: HG 407.
    9. London, BL Harley 2904: HG 430.
    10. London, Lambeth Palace Library 427: HG 517.
    11. Salisbury, Cathedral Library 150: HG 740.
    12. Salisbury, Cathedral Library 180: HG 754.
    13. Florence, Biblioteca Medicea Laurenziana 1 (Amiatinus): HG 825.
    14. Rome, Vatican City, Biblioteca Apostolica Vaticana Reg.lat. 12: HG 912.
*Lists – Refs*    none.

Composed originally in Hebrew and translated in the Septuagint, *Psalm 151* draws much of its content from 1 Samuel, purporting to be spoken by David after his fight with Goliath. In the *Codex Amiatinus* it is introduced as "psalmus dauid proprie extra numerum." The psalm is also included in the Psalterium Romanum (see **LITURGY, PSALTERS**), which was brought to Canterbury by Augustine (Weber 1953 p ix), but the *Psalm* does not occur in several English manuscripts of this psalter, including New York, Pierpont Morgan Library M 776 (HG 862); Cambridge, University Library Ff.1.23 (HG 4); and Berlin, Staatsbibliothek Preussischer Kulturbesitz Hamilton 553 (HG 790). It does occur in the Additional manuscript listed above (the *Bosworth Psalter*), but without an Old English gloss (Morrell 1965 p 129). The *Vespasian Psalter*, in its original plan, deliberately omitted this *Psalm*, but it "was added by the 4th hand on an inserted leaf" (*EEMF* 14.46) and has been glossed. NRK (203) suggests that the Latin text is "probably by the same hand" as the Old English glosses, which he dates to the mid-ninth century. Morrell (1965 pp 104, 111, 114, 118) records the presence of *Psalm 151* in some Gallican Psalters with Old English glosses (nos. 5, 8, 10, and 11 above), although in these cases the psalm is apparently not glossed. Mearns (1914 pp 94–95) notes simply that this psalm "is in many of the earlier Psalters," and in addition to those already noted, he includes references to two more Gallican Psalters listed in HG (nos. 6 and 9 above). James's catalogue (1911–12 vol 2) notes the *Psalm* in the three Corpus manuscripts (the beginning is imperfect in Corpus 272), Schenkl (1891–1908 no. 3772) in the second Salisbury manuscript (no. 12 above), and Wilmart's catalogue (1937–45 vol 1) in the Vatican manuscript. On the Salisbury manuscripts, see also Webber (1992 pp 77–79).

**Song of David**: *CAVT* 152; *RBMA* 105. See PSEUDO-PHILO BIBLICAL ANTIQUITIES.

**Apocryphon of Ezechiel**: *CAVT* 244; *ILRJH* 24; *OTP* 1.487–95.

Marchand (1991) has proposed that the "Apocryphon of Ezechiel" is the source for lines 4–11 of the Old English poem that has traditionally been called *The Partridge* (*Part*, A3.18; ed. *ASPR* 3; he also cites other Old English texts). He defines this text as a single verse, "in quacumque hora peccator ingemuerit et conversus fuit, salvus erit," which, citing earlier scholarship, he claims "was connected . . . with an Ezechiel apocryphon found in Clement of Rome and other early fathers" (p 607). Five fragments are considered part of this work (Mueller 1994); Marchand's verse does not appear among them. James (1914 pp 240–41) considers his verse "a loose quotation" of Ezechiel 33.11 "perhaps conflated with the Old Latin" of Isaias 30.15; see also Ezechiel 18.21.

**Sibylline Oracles** [ANON.Sib.]: *ANT* pp 613–15; *BPR* pp 795–849; *CANT* 319; *CAVT* 274; *CPG* 1352; *ILRJH* 32; *NTA* 2.652–85; *NTAP* 88; *OTP* 1.317–472; *RBMA* 122.
 ed.: *GCS* 8.1–226.

Surviving primarily in Greek, the *Sibylline Oracles* span the pagan, Jewish, and Christian traditions, having been written between the second century B.C. and the seventh century A.D. According to Collins (*OTP* 1.318), "the most characteristic feature" of these works "is the prediction of woes and disasters to come upon mankind." The Latin tradition, as Bischoff (1951) has shown, is dominated by the discussions of **LACTANTIUS** and particularly **AUGUSTINE**, who in DE CIVITATE DEI XVIII.23 (*CCSL* 48) includes a Latin translation of a Greek acrostic poem and a collection of oracles drawn from Lactantius. See also the following entry for another translation of the acrostic poem, and Bischoff (1951) for other Latin fragments, including one printed among the "dubia" of **BEDE** (*PL* 90.1181–86; *RBMA* 124). Lendinara (2003 pp 96–98) notes versions of the poem in Cambridge, Corpus Christi College 173 (HG 53); Cambridge, Corpus Christi College 448 (HG 114); London, BL Royal 15.B. XIX (HG 493); and Boulogne-sur-Mer, Bibliothèque Municipale 189 (HG 805).

In CATHOLIC HOMILIES II, 1 (*ÆCHom* II, 1; B1.2.2; ed. Godden, *EETS* SS 5.9),
ÆLFRIC follows his source, QUODVULTDEUS's CONTRA IUDAEOS, PAGANOS
ET ARIANOS (as Cross 1963 pp 14–15 noted), and remarks that a heathen prophetess
named "Sibylla" foretold Christ's Nativity, Passion, Resurrection, Ascension, and
Second Coming; see also Godden, *EETS* SS 18.346–53. Ælfric expands this remark in
his discussion of the Old Testament canon in his *Letter to Sigeweard* (*ÆLet* 4, B1.8.4.3;
ed. Crawford, *EETS* OS 160.46), where he identifies the Sibyls as ten virgins who
prophesied Christ to the heathens; in doing so, he was apparently following a tradition
about the Sibyls represented in ISIDORE's ETYMOLOGIAE VIII.8 (ed. Lindsay 1911;
see Biggs 2005a pp 484–85).

Grau (1908 pp 51 and 67) cites Augustine's translation of the acrostic poem and a
passage in the Greek text as possible sources for *Christ III* (*ChristC*, A3.1; 964–70a and
1195; ed. Cook 1909); neither, however, is conclusive (see Biggs 1986 pp 13 and 24).
Geffcken (*GCS* 8) edits the Greek text. English translations appear in *OTP* 1.335–472
and *NTA* 2.709–45.

**Versus sibyllae de iudicio** [ANON.Sib.ver.]: *ICL* 8497; see previous entry.
    ed.: Bulst 1938 pp 105–06.

*MSS – A-S Vers*    none.
*Quots/Cits*    1. Sib.ver. 12: ALDH.Metr. 93.33.
    2. Sib.ver. 14: ALDH.Metr. 93.22.
    3. Sib.ver. 28: ALDH.Metr. 79.24.
*Refs*    none.

This thirty-four-line poem, beginning "Iudicio tellus sudabit maesta propinquo,"
is an independent translation of the same acrostic poem included by AUGUSTINE in
DE CIVITATE DEI (see previous entry). It survives in only one manuscript and is
apparently quoted only by ALDHELM (DE METRIS; ed. *MGH* AA 15), who names
his source on three occasions; for other possible borrowings in his work, see Orchard
(1994 pp 195–200). Bulst (1938 pp 109–11) associates it with the school of
THEODORE OF CANTERBURY and HADRIAN; Lapidge (in Bischoff and
Lapidge 1994 pp 184–85) agrees, adding that it is "unlikely" that "a complete Greek
text of *Oracula Sibyllina*" was known at the school. Lapidge (in Lapidge and Rosier
1985 p 265 note 8) considers it unlikely that Aldhelm translated the poem himself
since his knowledge of Greek was limited (see also Orchard 1994 pp 197–98, who
reaches the same conclusion on metrical and other grounds). Lapidge (in Bischoff and
Lapidge 1994 p 185 note 219) speculates that "a copy of the poem may have formed
part of the sylloge of Milred of Worcester (d. 775), although certainty is impossible."
See MILRED OF WORCESTER and Lendinara (2003).
**Pseudo-Methodius Revelations** [ANON.Rev./PS.METH.1]: *BPR* pp 317–20; *CAVT*
254; *CPG* 1830; *RBMA* 124,4–8.
    ed.: Aerts and Kortekaas 1998 1.71–199.

*MSS*      Salisbury, Cathedral Library 165: HG 749.
*Lists – A-S Vers*      none.
*Quots/Cits*      see below.
*Refs*      see below.

    The original version of the *Revelations* is a Syriac apocalypse divided into historical and prophetic sections. It recounts the Creation, Fall, and Flood, followed by the succession of empires, the Arab invasions, the eventual triumph of the Last Roman Emperor, the coming of the Antichrist, and the end of the world. Composed around 690 (Reinink 1993 1.xii–xxix), it was translated into Greek around 700–710 and into Latin around 732 (Aerts and Kortekaas 1998 1.1–35), and thence into various vernaculars, directly influencing **ADSO**'s **DE ORTU ET TEMPORE ANTICHRISTI** (Verhelst 1973 pp 94–97), the *Visions of Daniel*, the medieval Alexander legend (Alexander 1985 pp 188–89), the *Cosmographia* of **AETHICUS ISTER** (*KVS* p 576), and possibly the Pseudo-Ephremian *Sermo de fine mundi* (Reinink 1996).

    Of the more than twenty-two pre-twelfth-century Latin manuscripts of the *Revelations*, which reflect four different recensions (Laureys and Verhelst 1988; Prinz 1985 pp 4–5), only Salisbury 165 (art. 2, fols 11–22; not in Laureys and Verhelst 1988, nor used by Aerts and Kortekaas 1998; see Webber 1992 pp 15–16 and 153; and Twomey forthcoming) and London, BL Royal 5.F.XVIII (see next entry), copied at Salisbury, are accepted as originating in England before 1100. With the exception of Salisbury 165, which is a first-recension text, all copies of the *Revelations* of established English origin, including later Middle English translations, are second-recension texts (see Twomey forthcoming).

    London, BL Cotton Claudius B.iv (the Old English *Hexateuch*, B8.1.4.1–6) contains Latin and late Old English notes to Genesis (B8.1.4.7) that cite "Methodius" but are drawn from Peter Comestor, *Historia scholastica* (ca. 1173), not from the *Revelations* (Stoneman 1984). Crawford (1923 and *EETS* OS 160.419–22) transcribes only the Old English notes; see nos. 1, 6, 7, 12, 13, and possibly 18. The Latin notes citing "Methodius" can be found in *EEMF* 18, fols 3v, 8, 12v, and 28. The Kentish characteristics of the Old English notes are cited as partial evidence of the manuscript's Canterbury provenance (*EEMF* 18.16; NRK 142).

    Hill (1987) notes that in preserving the tradition of a fourth son of Noah, the *Revelations* may be relevant to the West-Saxon royal genealogies; see also the **CAVE OF TREASURES**. The text of the Syrian original is printed by Reinink (1993). The first Greek and first Latin recensions are in the facing-page edition of Aerts and Kortekaas (1998). All four Greek recensions are in Lolos (1976). An earlier text of the first Latin recension is in Sackur (1898).

Michael W. Twomey

**Pseudo-Methodius Revelations** [ANON.Rev./PS.METH.2]: *BPR* pp 317–20; *CAVT* 254; *CPG* 1830; *RBMA* 124,4–8.
    ed.: Prinz 1985 pp 6–17.

*MSS*      London, BL Royal 5.F.XVIII: HG 463.5.
*Lists – A-S Vers*    none.
*Quots/Cits*     see previous entry.
*Refs*      see previous entry.

With the exception of Salisbury 165 (see previous entry), all copies of the *Revelations* of established English origin, including later Middle English translations, are second-recension texts (Twomey forthcoming). Royal 5.F.XVIII (art. 2, fols 29v–32v) was copied at Salisbury (Webber 1992 pp 13, 16, 145–46, and 153).

Prinz groups the Royal manuscript with four others including Oxford, St. John's College 128, which he dates, citing a private communication from Bernhard Bischoff, to the second half of the twelfth century (p 4 note 17); Hanna (2002 p 179) considers it to be from the beginning of the twelfth century. D'Evelyn (1918 pp 192–203) prints this manuscript, listing variants from Oxford, Bodleian Library Bodley 163, a composite manuscript, quite possibly from Peterborough Abbey. The first part of Bodley 163 was known in Anglo-Saxon England (HG 555). The *Revelations* occurs in the second part (fols 245r–248v). Ker (1964 p 151; not in Watson 1987) dated the manuscript to the eleventh century without distinguishing the parts; part two has most recently been dated to the early-twelfth century (Friis-Jensen and Willoughby 2001 p 6).

Michael W. Twomey

# APOCRYPHA ABOUT CHRIST AND MARY

Considered here are texts related to the lives of Jesus and Mary, some of which might justifiably be referred to as "gospels" since, to use Elliott's phrase but in a wider context, they "developed from, or were inspired by, the canonical Gospels" (*ANT* p 47). The order of presentation follows the chronology of the Bible, with some attention given to thematic relationships among the texts: narratives of Christ's birth and childhood, or "Infancy Gospels" (the PROTEVANGELIUM OF JAMES, the GOSPEL OF PSEUDO-MATTHEW, and DE NATIVITATE MARIAE; see *AG* p 64); narratives of Christ's death and resurrection (the GOSPEL OF BARTHOLOMEW, the GOSPEL OF NICODEMUS, and the VINDICTA SALVATORIS); and narratives of Mary's death and Assumption (the TRANSITUS OF PSEUDO-MELITO [B²] and TRANSITUS W). For the LETTERS OF CHRIST AND ABGAR, see APOCRYPHAL EPISTLES. For the TRINUBIUM ANNAE, see MISCELLANEOUS. For the *Inventio capitis Iohannis Baptistae* (*BHL* 4290–91) see the entry for IOHANNES BAPTISTA in ACTA SANCTORUM.

While a passage at the beginning of BEDE's COMMENTARIUS IN LUCAM (*CCSL* 120.19) might suggest that he knew a variety of apocryphal gospels, other sources, especially JEROME's preface to his COMMENTARII IN EVANGELIUM MATTHAEI (*CCSL* 77.1), may have provided his information (see Biggs 2003 pp 15–16). Following the homily for the sixteenth Sunday after Pentecost in the CATHOLIC HOMILIES II, ÆLFRIC includes a brief note on the birth of the Virgin ("De Maria") in which he condemns apocryphal traditions (*ÆCHom* II, 36.2; ed. Godden, *EETS* SS 5.271), while recording some material derived ultimately from them. Similarly, in his homily for the Nativity of the Blessed Virgin Mary (*ÆHomM* 8; *BaP* 3.24–48 lines 1–9), he again states that he will avoid apocrypha; on these passages, see Biggs (forthcoming). According to Clayton (1998 pp 114–15), "the feast of the conception of the Virgin was introduced in Winchester *c.* 1030," and the resulting liturgical texts draw on apocryphal traditions.

**Protevangelium of James** [ANON.Proteuang.Iac.]: *AG* pp 65–72; *ANT* pp 48–67; *BHG* 1046; *CANT* 50; *NTA* 1.421–39; *NTAP* 35; *RBMA* 141.
    ed.: *NTA* 1.426–37.

*MSS*    see next entry.
*Lists – Quots/Cits*    none.

*Refs*      ? for Ælfric, see the headnote to APOCRYPHA ABOUT CHRIST AND MARY
above.

This Greek apocryphon, compiled about A.D. 180 x 200, very likely in Egypt
(*CCSA* 9.4; Cothenet 1988), contains the earliest written account of the Nativity and
dedication of Mary, providing the names for her parents. It also recounts the miracles
attending the births of John the Baptist and Christ, the flight of John and Elizabeth
from Herod, and the murder of Zacharias. It survives in 140 Greek manuscripts, and
translations exist in at least seven other Eastern languages. No complete Latin translation remains, but various parts of the work occur in several contexts (see Kaestli
1996); see the following entry for a version of chapters 1–8.1. It was condemned in the
**GELASIAN DECREE** (ed. Dobschütz, *TU* 38/4 line 271; see *ANT* p 86).

Ties with Old English literature are not well established. Hill (1972a) proposed
the *Protevangelium* as the source for a passage in the Exeter Book poem *Descent into
Hell* (*Hell*, A3.26; ed. *ASPR* 3, lines 99–106) on the stasis of the Jordan River, but see
Hall (1989–90 pp 75–80) for an alternative interpretation which links the Jordan's
stasis instead to an exegetical tradition rooted in commentary on Psalm 113.3. Remly
(1974) advanced this apocryphon as the source for a passage in *Vercelli Homily* 10
(*HomS* 40.3, B3.2.40.6; ed. Scragg, *EETS* OS 300.203); Scragg's notes on lines 122
and 127 (*EETS* OS 300.215) explain the allusions without mentioning the apocry-
phon. The influence of the *Protevangelium* or another "Infancy Gospel" has also been
proposed for the Joseph-Mary dialogue (lyric 7) in the *Advent Lyrics* (*ChristA*, A3.1; ed.
*ASPR* 3). Cook (1909 p 99) refers to the *Protevangelium*, the **GOSPEL OF PSEUDO-
MATTHEW**, the **DE NATIVITATE MARIAE**, and the *History of Joseph the Carpenter*
(*ANT* pp 111–17; *CANT* 60; *NTAP* 46; at present there is no evidence of this work in
Anglo-Saxon England) in the notes to lines 186 ff. and 190 ff.; for further bibliography,
see Reinsch (1879 p 124). Burlin (1968 p 117) discounts the *Protevangelium* as the
direct source, concentrating instead on the possibility of an intermediary homily. Hill
(1977b p 14), who identifies a liturgical source, notes that the "development of the
dialogue no doubt owes something to the quasi-dramatic texts which A. S. Cook has
cited as analogues."

Two miniatures in the *Caligula Troper* (see **LITURGY**, **TROPERS**; *IASIM* 202.7
and 8) depict apocryphal legends of the conception and birth of Mary. In one an angel
announces Mary's birth to Joachim; Clayton (1998 p 113) argues that "the animals
depicted with Joachim point to this cycle having been derived from one designed to
accompany the Greek *Proteuangelium*" and that "the hexameters accompanying the
Annunciation illustration could be read as implying that Anna was already pregnant
when the angel appeared to Joachim, a reading in accordance with both the
*Proteuangelium* and the *Pseudo-Matthew*." For the second miniature, see *De Nativitate
Mariae*.

The edition designated above is a translation based on the editions of the Greek
by Tischendorf (1876) and de Strycker (1961), taking into account the evidence of a
fourth-century papyrus discovered in 1958. A new edition of the Greek text by A. Frey
is forthcoming in *CCSA*. Other evidence for early circulation of a Latin version in the
British Isles is offered by McNamara (1975), who draws attention to several distinc-

tively Insular features of the *Protevangelium* in Montpellier, École de Medicine 55 (eighth/ninth century), concluding that Ireland in particular was "connected with the transmission, or even the formation of this Latin rendering of the *Protevangelium*" (p 39; see also pp 42–47 and 49). See also McNamara (*CCSA* 13 and 14).

Thomas N. Hall

**Protevangelium of James** [ANON.Proteuang.Iac.serm.]: *BHL* 5342c.
  ed.: Clayton 1998 pp 319–22.

*MSS*      Cambridge, Pembroke College 25: HG 131.
*Lists – Quots/Cits*      none.
*Refs*      ? for Ælfric, see the headnote to APOCRYPHA ABOUT CHRIST AND MARY above.

As noted by Clayton (1986a p 289) and Cross (1987a p 37 item 51), a Latin version of chapters 1–8.1 was known in England from its inclusion in a sermon on the Nativity of Mary in Pembroke 25 (see HOMILIARIES, HOMILIARY OF SAINT-PÈRE DE CHARTRES). For other manuscripts of this sermon and its relationship to other versions of the apocryphon, see Kaestli (1996) and Clayton (1998 pp 315–17).

Thomas N. Hall

**Gospel of Pseudo-Matthew** [ANON.Euang.Ps.Mt.]: *AG* pp 78–81; *ANT* pp 84–99; *BHL* 5334–42; *CANT* 51; *NTA* 1.458; *NTAP* 53; *RBMA* 168.
  ed.: *CCSA* 9.277–481.

*MSS*      see next entry.
*Lists*      none.
*A-S Vers*      1. *LS* 18 (B3.3.18).
       2. ? *Mart* (B19.gx): see next entry
*Quots/Cits*      HomU 10 (*VercHom* 6, B3.4.10): see below.
*Refs*      ? for Ælfric, see the headnote to APOCRYPHA ABOUT CHRIST AND MARY above.

The *Gospel of Pseudo-Matthew* is a re-working of chapters 1–17.2 of the PROTE-VANGELIUM OF JAMES to which has been added an account of the flight into Egypt (chapters 18–24; see Clayton 1998 p 19). A final section (chapters 25–42), missing in most manuscripts but included by Tischendorf (1876 pp 93–111), is drawn from the *Infancy Gospel of Thomas* (*AG* pp 73–78; *CANT* 57; *RBMA* 175,2–23; there is no independent evidence for the knowledge of this work in Anglo-Saxon England), narrating the eccentric childhood miracles of Christ; Gijsel excludes this material from his edition (*CCSA* 9; see pp 40–42). Rather than trying to reconstruct the text of the author who adapted the *Protevangelium of James* probably in the first quarter of the seventh century (*CCSA* 9.67), Gijsel edits the two Carolingian versions of the text, which differ, for example, in their prologues. On possible references to this work in the **GELASIAN DECREE**, see *ANT* p 86. The attribution to **PASCHASIUS RAD-BERTUS** (see Canal-Sánchez 1968 p 473) is no longer accepted.

One partial translation exists in Old English in an anonymous sermon on the Nativity of Mary (*LS* 18, B3.3.18; ed. Clayton 1998 pp 164–90, replacing *BaP* 3.117–37). The text translates chapters 1–12 of *Pseudo-Matthew* beginning with the infertile marriage of Anne and Joachim and continuing through the doubting of Mary. Source relationships are detailed in Clayton (2000).

A series of translated excerpts is also incorporated into *Vercelli Homily 6* (*HomU* 10; ed. Scragg, *EETS* OS 300). Developing the work of Förster (*BaP* 12.134–36), Scragg (*EETS* OS 300.126) notes that lines 55–58 "relate the birth of Christ in a single sentence taken from the middle of chapter 13 of the *Euangelium* [*pseudo-Matthaei*]" and that lines 59–80 contain a "selective" translation of chapters 17–24; see also Atherton (1996). Scragg's claim, however, that lines 81–83 and 83–85 rely on chapters 25 and 42 is contested by Biggs (2002). Cross and Hill (1982 p 80) note that in specifying Mary's age as fourteen at the time of Christ's birth, the Old English prose **SOLOMON AND SATURN** (*Sol I*, B5.1) agrees with *Pseudo-Matthew* and **DE NATIVITATE MARIAE** as well as the *History of Joseph the Carpenter* (*ANT* pp 111–17; *CANT* 60; *NTAP* 46), a text apparently unknown in Anglo-Saxon England. Citing Napier (1889), they note that this detail can be found in a number of "snippets" in Old English manuscripts.

The account of Mary's birth (chapters 1–6.3) circulated independently in Anglo-Saxon England (see the following entry). It is possible, then, that the discussion in the **OLD ENGLISH MARTYROLOGY**, which relies on these chapters, is drawn specifically from this source; see the following entry. Clayton (1990b) asserts that chapter 2 is the "certain, direct source" for lines 10–19 in **ÆLFRIC**'s homily for the Nativity of the Blessed Virgin Mary (*ÆHomM* 8 [Ass 3], B1.5.8; ed. *BaP* 3.24–48); see, however, Biggs (forthcoming).

Elsewhere, two episodes from *Pseudo-Matthew* (from chapters 23 and 24) are paralleled in a sermon on the Nativity of the Innocents in Pembroke 25 (see Cross 1987a p 23, item 11; Cross 1987b p 64; and **HOMILIARIES, HOMILIARY OF SAINT-PÈRE DE CHARTRES**). A Latin gloss to Psalm 148.10 in Rome, Vatican City, Biblioteca Apostolica Vaticana Pal.lat. 68 (HG 909; **GLOSSA IN PSALMOS**, see **HIBERNO-LATIN BIBLICAL COMMENTARIES**, no. 10; see Wright 1990a) quotes from *Pseudo-Matthew* 18.1 (McNamara 1986 p 308). Also relevant is Saxl's argument (1943 pp 4–5) for at least indirect influence of an Infancy Gospel, probably *Pseudo-Matthew*, on the Flight into Egypt (or out of Egypt) panel on the Ruthwell Cross, a suggestion endorsed by Swanton (1996 pp 15–16).

For the first illustration in the *Caligula Troper*, see the main entry on the **PROTEVANGELIUM OF JAMES**. For early Irish knowledge of this work, see McNamara

(1975 p 48); note too that the *Gospel of Thomas* circulated in Ireland. For further discussion of the Old English evidence, see Healey (1985 pp 102–03).

Thomas N. Hall

**Gospel of Pseudo-Matthew** [ANON.Euang.Ps.Mt.serm.].
    ed.: Clayton 1998 pp 323–27.

*MSS*        London, BL Cotton Nero E.i: HG 344.
*Lists*      none.
*A-S Vers*    ? *Mart* (B19.gx).
*Quots/Cits*   none
*Refs*       ? for Ælfric, see the headnote to APOCRYPHA ABOUT CHRIST AND MARY
          above.

The story of the birth of Mary, taken from chapters 1–6.3 of *Pseudo-Matthew*, is preserved as a Latin sermon in the COTTON-CORPUS LEGENDARY (see Cross 1985b pp 125–26, who shows that this sermon also appears in ninth-century continental manuscripts; and Jackson and Lapidge 1996 p 136). Kotzor (1981 2.348–49) notes that the details concerning the birth of Mary in the OLD ENGLISH MARTYROLOGY (B19) could have derived from this version. See also Cross (1985a p 248), Clayton (1998 pp 107–08), Rauer (2000), and Lapidge (2005).

Thomas N. Hall

**De Nativitate Mariae** [ANON.Nat.Mariae]: *BHL* 5343–45; *CANT* 52; *NTAP* 50; *RBMA* 160.
    ed.: *CCSA* 10.269–333.

*MSS*        1. Durham, Cathedral Library A.III.29: HG 222.
          2. Salisbury, Cathedral Library 179: HG 753.
*Lists – Quots/Cits*        none.
*Refs*       ? for Ælfric, see the headnote to APOCRYPHA ABOUT CHRIST AND MARY
          above.

*De Nativitate Mariae*, a revision of the GOSPEL OF PSEUDO-MATTHEW, dates not from the Carolingian period (it has been frequently attributed to PASCHASIUS RADBERTUS), but according to Beyers (*CCSA* 10.32–33) to the tenth or early eleventh century. The first proof of the existence of the apocryphon is in an early eleventh-century sermon by FULBERT OF CHARTRES (SERMO 4, DE NATIVI-TATE MARIAE, lines 6–29 [*PL* 141.320]; see *CCSA* 10.32). Fassler (2000 p 401) has even suggested that it may have been Fulbert himself who composed the *De Nativitate Mariae*, although she concedes that there is no hard evidence to support such an ascription.

*De Nativitate Mariae* was clearly known in Winchester in the eleventh century. The Durham manuscript, a version of the HOMILIARIUM of PAUL THE DEACON, has Winchester connections, as it contains texts for the two feasts of SWITHUNUS and for the feasts of BIRINUS and ÆTHELDRYTHA (see ACTA SANCTORUM). The author of the benediction for the feast of the Conception of the Virgin in the *Canterbury Benedictional* (*HBS* 51.118–19; see LITURGY, PONTIF-ICALS AND BENEDICTIONALS) appears to have known the text also since he refers to the angel's announcement of Mary's name before her birth, a detail that seems to depend on the *De Nativitate Mariae* (Clayton 1998 p 115). Prescott (1987) argues that the *Canterbury Benedictional* was probably composed in Winchester. On the Salisbury manuscript, dated to the end of the eleventh century, see Webber (1992 pp 8–21 and 153–54).

For a possible use of the text in the Old English prose SOLOMON AND SATURN (*Sol I*, B5.1), see the first entry above on the *Gospel of Pseudo-Matthew*.

Mary Clayton

**Questions of Bartholomew** [ANON.Quaest.Bart.]: *AG* pp 99–102; *ANT* pp 652–68; *CANT* 63; *NTA* 1.537–51; *NTAP* 17; *RBMA* 135.
    ed.: Moricca 1921 and 1922.

*MSS – Quots/Cits*      none.
*Refs*      BEDA.Comm.Luc. I.22: see below.

In the preface to his COMMENTARII IN EVANGELIUM MATTHAEI (*CCSL* 77.1), JEROME mentions Bartholomew in a list of authors supposed to have written gospels, and the GELASIAN DECREE (ed. Dobschütz, *TU* 38/4 line 275) also refers to *Evangelia nomine Bartholomaei*. Jerome's reference, however, may be taken from ORIGEN's first homily on Luke, while the *Gelasian Decree* may in turn depend on Jerome. Two surviving works have been identified with the *Gospel of Bartholomew*: a Coptic BOOK OF THE RESURRECTION OF CHRIST BY BARTHOLOMEW and the *Questions of Bartholomew* extant in Greek, Slavonic, and Latin. Kaestli (1988) urges that the latter work should be designated *Questions of Bartholomew* (as in the Slavonic and in one of the Latin manuscripts) rather than "Gospel of Bartholomew" (see pp 8–9), and suggests that the gospel mentioned by Jerome and the *Gelasian Decree* may be a different work, perhaps attested in other scattered allusions and citations (p 9 note 14; see also Cherchi 1984). Kaestli concludes that the Coptic work has "only a few motifs in common" with the *Questions of Bartholomew*, "and they cannot be two recensions of the same original writing" (English Summary, p 6). Regarding the relationships of the various versions of the *Questions of Bartholomew*, Kaestli stresses that the conclusions of Wilmart and Tisserant (1913) must be reassessed in light of the evidence of the complete Latin text published by Moricca (1921 and 1922). *ANT* and *NTA* include eclectic English translations of the *Questions of Bartholomew*, conflating the various versions; for criticisms of the previous editions, see Kaestli (1988 pp 18–21). For annotated French translations, see Kaestli and Cherix (1997) and Kaestli (1997).

Two manuscripts preserve Latin translations of the *Questions of Bartholomew*: Rome, Vatican City, Biblioteca Apostolica Vaticana Reg.lat. 1050 (ninth century), which contains three fragments of the text (1.21–30, 4.7–29, and 4.51–54), edited by Wilmart and Tisserant (1913), and Rome, Biblioteca Casanatense 1880 (tenth century), the only complete version, edited by Moricca (1921 and 1922).

Bartholomew's exalted role as interlocutor and visionary seems to be due to his identification with Nathanahel in John 1.47. After witnessing the angels descending upon Christ at the Crucifixion (cf. John 1.51), Bartholomew puts questions to Christ, to Mary, and to Satan. In response, Christ relates his harrowing of hell; Mary relates how she conceived Jesus; Christ shows the apostles the abyss; Beliar/Satan is compelled to tell Bartholomew the names of the angels of the winds and the elements and recounts the creation of Adam and the fall of the angels who refused to worship Adam; and Christ identifies the most grievous sins.

BEDE's reference in his COMMENTARIUS IN LUCAM (*CCSL* 120.19) to a gospel written by Bartholomew depends on Jerome's *Commentarii in Evangelium Matthaei* (*CCSL* 77.1).

Gollancz (1927 p civ) suggests that the devils' reference to a "son" of Satan in *Christ and Satan*, lines 63–64 (*Sat*, A1.4; ed. *ASPR* 1) may depend on the *Questions of Bartholomew*, in which Satan has a son named Salpsan. Other plausible explanations have been offered for the allusion (see Clubb 1925 pp 62–63; Finnegan 1977 p 27; and Hill 1977c pp 323–35), but Morey (1990 p 401) supports Gollancz's suggestion and argues that the *Questions* may also lie behind the poem's statement in line 20a that Adam was created before the fall of Lucifer. Anlezark (2003 pp 127–28) suggests that passages in *Solomon and Saturn II* (*MSol*, A13; ed. Menner 1941; SOLOMON AND SATURN) referring to Lucifer's intent to propagate himself with other fallen angels (lines 446–47a) and to the *bearn heofonwara* (line 455b) who fell with him may also reflect the influence of the *Questions*. Doane (1991 p 98) cites a speech by the bound Satan in "The Gospel of Bartholomew" (44, trans. James 1924 p 177) as "closely resembling" *Genesis B* (*GenB*, A1.1; ed. *ASPR* 1) lines 368ff. in that Satan states that he sends subordinate demons to tempt humans.

Grant (1982 pp 43 and 46) cites the "Gospel of Bartholomew" among other apocryphal texts for the archangel Michael's participation in creation and struggle with Satan in an anonymous homily on Michael, *LS* 24 (MichaelTristr, B3.3.24; ed. Grant 1982 pp 56–77).

Henderson (1986 p 81 note 33) refers to the "Gospel of Bartholomew" (i.e. the *Questions of Bartholomew*, translated by James 1924 pp 174–75) as a possible source for Bartholomew's power over the devils in *Guthlac A* (*GuthA*, A3.2; ed. Roberts 1979); but see Hill (1979 p 185 note 1) for another possible source in PSEUDO-ISIDORE, DE ORTU ET OBITU PATRUM (where the section on Bartholomew is dependent on PSEUDO-ABDIAS APOSTOLIC HISTORIES according to Dumville 1973 p 314).

Wright (1987 pp 142–43) cites a passage from the *Questions of Bartholomew* (p 512) as a possible source for a description of the creation of Adam (DE PLASMATIONE ADAM) found in four early manuscripts, including an Anglo-Saxon missionary manuscript known as the *Vocabularius Sancti Galli* (St. Gall, Stiftsbibliothek 913, second half of the eighth century, "by a scribe trained in the Anglo-Saxon tradition," *CLA* 7.976; ed. Baesecke 1933 p 8). Wright (1987 pp 142–43) draws attention to a similar description of the creation of Adam in the probably Irish *Fragmentum Pragense* (*CPL* 2255; *KVS* An creat; ed. *PLS* 2.1484–85), where it is accompanied by allusions to the creation of the angels from fire and water and to the prior creation of Satanahel, both motifs also found in the *Questions of Bartholomew*.

Charles D. Wright

**Book of the Resurrection of Christ by Bartholomew** [ANON.Res.Christ. Bart.]: *AG* pp 102–04; *ANT* pp 668–72; *CANT* 80; *ILRJH* pp 51–52; *NTA* 1.553–57; *NTAP* 16; see *RBMA* 135.
     ed.: Budge 1913 pp 1–48.

*MSS – Refs*          none.

The *Book of the Resurrection of Christ* survives only in Coptic, including the nearly complete London, BL manuscript (Oriental 6804) edited by Budge and a series of fragments, some of which include material not paralleled in the London text that may belong rather to the *Gospel of Gamaliel*. Budge (1913 pp 70–130) includes an English translation; for annotated French translations based on the London manuscript but taking into account the fragments, see Kaestli and Cherix (1997) and Kaestli (1997). On the relationship between this work and the "Gospel of Bartholomew," see the QUESTIONS OF BARTHOLOMEW.

The London version begins with the burial of Jesus by Joseph of Arimathea. Death, accompanied by his six sons in the form of serpents, comes to the tomb of Jesus but flees when Jesus reveals his face and laughs at him. Jesus then harrows hell, leaving it empty but for three souls (Herod, Cain, and Judas, according to a Paris fragment). He appears to the three Marys and other women in the garden of Philogenes, and ascends to heaven with Adam and the other redeemed souls, whose glorious reception is witnessed by Bartholomew in a vision. A new section describes how Jesus in the seventh heaven has the Father bless each of the apostles. Jesus now appears to them at Galilee, but Thomas has returned home to resurrect his dead son Siophanes, whom he makes bishop of a group of converts. When Thomas rejoins the other apostles at the Mount of Olives, he doubts their account of the resurrected Christ's appearance, so Jesus appears again and has Thomas touch his wounds. After

Jesus ascends to heaven, the apostles celebrate the Eucharist and then separate to preach.

Heimann (1966 p 41) states that the six dragons springing from the head of Satan/Mors in the Vita-Mors drawing of the *Sphaera Apulei* in the *Leofric Missal* (Oxford, Bodleian Library Bodley 579, fol 50; reproduced in Temple 1976 plate 56; see also **LITURGY, MASSBOOKS**) "are clearly the six sons of Death mentioned in the apocryphal Coptic *Book of the Resurrection of Christ*," and proposes the same source for another drawing in the *Stuttgart Psalter* (p 44). Deshman (1977 p 167) accepts Heimann's identification, but Jordan (1986 p 293; see also p 314 note 32) dismisses it with the comment that "there is no evidence that the work was ever known in the West during the Middle Ages," referring instead to a cryptic allusion in **ALDHELM**'s **AENIGMATA** (Riddle 81, *De Lucifero*; ed. *MGH* AA 15.134–35) to Lucifer's "six companions" (*comites*); but this allusion is explained as the six *sidera errantia* in a gloss in London, BL Royal 12.C.XXIII (HG 478; ed. Stork 1990 p 203).

Charles D. Wright

**Gospel of Nicodemus** [ANON.Euang.Nic.]: *AG* pp 88–97; *ANT* pp 164–204; *CANT* 62; *DB* 3.544–47; *NTA* 1.501–36; *NTAP* 57; *RBMA* 179,4–27.
    ed.: Cross 1996 pp 138–246.

*MSS*      1. London, BL Royal 5.E.XIII: HG 459.
        2. Saint-Omer, Bibliothèque Municipale 202: HG 930.5.
*Lists*      1. Exeter: ML 10.14.
        2. Exeter: ML 10.21.
*A-S Vers*      1. *NicA* (B8.5.2.1).
        2. *NicB* (B8.5.2.2).
        3. *NicC* (B8.5.3.1).
*Quots/Cits – Refs*      none.

The title *Gospel of Nicodemus*, used in the later Middle Ages (e.g. Vincent of Beauvais, *Speculum historiale* VII.40), has been applied in different ways to the various recensions of the work distinguished in the scholarship. Since translations of Greek recension A (Tischendorf 1876) exist in several oriental languages, scholars generally agree that it represents the original version, but they disagree on when it was composed; see Hall (1996 p 37: between the second and fourth centuries), Izydorczyk and Dubois (1997 p 40: prior to the latter half of the fourth century), and *ANT* (fifth-sixth century). A fifth-century palimpsest in Vienna (*CLA* 10.1485; ed. Philippart 1989) preserves fragments of a Latin translation. This version, known as the *Commentaries of Nicodemus* (the titles *Acta Pilati* and *Gesta Pilati* are sometimes applied to this part and sometimes to the whole work), retells the trial, Passion, Resurrection, and Ascension of Christ. To it was added the "Descensus ad inferos"; Hall (1996 p 45) suggests that this part of the work "had already achieved a more or less fixed state by the end of the third century"; see also O'Ceallaigh (1963) and Collett (1981). It claims to be by Karinus and Leucius, two "eyewitnesses" who arose at the Crucifixion (Matthew 27.52–53). At least three Latin recensions of this work can be identified, although the precise relationships between them have yet to be determined (Izydorczyk and Dubois 1997 p 30). Of main interest to Anglo-Saxonists is Latin recension A, which appends a letter from Pilate to the emperor Claudius. Hall (1996 p 46) notes that the most common name for the apocryphon in Latin manuscripts from the ninth to the thirteenth century is *Gesta Salvatoris*.

The London manuscript, written in the mid- to late-ninth century probably in Brittany, was in England by the tenth century (see Petitmengin 1993 pp 622–26, Hall 1996 pp 48–49, and Ambrose 2005 pp 208–14); Cross (1996) provides some variant readings from it. It omits the prologue and the manuscript ends as a palimpsest shortly before the end of chapter 27. The Saint-Omer manuscript, probably copied at Saint-Bertin in the late-ninth century, appears to have been in England by the middle of the eleventh century (Cross and Crick 1996 p 17), and is probably the manuscript referred to in Leofric's donation list to Exeter (ML 10.21; see Cross and Crick 1996 p 35). This manuscript was used for the Old English translation of the work preserved in Cambridge, University Library, Ii.2.11 (*NicA*; ed. Cross 1996 pp 139–247), itself recorded in the Exeter donation list (ML 10.14).

Writing before Cross's discovery of the significance of the Saint-Omer manuscript, Campbell (1982 p 114) claimed that each of the three Old English versions "seems to descend independently from the translator's autograph." The earliest manuscript is the one that contains *NicA*; in it the apocryphon follows the canonical Gospels (see Marx 1997 pp 208–10). Cross (1996 p 134) notes that *NicB* (London, BL Cotton Vitellius A.xv; ed. Hulme 1898) "corresponds with A very closely in idea and often in word," yet it is missing approximately two printed pages at its beginning. *NicC* (London, BL Cotton Vespasian D.xiv; ed. Hulme 1903–04 pp 591–610) abridges the material for presentation as a homily. For editions and discussion of these versions, see also Allen (1968).

In addition to the direct use of Latin recension A, scholars have often cited the *Gospel of Nicodemus* when discussing examples of the Harrowing; see Clubb (1925 p 98); Crotty (1939 pp 349–52); and Allen and Calder (1976 pp 175–76). The motif is popular in Old English poetry and prose from at least as early as the time of **BEDE** (see, for example, his **RETRACTATIO IN ACTUS APOSTOLORUM**; ed. *CCSL* 121 2.120–30). The issue, however, is complicated both by the evolution of orthodox Church doctrine and by popular developments of the theme.

Independent of the *Gospel of Nicodemus* proper, but of particular interest to Anglo-Saxonists, is **PSEUDO-AUGUSTINE, SERMO 160** (*PL* 39.2059–61) on the Harrowing, proposed by Förster (1906 pp 301–07) as a source for *Blickling Homily 7* (*HomS* 26, B3.2.26; ed. Morris, *EETS* OS 58, 63, 73). Building on this argument, Dumville (1972 p 375) postulates a lost Latin homily that drew on *Sermo 160* as a source for the discussion of the Harrowing in the ninth-century section of the *Book of Cerne* (ed. Kuypers 1902 pp 196–98; see Brown 1996) and *Blickling 7*. This tradition may also underlie the entry on the Harrowing in the **OLD ENGLISH MARTYR-OLOGY** for March 26 (B19.bn; ed. Kotzor 1981; see **MARTYROLOGIES**, Rauer

2000, and Lapidge 2005); and it may also be related to an anonymous homily on Easter Day in Oxford, Bodleian Library Junius 121 (*HomS* 28, B3.2.28; ed. Luiselli Fadda 1972), but Campbell (1982 p 140) thinks not.

Similarly, the Harrowing makes up the first part of an anonymous homily for Easter Day preserved in two versions, one in Cambridge, Corpus Christi College 41 (*NicD*, B8.5.3.2; ed. Hulme 1903–04 pp 610–14), and the other in Cambridge, Corpus Christi College 303 (*NicE*, B8.5.3.3; ed. Hulme 1903–04 pp 610–14). The immediate source has not yet been found, although the phrase "an þissum bokum" implies that the homilist worked from written sources, and the connection of CCCC 41 to the Leofric donation (NRK 32) may indicate some link to *NicA* (ML 10.14). Moreover, a discussion of the Harrowing appears in another homily for Easter Day in Cambridge, Corpus Christi College 162 (*HomS* 27, B3.2.27; ed. Lees 1986 pp 117–23).

Descent loci in Old English poetry include the *Descent into Hell* (*Hell*, A3.26; ed. *ASPR* 3); *Christ I, II*, and *III* (*ChristA–C*, A3.1; ed. Cook 1909); *Christ and Satan* (*Sat*, A1.4; ed. Finnegan 1977), and *Guthlac B* (A3.2; ed. Roberts 1979).

Campbell's study (1982) is the most comprehensive for the Old English material, although his thesis — that little convincing evidence has been advanced for the knowledge of the *Gospel* before the translations (*NicA, B*, and *C*) — as a negative one leaves the question open. Healey (1985) is more willing to see the direct influence of the *Gospel* in a variety of texts; see also the bibliographical essay by Pelteret in Woods and Pelteret (1985 pp 164–65). Hulme (1898) prints *NicA* and *NicB*; Allen 1968 prints *NicA* and variants from *NicB* and *C*, as well as a Latin text based on Tischendorf (1876). *NicA* also appears in Crawford (1927) and *NicC* in Warner (*EETS* OS 152.77–88). Kim (1973) edits the Latin text from a tenth-century manuscript; see also Collett (1981), who edits an example of recension A in Oxford, Bodleian Library Fairfax 17 (twelfth century) and of recension B in Cambridge, Corpus Christi College 288 (thirteenth century). Izydorczyk (1993) lists 424 surviving manuscripts that contain the work.

Frederick M. Biggs and James H. Morey

**Vindicta Salvatoris** [ANON.Vin.Sal.]: *AG* pp 97–98; *BHL* 4221; *CANT* 70; *LTK* 8.505–06; *NTAP* 87; *RBMA* 180.
    ed.: Cross 1996 pp 248–92.

*MSS*    Saint-Omer, Bibliothèque Municipale 202: HG 930.5.
*Lists*    none.
*A-S Vers*    1. *VSal* 1 (Ass 16, B8.5.4.1).
    2. *VSal* 2 (Ass 17, B8.5.4.3).
*Quots/Cits – Refs*    none.

Once upon a time there was a king of Aquitaine named Titus who suffered from cancer but was healed and later baptized by a converted Jew named Nathan, who had served under Pontius Pilate. Eager to prove his devotion to his new faith, Titus sets out for the Holy Land accompanied by his general Vespasian and seeks to avenge the death of Christ by massacring all the Jews in Jerusalem. In Jerusalem, Titus encounters Veronica, the woman once healed of an issue of blood by Christ, and Veronica uses a linen cloth imprinted with a likeness of Christ's face to heal the emperor Tiberius of leprosy. During this time, an officer of Tiberius named Volosianus tries Pilate in Damascus and subjects him to a painful death.

Variations of this story circulated throughout medieval Europe, building on details from what eventually emerged as four distinct legends: the destruction of Jerusalem by Titus and Vespasian, Veronica and her miraculous cloth, the disease and cure of Tiberius, and the death of Pilate. The first derived from **RUFINUS**'s translation of **JOSEPHUS**'s **DE BELLO JUDAICO**; the second from a scene in the *Acta Pilati* portion of the **GOSPEL OF NICODEMUS** in which Veronica makes an appearance during the trial of Christ before Pilate and identifies herself as the woman healed of a hemorrhage; the third from the *Cura sanitatis Tiberii* (*BHL* 4218; *CANT* 69), which is often copied as an appendix to the *Gospel of Nicodemus* and which sometimes includes an epilogue describing the imprisonment and death of Pilate. Three of these four legends are thus intimately connected with the transmission of the *Gospel of Nicodemus*, which helps explain why the *Vindicta Salvatoris* itself is often copied as a companion to the *Gospel of Nicodemus*, as in the Saint-Omer manuscript and in all three manuscripts containing Old English translations. It is unknown when or where these various legends came together in the form of the *Vindicta Salvatoris*. Dobschütz (*TU* 18.277\*) speculates that it was composed between 700 and 720 in Aquitaine, where the encounter between Titus and Nathan is said to take place.

The Saint-Omer manuscript is a homiliary produced at the abbey of Saint-Bertin at Saint-Omer in western Flanders in the late-ninth century (see **HOMILIARIES**); its copy of the *Vindicta Salvatoris* is the earliest known. The manuscript reached England by the middle of the eleventh century, when it was used as the basis for an Old English translation made at Exeter very likely during the episcopacy of Leofric (ca. 1050–72); for an argument that Saint-Omer 202 did *not* provide the immediate source for the Old English translation, however, see Lindström (2005). This translation (*VSal* 1; ed. Cross 1996 pp 249–93) survives in two manuscripts; another text (*VSal* 2), which faithfully parallels the opening of *VSal* 1 but ends with a confused summary of the Titus and Vespasian episode, was printed by Assmann (*BaP* 3.193–94).

Several charms invoke Veronica by name (Storms 1948 pp 56, 233, and 291; Grattan and Singer 1952 pp 34 and 50; Jolly 1996 pp 149, 150, and 163; see **MAGICAL WRITINGS**), but have nothing more in common with the *Vindicta Salvatoris*. Schönbach (1876 p 199 note) unconvincingly suggests that **CYNEWULF** alludes to the *Vindicta Salvatoris* in **JULIANA** 302–06. I have not been able to substantiate Ogilvy's assertion (*BKE* p 71) that "Aelfric's Saints' Lives 16 [presumably ÆLS (Memory of Saints); B1.3.17] rests upon the *Vindicta Salvatoris*."

Tischendorf (1876 pp 471–86) edits the Latin from two fourteenth-century manuscripts and in his apparatus presents variants from the two Old English versions but in Latin translation; see Schönbach (1876 pp 183–86). Tischendorf's edition was translated into English by Walker (1870 pp 245–55) and into Spanish by Santos Otero (1999 pp 507–26). Other Latin manuscripts are listed by Dobschütz (*TU* 18.276\*–77\*), Goodwin (1851), and *BHL* 4221. A new edition is currently in preparation by Zbigniew Izydorczyk and Rémy Gounelle. For fuller discussion of the background of the *Vindicta Salvatoris* and its relation to other medieval apocrypha, see Hall (1996 pp 58–81).

Thomas N. Hall

**Transitus of Pseudo-Melito (B²)** [ANON.Trans.B²/PS.MEL.]: *BHL* 5251–52a; *CANT* 111; *NTAP* 51; *RBMA* 164,5.1; see also *AG* pp 192–204.
  ed.: Haibach-Reinisch 1962 pp 63–87.

*MSS – Lists*        none.
*A-S Vers*        1. *LS* 20 (AssumptMor, B3.3.20).
      2. *LS* 21 (AssumptTristr, B3.3.21).
*Quots/Cits*      1. Trans.B² 70.5–11: BEDA.Retract.Act. VIII.28–33.
      2. Trans.B² 71.3–5: BEDA.Retract.Act. VIII.9–11.
*Refs*        1. BEDA.Retract.Act. XIII.2.7–19.
      2. ? *ÆCHom* I, 30 (B1.1.32) 436.6–20: see below.
      3. ? *ÆCHom* II, 34 (B1.2.36) 115–33: see below.

Apocryphal texts discussing the death and Assumption of the Virgin appear, at the latest, by the fifth century. Because of their complex textual histories in several different languages, the versions have yet to be fully sorted out into separate traditions (see Clayton 1999), but the two Latin versions that were certainly known to the Anglo-Saxons (*B²* and **TRANSITUS W**) apparently both descend from a lost Greek version of the fifth century via a Latin text of the fifth to seventh century (see Clayton 1986b pp 25–26, 1990a pp 153–55, and 1998 pp 69–76).

The influence of the *Transitus* texts can be discerned in Anglo-Saxon art. A carved stone slab in Wirksworth, Derbyshire (published by Clayton 1990a illustration 3; see also Clayton 1998 pp 104–07), which Hawkes (1995) dates to the late-eighth or early-ninth century, includes a representation of the dead Mary on a bier carried by two apostles (Peter and Paul, according to the apocryphal tradition), preceded by another figure carrying a palm (John). Attached by his hands to the bier is the Jew who wished to burn Mary's body and in a circle or cloud above are six heads, presumably angels. The next scene may depict Christ handing Mary's soul to Michael or an angel returning with Mary's soul so Christ can reunite it with her body (Clayton 1998 pp 105–06). The *Benedictional of Æthelwold* (London, BL Additional 49598, fol 102v; *IASIM* 111.25; see **LITURGY, PONTIFICALS AND BENEDICTIONALS**), a Winchester manuscript of 971 x 984, includes a miniature of the feast of Mary's Assumption which depicts nine apostles, while above them Mary lies on a bed, attended by three women, and the hand of God, flanked by four angels, lowers a crown (Clayton 1998 pp 108–10). A simplified version of this miniature is found in the *Benedictional of Archbishop Robert* (Rouen, Bibliothèque Municipale 369, fol 54v; see LITURGY, PONTIFICALS AND BENEDICTIONALS).

In his Assumption homilies in both CATHOLIC HOMILIES I and II, ÆLFRIC objects to the circulation of unauthorized apocryphal accounts: he was presumably referring to *B²* or to *W*, or to both.

*Transitus B²*, which purports to be the work of Melito (thus the attribution to Pseudo-Melito), has been dated to the fifth century by Haibach-Reinisch (1962 pp 44–47), but more recently to the end of the sixth or the seventh century (Mimouni 1995 p 272; Clayton 1998 p 85). It is a self-conscious attempt to improve a previous deficient account of Mary's death, emphasizing the Assumption more than any other apocryphal narrative (Clayton 1999 pp 89–92).

In his RETRACTATIO IN ACTUS APOSTOLORUM (ed. *CCSL* 121), BEDE quotes directly from this version, objecting that its chronology is incompatible with the Acts of the Apostles and recognizing its false attribution to Melito (Clayton 1998 pp 102–03; see also Acerbi 1996 p 128).

Haibach-Reinisch (1962 pp 312–13) suggests that *B²* was disseminated in southern Germany by Anglo-Saxon missionaries. This version is probably the basis for the account of the Virgin's Assumption given by the Anglo-Saxon nun HYGEBURG (VITA WILLIBALDI, ed. *MGH* Scriptores 15.97.32–98.7), who wrote in Heidenheim, Germany around 780 (Clayton 1998 pp 103–04). Since it contains details that do not agree with any published apocryphon, it may be based on hearsay.

A vernacular homily on the Assumption in Cambridge, Corpus Christi College 41 (*LS* 21; ed. Clayton 1998 pp 216–28; previously ed. by Tristram 1970 and Grant 1982) is an abbreviated version of *B²* (Clayton 1998 p 213 and 1999 p 94). A second homily on this topic (*LS* 20; ed. Clayton 1998 pp 246–72; previously ed. by Morris as *Blickling Homily* 13, *EETS* OS 58, 63, 73) follows its rendering of *Transitus W* with three chapters (15, 16, and 17) from this work (Clayton 1999 pp 94–98; see also Faerber 1999). Kabir (2001a p 59) draws two possible explanations from Clayton's work for the combining of these texts ("the homilist's desire to describe Mary's end in the fullest detail possible, and his need to clarify the ambivalences and reconcile the contradictions within the *Transitus* narratives available to him"), and adds a third, "his attempt to create a vernacular Assumption narrative more in keeping with popular Anglo-Saxon conceptions of the interim paradise than either Latin text he had before him."

In their commentary on question 17 in the Old English prose SOLOMON AND SATURN (*Sol I*, B5.1), Cross and Hill (1982 p 81) cite a Syriac *Transitus B. Virginis* for the comment that Mary lived for sixteen years following the Ascension. The Old English homily *LS* 21 (ed. Clayton 1998 p 216) specifies three years; in her note, Clayton (p 230) comments that "*Transitus B²* reads *secundo igitur anno*, with one manuscript reading *quarto decimo*." Citing Napier (1889), Hill and Cross (p 80) also note that sixteen years are indicated in "a number of snippets in Old English manuscripts." On the various ages assigned to Mary in Anglo-Saxon texts, see also Hall (1988).

Clayton (1998 pp 334–43) reprints Haibach-Reinisch's edition (1962) but without the apparatus. For the knowledge of the *Transitus Mariae* in Ireland, see McNamara (1975 pp 122–23) and Willard (1937a pp 341–64).

Mary Clayton

**Transitus W** [ANON.Trans.W]: *BHL* 5352b–n; *CANT* 114; *NTAP* 51; *RBMA* 164,6.1.
    ed.: Clayton 1998 pp 328–33.

*MSS*    Cambridge, Pembroke College 25: HG 131.
*Lists*    none.
*A-S Vers*    *LS* 20 (AssumptMor, B3.3.20): see below.
*Quots/Cits*    none.
*Refs*    1. ? *ÆCHom* I, 30 (B1.1.32) 436.6–20: see previous entry.
    2. ? *ÆCHom* II, 34 (B1.2.36) 115–33: see previous entry.

According to Wenger (1955 p 66) this work was composed in the seventh or eighth century; however, since it corresponds more closely than any other Latin *Transitus* to **GREGORY OF TOURS**'s account of Mary's death, it or its source was probably circulating by the end of the sixth century (Clayton 1999 pp 88–89). There are two versions, which differ mainly in their conclusions. In both, the apostles gather at the sepulchre. Christ arrives and commands Michael to receive the body of Mary into the clouds. The apostles are received into the clouds, and Christ commands the clouds to go to paradise. One ends with Mary's body being placed in paradise, while the other then specifies that her soul is replaced in her body.

The Cambridge manuscript contains a variant, abbreviated text of *Transitus W* (Clayton 1998 p 317) as represented by the edition of Wilmart (1933), which includes readings from nine manuscripts. While other copies of the **HOMILIARY OF SAINT-PÈRE DE CHARTRES**, of which the Cambridge manuscript is an example (see Cross 1987a and **HOMILIARIES**), do not contain this text, it was apparently part of the original collection (Cross 1987a p 51).

A homily on the Assumption (*LS* 20; ed. Clayton 1998 pp 246–72; previously edited by Morris as *Blickling Homily* 13, *EETS* OS 58, 63, 73) translates this work, omitting chapter 6, before concluding with three chapters drawn from **TRANSITUS B²**, a *Magnificat*, and beatitudes. Clayton (1998 pp 278–97) compares the Old English to readings printed in Wilmart (1933); see also Clayton (1999 pp 94–98) and Faerber (1999).

Marocco (1950) prints two fragmentary versions, and Mimouni (1995 p 281 note 85) lists three more manuscripts.

Mary Clayton

# APOCRYPHAL ACTS

From the New Testament, the Anglo-Saxons would have known of the apostles as the twelve disciples chosen by Christ to spread his message; for meanings of "apostle" in the early Church, see *NTA* 2.1–27. The names, however, differ in the canonical lists (Matthew 10.1–42, Mark 3.13–19, Luke 6.12–16, and Acts 1.13–26); see the *NCE* 1.572. For the veneration of the apostles in Anglo-Saxon England, see Thacker (2000) and O'Leary (2003).

Of the five early apocryphal *Acts* (John, Peter, Paul, Andrew, and Thomas) composed in the second and third centuries, only the *Acts of Peter* (in its Latin form known as the ACTUS VERCELLENSES) has been mentioned as a possible source for an Anglo-Saxon author, although they did use the PSEUDO-CLEMENT RECOGNITIONS (included in this section), disseminated through RUFINUS's translation. Instead, most of their additional information about the apostles would have derived from retellings of their legends, particularly their martyrdoms (*passiones*), adapted to hagiographic conventions; these generally date to between the third and sixth centuries. For the *Revelatio Stephani* (*BHL* 7851) see the entry for STEPHANUS DIACONUS PROTOMARTYR under ACTA SANCTORUM.

One indication of the apostles' special status is to be found in works devoted exclusively to them (see Philippart 1977 pp 16–18 and 87–92). The large collection known as the PSEUDO-ABDIAS APOSTOLIC HISTORIES is treated here first. Three others — the BREVIARIUM APOSTOLORUM, the NOTITIA DE LOCIS APOSTOLORUM, and the NOMINA LOCORUM IN QUO APOSTOLI REQUIESCUNT — are included under MISCELLANEOUS. This general tradition is represented in the Old English poem *Fates of the Apostles* (*Fates*, A2.2; ed. Brooks 1961; see CYNEWULF). Entries on individual apostles, or sometimes two together, follow the *Apostolic Histories* in alphabetical order. For the apocryphal EPISTLE OF PAUL TO THE LAODICEANS, see APOCRYPHAL EPISTLES.

BEDE (RETRACTATIO IN ACTUS APOSTOLORUM I.13; *CCSL* 121.106) refers to "historiae" containing "passiones apostolorum," which he asserts are held by most to be apocryphal (see also O'Leary 2003 p 113). The detail Bede cites is identified in the *CCSL* as the *Pseudo-Abdias Apostolic Histories*. While Bede need not be referring specifically to this work, because he does so prompted by the names Simon and Jude, he may be recalling it since it is following the section on them that Abdias is mentioned as its author (see Biggs 2003 pp 13–14). Similarly the "passiones apostolorum" in the Exeter List (ML 10.42) could refer to the *Apostolic Histories*, to the anonymous *Breviarum Apostolorum*, or to collections such as those in Würzburg, Universitäts-bibliothek M.p.th.f.78 (*CLA* 9.1425; Anglo-Saxon majuscule and minuscule, written

according to Lowe "in an Anglo-Saxon center on the Continent, perhaps in the
Würzburg region") and Brussels, Bibliothèque Royale II 1069 (*CLA* 10.1551; also
"written in an Anglo-Saxon center on the Continent"). Apocryphal traditions about
the apostles circulated as well in other works; see in particular the two collections by
ISIDORE and PSEUDO-ISIDORE called DE ORTU ET OBITU PATRUM.

For an overview of research on the *Apocryphal Acts*, see Bovon, van Esbroeck, et al.
(1981); MacDonald (1986a); Bovon, Brock, and Matthews (1999); Bovon (2003);
and the article on "Apocryphes" in the *DS*.

**Pseudo-Abdias Apostolic Histories** [ANON.Hist.apost./PS.AB.]: *CANT* 256; *NTAP*
7; *RBMA* 192; see *CCSA* 2.750–58.
ed.: Fabricius 1719 2.402–742.

*MSS*        none.
*Lists*       ? see APOCRYPHAL ACTS (above).
*A-S Vers*    none.
*Quots/Cits*  see below.
*Refs*        ? see APOCRYPHAL ACTS (above).

This collection, also known as the *Virtutes Apostolorum*, was compiled in Gaul in
the sixth century (Kaestli 1981 p 52). In Fabricius's edition, it contains the following
sections: 1 Peter; 2 Paul; 3 Andrew; 4 James the Great; 5 John; 6 James the Less, Simon,
and Jude; 7 Matthew; 8 Bartholomew; 9 Thomas; and 10 Philip. This edition reprints
the edition of Lazius (1551). According to Kaestli (1981 p 52), however, the edition
of Nausea (1531) is closer to the manuscripts; it lacks the prologue and epilogue, and
its sections follow a different order.

Some of the sections are drawn from *Acts* (or *Martyrdoms*) that still exist, and so,
as Cross (1979b p 17) points out, it is often impossible to determine whether this
collection has been used. Nor is it certain if the entire collection was known in Anglo-
Saxon England (see the headnote to APOCRYPHAL ACTS above for possible general
references), although the possibility that ÆLFRIC consulted it for his CATHOLIC
HOMILIES was suggested by Förster (1892 pp 43–45; see also Zettel 1979 p 4). In
considering his homily on Simon and Jude (II, 38, B1.2.41), Godden (*EETS* SS
18.613) distinguishes between the transmission of these texts in separate legendaries
(represented by Mombritius 1910) and in the *Apostolic Histories*, and writes that, "the
format of the Abdias compilation leaves no traces on this or other apostolic narratives
by him, and the account of Abdias and his writings is given at the end of his piece, as
in Mombritius, whereas in the Ps-Abdias collection it is given in a preface at the head
of the whole work," concluding that Ælfric "probably" did not know the *Apostolic
Histories*.

If a *Martyrdom* that has been discussed as a possible source for an Anglo-Saxon
text exists independently of the *Apostolic Histories*, it is discussed later in this section

(with a cross-reference at this point). Some relevant versions, however, are unique to *Pseudo-Abdias*.

Andrew (see *BHL* 430; *CANT* 232): Herzfeld (*EETS* OS 116.xlii) identifies the account of Andrew's passion (502–15) as the source for the **OLD ENGLISH MARTYROLOGY** entry on Andrew (B19.hg; ed. Kotzor 1981; see also Lapidge 2005). Cross (1979b pp 27–28), who notes that this entry in the *Martyrology* also draws on the **MARTYRDOM OF ANDREW**, finds a specific detail drawn from *Apostolic Histories* that does not occur in the *Martyrdom*, the identification of Maximilla, who buries the apostle, as the wife of Egeas (260.15). Rauer (2000) considers the entire passage (260.9–17) as possibly drawing on this work or the *Martyrdom*. Cross (1979a pp 170–71) also discusses *Pseudo-Abdias* as a possible source for details about Andrew in *Fates of the Apostles* (A2.2; lines 16–22; ed. Brooks 1961), but none is restricted to this source. See also the **ACTS OF ANDREW AND MATTHIAS**.

Bartholomew: see the **MARTYRDOM OF BARTHOLOMEW** and the **QUESTIONS OF BARTHOLOMEW**.

James the Great: see the **MARTYRDOM OF JAMES THE GREAT**.

James the Less (*BHL* 4089; *CANT* 275): Cross (1979b pp 29–31) notes that this account relies on **EUSEBIUS-RUFINUS**'s **HISTORIA ECCLESIASTICA** (ed. Mommsen, *GCS* 9), and so is a possible source for the *Old English Martyrology* entry (B19.ds; ed. Kotzor 1981; see Rauer 2000 and Lapidge 2005); similarly Cross (1979a p 174) considers this account a possible source for material on James in **CYNEWULF**'s *Fates* (A2.2; lines 70–74; ed. Brooks 1961). See also the **MARTYRDOM OF JAMES THE LESS**.

John (*BHL* 4316; *CANT* 219; *NTA* 2.155; also ed. *CCSA* 2.799–834): item 10 of Cambridge, Pembroke College 25 (see **HOMILIARIES, HOMILIARY OF SAINT-PÈRE DE CHARTRES**, and Cross 1987a p 22) is largely drawn from the account of John's death in the *Apostolic Histories* (581.3–589.14). Herzfeld (*EETS* OS 116.xxxvi) cites this work as the source for the entry in the *Old English Martyrology* (B19.e; ed. Kotzor 1981; see also Lapidge 2005), but Cross (1979b pp 34–37) qualifies this suggestion, offering one detail, John's failure to turn pale even after drinking the poison (7.6), occurring only in this source; Rauer (2000) identifies it as one of several possible sources. Item 61 in the *Book of Cerne* (ed. Kuypers 1902 p 157; see Brown 1996 p 138 and **PRAYERBOOKS**) is a prayer attributed to John when he drank a poisoned cup at Ephesus, drawn from either this source or the **PSEUDO-MELITO MARTYRDOM OF JOHN**. This prayer, with an Old English gloss, is the first addition to the *Durham Collectar* after its removal to Chester-le-Street around 970 (ed. *SS* 140.125; see *EEMF* 16.48). Rosser (2000) lists the work as a certain source, along with others, for two passages (lines 26b–27a and 30–33a) in *Fates of the Apostles* (*Fates*, A2.2; ed. Brooks 1961).

Matthew: see the MARTYRDOM OF MATTHEW.

Paul: see the MARTYRDOM OF PAUL.

Peter: see the MARTYRDOM OF PETER.

Philip: see the MARTYRDOM OF PHILIP.

Simon and Jude: see the MARTYRDOM OF SIMON AND JUDE.

Thomas (*BHL* 8140): apparently not known in Anglo-Saxon England, but see the
MARTYRDOM OF THOMAS.


**Acts of Andrew:** *NTAP* 9; *RBMA* 198.

Ogilvy (*BKE* p 68) incorrectly reports that Förster (1893 pp 202–06) identified
this work as the source of *Blickling Homily* 18 (*LS* 1.2; ed. *EETS* OS 58, 63, 73):
Förster in fact showed that the ACTS OF ANDREW AND MATTHIAS is the source of this
homily. Worcester, Cathedral Library F.91 (HG 762), which Ogilvy also mentions,
actually contains chapters 21–37 of **GREGORY OF TOURS**'s DE MIRACULIS
ANDREAE (*BHL* 430; see Thomson 2001 p 58, who dates the hand of these folios to
the beginning of the twelfth century).


**Acts of Andrew and Matthias** [ANON.Act.Andr.Matth.]: *CANT* 236; *NTA* 2.443–
47; *NTAP* 10; *RBMA* 201 (*Andrew* is incorrectly listed in vol 8 [198,9.1]).
      ed.: Blatt 1930 pp 33–95.

*MSS – Lists*          none.
*A-S Vers*        1. *And* (A2.1).
         2. *LS* 1.1 (AndrewBright, B3.3.1.1).
         3. *LS* 1.2 (AndrewMor, B3.3.1.2).
*Quots/Cits – Refs*         none.

This originally Greek legend (written according to the *RBMA* in Egypt around
the turn of the fifth century, but dated perhaps earlier in the *NTA*) relates the
adventures of two apostles (Andrew and Matthias or Matthew) among a race of
cannibals. On the relationship of this work to the ACTS OF ANDREW (with
implications for dating), see Flamion (1911), the exchange between MacDonald
(1986a and 1990) and Prieur (1986 and *CCSA* 5.32–35), as well as Hilhorst and
Lalleman (2000).

In a study of the sources of the Old English *Andreas* (*And*; ed. Brooks 1961), Schaar (1949) distinguishes two main traditions of the legend, the "detailed and fantastic" and the "shorter and less miraculous" (p 15). He includes the Greek versions, the Latin prose version in the Casanatense Library, and *Andreas* in the former group, and the Latin poetic version and the Old English prose versions (*LS* 1.1 and 1.2; ed. Cassidy and Ringler 1971 pp 205–19 and Morris, *EETS* OS 58, 63, 73) in the latter. He also notes that the Greek versions sometimes contain details relevant to *Andreas* not found in the Latin versions (p 23). Brooks (1961) asserts that the Latin poetic version "is in fact so free a rendering that it cannot be considered the source of any of the existing Old English versions" (p xvii), although he acknowledges that in using the proper names Achaia, Mirmidonia, and Plato, it contains details not found in either the Greek versions or in the Casanatense manuscript. Baumler (1985) adds further general similarities between the Latin poetic version and *Andreas*.

Cassidy and Ringler (1971 p 205) note that the Old English prose version found in Cambridge, Corpus Christi College 198 (*LS* 1.1) is "a very lightly abridged form of the text" in *Blickling Homily* 18 (*LS* 1.2), but it "cannot be derived" directly from the earlier manuscript. The editors also assert that the *Bonnet Fragment* is closer to their text than is the Latin version in the Casanatense manuscript, and they print this version, with one omission, in the apparatus of the text. Baumler (1985 p 71) suggests that there may have been "more than one model" for the Cambridge and Blickling versions.

The surviving Greek versions have been edited by Tischendorf (1851 pp 132–66) and by Bonnet (in Lipsius and Bonnet 1891–1903 vol 2/1); Tischendorf's text is translated by Walker (1870). Blatt (1930) edits two Latin versions: one in prose found in the twelfth-century manuscript Rome, Biblioteca Casanatense 1104 (translated by Allen and Calder 1976 pp 15–34); and the other in verse found in the eleventh-century manuscript Rome, Vatican City, Biblioteca Apostolica Vaticana Vat.lat. 1274. The "Bonnet Fragment" (in Rome, Biblioteca Vallicelliana plut. I, tom. iii, an eleventh-century palimpsest), is also in prose; Blatt prints it opposite the Casanatense text (pp 13–15). A shorter Latin prose account occurs in the University of Bologna manuscript 1576; it has been edited by Baumler (1985 pp 90–112), who dates the manuscript to the eleventh century. Finally, much condensed Latin versions occur in the PSEUDO-ABDIAS APOSTOLIC HISTORIES (ed. Fabricius 1719 2.457–59) and in GREGORY OF TOURS's DE MIRACULIS ANDREAE (*MGH*.SRM 1.827–28; *CCSA* 6.569–73). See also MacDonald (1990 pp 70–68) for a reconstruction of the text from a comparison of the Greek and Latin (including Old English) traditions; he offers a facing-page English translation.

For further discussions of *Andreas*'s relationship to its sources, see Hill (1968), Szittya (1973), Walsh (1977 and 1981), Earl (1980), Biggs (1988), and Boenig (1991). For a translation into French of the prose version *LS* 1.1 and further discussion of the tradition, see Faerber (2005 pp 199–216).

**Martyrdom of Andrew** [ANON.Pas.Andr.]: *BHL* 428; *CANT* 226; *RBMA* 199,6.
   ed.: Lipsius and Bonnet 1891–1903 2/1.1–37.

*MSS – Lists*       none.
*A-S Vers*       *ÆCHom* I, 38 (B1.1.40) lines 169–348.
*Quots/Cits*    1. Pas.Andr. 33.4–34.4: *Mart* (B19.hg) 10–11.
      2. Pas.Andr. 35.1–3: *Mart* (B19.hg) 10–11.
*Refs*    none.

The *Martyrdom*, identified in *CANT* as the *Epistula presbyterorum et diaconorum Achaiae*, recounts the conflict between Andrew and Aegeas, the ruler in Achaia who attempts to force the Christians to worship idols; in it, Andrew is eventually put to death on a cross. It is a Latin redaction of the end of the ACTS OF ANDREW made in the sixth century (*CCSA* 6.13).

Zettel (1979 p 32) identifies the *Martyrdom* as item 139 in his reconstructed COTTON-CORPUS LEGENDARY (see also Jackson and Lapidge 1996). Although it does not occur in either the Cotton or the Corpus manuscript, it is included in Oxford, Bodleian Library Bodley 354 (twelfth century), and in the table of contents in Salisbury, Cathedral Library 222 (olim Oxford, Bodleian Library Fell 1; HG 623; see Webber 1992 pp 156–57). Godden (*EETS* SS 18.319) notes that the version in Bodley 354 is similar to that printed by Mombritius (1910 1.104–07), but that in Hereford, Cathedral Library P.7.vi, which Zettel (1979 pp 166–71 and 244–46) found to be closer to ÆLFRIC's homily on Andrew (*ÆCHom* I, 38; ed. Clemoes, *EETS* SS 17), is "virtually identical" to Lipsius and Bonnet.

Förster (1892 pp 21–22) identifies the *Martyrdom* as Ælfric's source for the second part of his homily on Andrew, which Godden (*EETS* SS 18.318) argues was probably written "around the time when he was completing work on the Second Series," but "transferred to the First before the latter was circulated." Godden (pp 324–29) further divides lines 170–348 into twenty-two passages, each with a specific source from the *Martyrdom*; Ælfric in general follows the order of his source although he omits some material (see Biggs 2005a and Faerber 2005).

Cross (1979b pp 27–28) cites it as a source for details, including the two noted above, about Andrew in the OLD ENGLISH MARTYROLOGY (B19.hg; ed. Kotzor 1981; see also Lapidge 2005), that are not found in the PSEUDO-ABDIAS APOSTOLIC HISTORIES; Rauer (2000) considers both possible sources. Cross (1979a pp 170–71) also identifies it as a possible source for CYNEWULF's comments about Andrew in *Fates of the Apostles* (A2.2; lines 16–22; ed. Brooks 1961).

Item 66 from the *Book of Cerne* (161.4–15; ed. Kuypers 1902) is taken with minor changes from the *Martyrdom* (24.8–26.1); see Kuypers (1902 p 233) and Brown (1996 pp 138–39). In addition to Lipsius and Bonnet and Mombritius, see also Fábrega Grau (1953 2.59–64).

**Martyrdom of Bartholomew** [ANON.Pas.Bart.]: *BHL* 1002; *CANT* 259; *NTA* 2.452–53; *NTAP* 18; *RBMA* 207,1.
   ed.: Mombritius 1910 1.140–44.

*MSS*    1. London, BL Cotton Nero E.i: HG 344.
      2. Salisbury, Cathedral Library 222 (olim Oxford, Bodleian Library Fell 1): HG 623.
*Lists*    none.
*A-S Vers*    *ÆCHom* I, 31 (B1.1.33).
*Quots/Cits*    1. Pas.Bart. 140.33–35: *Mart* (B19.gb) 186.9–12.
      2. Pas.Bart. 143.26–35: *Mart* (B19.gb) 186.12–13.
      3. Pas.Bart. 144.1–37: *Mart* (B19.gb) 186.15–188.7.
*Refs*    none.

The *Martyrdom* appears in the PSEUDO-ABDIAS APOSTOLIC HISTORIES (ed. Fabricius 1719 2.669–87) and so can be dated to the sixth century or possibly earlier. Bonnet (1895) has demonstrated that the known Greek text depends on the Latin. It tells how, by overthrowing idols in India, Bartholomew is able to convert one king, Polymius, before his brother, Astriges, has the apostle martyred.

Zettel (1979 p 24) identified this work as item 89 in his reconstructed **COTTON-CORPUS LEGENDARY** (see Jackson and Lapidge 1996): it occurs in both the London and Salisbury manuscripts; on the latter, see Webber (1992 pp 156–57). Förster (1892 p 21) notes ÆLFRIC's use of this work for the first part of his homily on Bartholomew (*ÆCHom* I, 31; ed. Clemoes, *EETS* SS 17.439–50), and Zettel (1979 pp 181–82) indicates several passages where readings from the Cotton manuscript are closer to Ælfric's version than the text in Mombritius. Godden (*EETS* SS 18.257–64) quotes from Mombritius, but he provides variants from Lipsius and Bonnet (1891–1903 2/1.128–50), the *Apostolic Histories*, and the Cotton-Corpus manuscripts that are closer to Ælfric.

Godden (*EETS* SS 18.87) also quotes a passage from this *Martyrdom* (142. 16–24) for comparison to a remark in Ælfric's homily on the first Sunday in Lent (*ÆCHom* I, 11; ed. *EETS* SS 17, lines 42–47) concerning Christ's fasting.

Herzfeld (*EETS* OS 116.xl) points out that the entry on Bartholomew in the **OLD ENGLISH MARTYROLOGY** (B19.gb; ed. Kotzor 1981; see also Lapidge 2005) draws on this account; see also Cross (1979b pp 19–20). Rauer (2000), who specifies the three borrowings noted above, lists them as "probable" direct sources. Cross (1979a pp 172–74) considers this work as a possible source for details concerning Bartholomew in CYNEWULF's *Fates of the Apostles* (A2.2; lines 42–49; ed. Brooks 1961).

**Pseudo-Clement Recognitions** [ANON.Recog./PS.CLEM.]: *BHL* 6644–45; *CANT* 209.5; *CPG* 1015.5; *NTA* 2.483–530; *NTAP* 21; *ODCC* pp 367–68; *RBMA* 208,3.
   ed.: *GCS* 51.3–387.

*MSS*       1. Oxford, Trinity College 60: HG 692.5.
            2. Salisbury, Cathedral Library 11: HG 701.
*Lists – A-S Vers*      none.
*Quots/Cits*       1. Recog. 6.2–3: ALDH.Pros.uirg. 257.7–8.
            2. Recog. 45.1–3: BEDA.Exp.Act.apost. V.xxxiv.71–73.
            3. Recog. 45.1–3: BEDA.Retract.Act. V.xxxiv.37–40.
            4. Recog. 23.21–24.9: BEDA.Comm.Gen. I.309–22.
            5. Recog. 191.4–11: BEDA.Temp.rat. V.61–69.
*Refs*       1. ALDH.Pros.uirg. 257.13–15.
            2. ALDH.Epist. 482.29; *MGH* AA.15.

Anglo-Saxons would have known the *Recognitions* through **RUFINUS**'s translation of a lost Greek text dated to the mid-fourth century (*NTA* 2.485). The work relates the story of Clement, who, separated from his family early in life, travels to meet Peter, becomes his disciple and witnesses his encounter with Simon Magus; he is finally reunited with his family. The narrative was adapted by various heretical groups (the *Recognitions* is posited to be a reaction to heretical expansions of the earlier *Homilies* [*CPG* 1015.4]), and although Rufinus's translation omits unorthodox passages, a version is still condemned by the **GELASIAN DECREE** (ed. Dobschütz, *TU* 38/4 lines 263–64).

The Salisbury manuscript is dated by Rehm (*GCS* 51.lxxvii) to the twelfth century. Webber (1992 pp 22–24 and 162) places its scribes in her second group, active early in the twelfth century. In addition to the Trinity College manuscript (identified as early-twelfth century in HG), Rehm lists a New College, Oxford fragment (included by Gneuss in his 1981 "Preliminary List," no. 679) and London, BL Royal 6.B.XIV as eleventh century; neither is included in HG. Ogilvy notes one other manuscript, London, BL Additional 18400, but it is included by Rehm (*GCS* 51.xxii) among the German manuscripts and is not in HG.

Ogilvy (*BKE* p 116) states that the "Clement" mentioned by **ALCUIN** in his **VERSUS DE SANCTIS EUBORICENSIS ECCLESIAE** (ed. Godman 1982 line 1552) is the author of this work. Lapidge (ML 1.12) identifies the reference as to Aurelius **PRUDENTIUS** Clemens, and the context of the name among Christian Latin poets supports his assertion; see also Godman (1982 p 125), who translates "Prudentius."

In his comments on Clement in his prose **DE VIRGINITATE** (*MGH* AA 15.257), **ALDHELM** quotes from the opening of this work and notes that Rufinus translated it from Greek into Latin. In commenting on Acts 5.34 in both his **EXPOSITIO ACTUUM APOSTOLORUM** and his **RETRACTATIO IN ACTUS APOSTOLORUM** (*CCSL* 121), **BEDE** turns to the *Recognitions* for information about Gamaliel. He uses other passages pertaining to Genesis in his commentary on this book (*CCSL* 118A.12) and in his **DE TEMPORUM RATIONE** (*CCSL* 123B.286; see also Acerbi 1996 p 133). He may draw on the *Recognitions* elsewhere in his didactic works; see *CCSL* 123.734. See also the **PSEUDO-CLEMENT LETTER TO JAMES**.

In addition to the edition by Rehm (*GCS* 51), the work also appears in *PG* 1.1207–1454.

**Pseudo-Clement Letter to James** [ANON.Epist.Iac./PS.CLEM.]: *BHL* 6646; *CANT* 209.3; *CPG* 1015.3; *NTA* 2.485 and 496–503; *RBMA* 209,1.

Ogilvy (*BKE* pp 116–17) suggests that this work "may have been used by **BEDE**" in explaining Laurence's succession to Augustine as archbishop of Canterbury by recalling Peter's designation of Clement as his successor in Rome (**HISTORIA ECCLESIASTICA** II.iv; ed. Colgrave and Mynors 1969 p 144 lines 16–22). Ogilvy notes, however, that Plummer (1896 2.82) adduces other sources including **RUFINUS**'s preface to the **PSEUDO-CLEMENT RECOGNITIONS** (4.29–5.10) and the **LIBER PONTIFICALIS** (ed. Duchesne 1955 1.123 lines 5–7), both works that Bede is known to have used elsewhere. On the role of the *Letter* in shaping this tradition, see Ullmann (1960), who mentions Bede's remarks and adds that **ALDHELM** also identifies Clement as the first pope in his prose **DE VIRGINITATE** (*MGH* AA 15.257 lines 3–5).

**Martyrdom of James the Great** [ANON.Pas.Iac.Mai.]: *BHL* 4057; *CANT* 272; *NTA* 2.477; *RBMA* 213,11.
    ed.: Mombritius 1910 2.37–40.

*MSS*    1. London, Bl. Cotton Nero E.i: HG 344.
    2. Salisbury, Cathedral Library 222 (olim Oxford, Bodleian Library Fell 1): HG 623.
    3. Paris, Bibliothèque Nationale lat. 10861: HG 898.
*Lists*    none.
*A-S Vers*    1. *ÆCHom* II, 31–32 (B1.2.34).
    2. *LS* 11 (James; B3.3.11).
*Quots/Cits*    1. Pas.Iac.Mai. 39.5–8: *ÆCHom* II, 1 (B1.2.2) 191–95.
    2. Pas.Iac.Mai. 39.10–12: *ÆCHom* II, 1 (B1.2.2) 195–200.
    3. Pas.Iac.Mai. 39.14–16: *ÆCHom* II, 1 (B1.2.2) 200–01.
    4. Pas.Iac.Mai. 39.17–19: *ÆCHom* II, 1 (B1.2.2) 204–05.
    5. Pas.Iac.Mai. 39.19–21: *ÆCHom* II, 1 (B1.2.2) 207–10.
    6. Pas.Iac.Mai. 39.23–27: *ÆCHom* II, 1 (B1.2.2) 210–13.
*Refs*    none.

The *Martyrdom* appears in the **PSEUDO-ABDIAS APOSTOLIC HISTORIES** (ed. Fabricius 1719 2.516–31) and so can be dated to the sixth century or possibly earlier. While preaching in Judea, James the Great overcomes a magician named Hermogenes but eventually is decapitated by King Herod.

Zettel (1979 p 23) lists this text as item 74 in his reconstructed **COTTON-CORPUS LEGENDARY** (see Jackson and Lapidge 1996): it occurs in the London and Salisbury manuscripts; on the latter, see Webber (1992 pp 156–57).

Förster (1892 p 23) notes that it is **ÆLFRIC**'s source for his homily on James (*ÆCHom* II, 31–32; ed. Godden, *EETS* SS 5.241–48). Godden (*EETS* SS 18.575) asserts that the version in the *Apostolic Histories* "is generally less close but occasionally provides a reading closer to Ælfric"; he quotes from Mombritius but provides variants from Fabricius and the Cotton-Corpus manuscripts. He comments that "Ælfric follows the narrative of his source fairly closely from beginning to end, but summarizes in one sentence (lines 122–24) the very long list of Old Testament testimonies to Christ given by the apostle in his sermon, which forms the central third of the Latin *Martyrdom* and plays a key role in the text's doctrinal concerns with the defeat of Judaism by Christianity," and offers some possible reasons for this change, including that he "may have already used (or decided to use) this material" in CATHOLIC HOMILY II, 1.

In discussing the *Martyrdom* as a source for Ælfric's homily on the nativity of Christ (*ÆCHom* II, 1; ed. Godden, *EETS* SS 5.3–11), Godden (*EETS* SS 18.347) notes that it "gives eleven of the prophecies . . . often in the same sequence, and shows the same habit of grouping them by topics such as the birth or ascension." In addition to the six quotations listed above, Godden notes other possible borrowings.

Handley (1974 p 245) notes that the *Martyrdom* is the source for the homily on James, art. 11 in London, BL Cotton Vespasian D.xiv (*LS* 11; ed. Warner, *EETS* OS 152.21–25), commenting that "the version preserved here includes much less legendary material than Ælfric's homily, concentrating on a conventional account of the basis of the Christian faith in which James defends his belief by adducing the evidence of the prophets concerning Christ's coming, relating the deeds of Christ and adjuring all his hearers to repent of their sins." Schmetterer (1981 pp 54–93) provides a list of 55 manuscripts that include the *Martyrdom*, and prints one, Munich, Bayerische Staatsbibliothek clm 3788, in the apparatus for the Old English text. Proud (2001) asserts that the Munich version is not always closer than that printed in Mombritius, the text she uses while providing variants from Fabricius and Lopez Ferreiro (1898–1911 1.392–401). See also Godden (*EETS* SS 18.575–76).

Herzfeld (*EETS* OS 116.xl) cites this account of James's martyrdom in relation to the OLD ENGLISH MARTYROLOGY entry (B19.ex; ed. Kotzor 1981; see also Lapidge 2005), but Cross (1979b pp 32–34; following Cockayne 1861) notes that the Bible is the primary source; Rauer (2000) does not list it. Cross (1979a p 172) mentions this work as a possible source for details about James in CYNEWULF's *Fates of the Apostles* (*Fates*, A2.2; lines 33b–37a; ed. Brooks 1961), but here, too, most are biblical.

In addition to the editions in Mombritius and Fabricius, the work also appears in Fábrega Grau (1953 2.111–16).

**Martyrdom of James the Less** [ANON.Pas.Iac.Min.]:  *BHL* 4093; *NTA* 2.478.
    ed.: Fábrega Grau 1953 2.100–01.

*MSS*      1. London, BL Cotton Nero E.i: HG 344.
       2. Salisbury, Cathedral Library 221 (olim Oxford, Bodleian Library Fell 4): HG 625.

*Lists – Refs*    none.

Like the account in the PSEUDO-ABDIAS APOSTOLIC HISTORIES (ed. Fabricius 1719 2.603–07), this brief *Martyrdom* is based on Hegesippus's account of the martyrdom of James, brother of Christ and bishop of Jerusalem, as transmitted by the EUSEBIUS-RUFINUS HISTORIA ECCLESIASTICA (23.4–18; ed. Mommsen, *GCS* 9). James's death is brought about by the Pharisees, who want him to speak out against Christ; he uses the occasion to preach the Gospel.

Zettel (1979 p 19) identifies the *Martyrdom* as item 45 of his reconstructed COTTON-CORPUS LEGENDARY (see Jackson and Lapidge 1996): it occurs in the London and Salisbury manuscripts; on the latter, see Webber (1992 pp 154–56). Cross (1979b pp 29–31) cites it, among others, for details in the OLD ENGLISH MARTYROLOGY on James (B19.ds; ed. Kotzor 1981; see Rauer 2000 and Lapidge 2005).

In addition to the text in Fábrega Grau, see also de Smedt, de Backer, van Ortroy, and van den Gheyn (1889 pp 136–37).

**Pseudo-Melito Martyrdom of John** [ANON.Pas.Io./PS.MEL.]: *BHL* 4320; *CANT* 220; *RBMA* 221; see also *CCSA* 2.764–95 and *NTA* 2.204–05.
    ed.: *PG* 5.1239–50.

*MSS*    Cambridge, Pembroke College 25: HG 131.
*Lists*    none.
*A-S Vers*    *ÆCHom* I, 4 (B1.1.5).
*Quots/Cits*    ALDH.Pros.uirg.: see below.
*Refs*    none.

Introduced by a letter that identifies "Melitus" as its author, the *Martyrdom* recounts the deeds and miracles of John, culminating in his death. Junod and Kaestli (*CCSA* 2.770–90) argue that this work, composed between the mid-fifth and the end of the sixth century, and the version in the PSEUDO-ABDIAS APOSTOLIC HISTORIES descend independently from a common source, although they are combined in some later manuscripts.

Item 9 of the Pembroke manuscript (see HOMILIARIES, HOMILIARY OF SAINT-PÈRE DE CHARTRES; and Cross 1987a p 22) includes the opening miracles from this work (1241.18–1243.22) in a slightly shortened form with a homiletic introduction and conclusion. The following homily, on John's assumption, is drawn largely from the account in the *Apostolic Histories* and opens with a passage that overlaps with the *Martyrdom* (1249.28–39).

Zettel (1979 p 33) lists this work as item 150 in his reconstructed COTTON-CORPUS LEGENDARY (see Jackson and Lapidge 1996); it occurs only in Oxford, Bodleian Library Bodley 354 (twelfth century).

In his prose DE VIRGINITATE, ALDHELM recounts the incidents of John restoring shattered gems (*MGH* AA 15.254 lines 15–17), resurrecting a woman (254 line 17–255 line 3), and drinking poison (255 lines 3–8), all recounted in the *Martyrdom* (1242.20–1243.15, 1241.33–17, and 1248.5–23). Cross (1979a p 165) asserts that BEDE "had available, and disliked, the Pseudo-Melitus account of John the Evangelist," but the exact comments in his RETRACTATIO IN ACTUS APOSTOLORUM (I.48–85 and VIII.13–14; *CCSL* 121) appear to be too general to support this claim.

Förster (1892 pp 17–18) notes ÆLFRIC's use of the *Martyrdom* in his homily on John's assumption (*ÆCHom* I, 4; ed. Clemoes, *EETS* SS 17.208–16); see also Zettel (1979 pp 160–62, 164–66, and 238–41). Godden (*EETS* SS 18.28) remarks that it "survives in many different versions and it is not easy to be sure which one [Ælfric] used," but he concludes that it was probably "the shorter type," that is this version. He quotes the work from the interpolated version printed by Mombritius (1910 2.55–61; *BHL* 4321), noting readings from Fabricius (1719 3.604–23, the same version as in the *PG*) and the Hereford manuscript representing the *Cotton-Corpus Legendary* discussed by Zettel (1979).

Godden (*EETS* SS 18.317–18) also notes that Ælfric mentions two episodes drawn from the full story of the evangelist in *Catholic Homily* I, 4 in his homily on Clement (*ÆCHom* I, 37, B1.1.39; lines 245–49).

In addition to *PG* and Fabricius (1719 3.606–23), the work is edited in Fábrega Grau (1953 2.102–10).

**Martyrdom of Mark** [ANON.Pas.Mc.]: *BHL* 5276; *NTA* 2.461–64; *RBMA* 224,2; see *CANT* 287.

    ed.: *AS* April 3.347–49.

*MSS*    1. London, BL Cotton Nero E.i: HG 344.
        2. Salisbury, Cathedral Library 221 (olim Oxford, Bodleian Library Fell 4): HG 625.
*Lists*    none.
*A-S Vers*    *ÆLS* (Mark, B1.3.16).
*Quots/Cits*    BEDA.Mart.: see below.
*Refs*    none.

Mark is not named as an apostle in the Bible, but his *Martyrdom* is treated here since it is often grouped with the others (Philippart 1977 p 89). It describes how Mark establishes the faith in Egypt, particularly in Alexandria, before he is martyred by being dragged through the streets of the city. Since PAULINUS OF NOLA (d. 431) refers to a detail, the saint's encounter with the cult of Sarapis, found in it, a Latin version may have existed in the fifth century (*NTA* 2.462).

Zettel (1979 p 19) identifies this work as item 43 of his reconstructed COTTON-CORPUS LEGENDARY (see Jackson and Lapidge 1996): it occurs in the London and Salisbury manuscripts; on the latter, see Webber (1992 pp 154–56).

Quentin (1908 pp 85–86) shows the *Martyrdom* to be the source for **BEDE**'s entry on Mark in his **MARTYROLOGIUM** (ed. Dubois and Renaud 1976). Love (2000a) documents the relationship between the two texts.

Ott (1892 pp 40–41) recognizes the *Martyrdom* as the source for **ÆLFRIC**'s account of Mark's death (*ÆLS* Mark; ed. Skeat, *EETS* OS 76 and 82). Zettel (1979 pp 224–26) suggests that Ælfric consulted it in the *Cotton-Corpus Legendary*. Jayatilaka (1997a) establishes the correspondences between the two texts.

In addition to *AS*, the work is printed in Mombritius (1910 2.173–75).

**Martyrdom of Matthew** [ANON.Pas.Mt.]: *BHL* 5690; *CANT* 270; *NTA* 2.460; *RBMA* 225,17.
    ed.: Talamo Atenolfi 1958 pp 58–80.

*MSS*    1. London, BL Cotton Nero E.i: HG 344.
        2. Salisbury, Cathedral Library 222 (olim Oxford, Bodleian Library Fell 1): HG 623.
*Lists*    none.
*A-S Vers*    *ÆCHom* II, 37 (B1.2.40) 80–225.
*Quots/Cits*    Pas.Mt. 58.12–80.14: *Mart* (B19.hf) 213.5–214.6.
*Refs*    none.

The *Martyrdom* appears in the **PSEUDO-ABDIAS APOSTOLIC HISTORIES** (ed. Fabricius 1719 2.636–68) and so can be dated to the sixth century or possibly earlier; it is not related to the Greek text (ed. Lipsius and Bonnet 1891–1903 2/1.217–62). After converting Ethiopia by driving out dragons and resurrecting the king's son, Matthew is eventually martyred at the altar when he attempts to prevent a succeeding king's marriage.

Zettel (1979 p 26) identifies this work as item 104 of his reconstructed **COTTON-CORPUS LEGENDARY** (see Jackson and Lapidge 1996): it appears in the London and Salisbury manuscripts; on the latter, see Webber (1992 pp 156–57).

Herzfeld (*EETS* OS 116.xli) cites it in discussing the entry on Matthew in the **OLD ENGLISH MARTYROLOGY** (B19.hf; ed. Kotzor 1981; see Lapidge 2005); see also Cross (1979b pp 23–25). Rauer (2000), who identifies virtually the entire work as the certain, direct source for much of the entry, refers to wording in Fabricius (1719 2.637) that does not appear in the edition cited above. Cross (1979a p 169) identifies the *Martyrdom* as a source for details about Matthew in **CYNEWULF**'s *Fates of the Apostles* (A2.2; lines 63–69; ed. Brooks 1961).

Förster (1892 p 24) notes that it is the source for **ÆLFRIC**'s discussion of Matthew's passion (*ÆCHom* II, 37; ed. Godden, *EETS* SS 5.275–79). Citing Zettel (1979 p 58), Godden (*EETS* SS 18.606) states that "the versions surviving in manuscripts of the *Cotton-Corpus Legendary* are not particularly close"; he considers Fabricius's edition (1719 2.636–68) to be "marginally the closest" to Ælfric, but he

also refers to Talamo Atenolfi and Mombritius (1910 2.257–63); see in particular his
note on lines 131–49.

Talamo Atenolfi edits the text from a single manuscript, Rome, Vatican City,
Biblioteca Apostolica Vaticana Vat.lat. 5771 and offers a facing-page translation into
Italian.

**Matthias:** *NTAP* 55; *ODCC* p 1064.

Selected to replace Judas (Acts 1.26), Matthias plays no further role in the Bible. A
gospel attributed to him but no longer extant is condemned by **ORIGEN**; three
passages from "traditions" ascribed to him have been identified (see *NTA* 1.382–86
and *CANT* 17). In his **COMMENTARIUS IN LUCAM**, **BEDE** (*CCSL* 120.19), following
**JEROME**'s **COMMENTARII IN EVANGELIUM MATTHAEI** (*CCSL* 77.1; see Biggs 2003
pp 15–16), includes the *Gospel of Matthias* in a list of apocrypha, but there is no
evidence that he knew the work itself or, indeed, that it was known in Anglo-Saxon
England. Andrew rescues Matthias (or Matthew) at the beginning of the **ACTS OF
ANDREW AND MATTHIAS**: in the Old English versions, he is identified as Matthew.

In his *Letter to Sigeweard* (*ÆLet* 4, B1.8.4.3; ed. Crawford, *EETS* OS 160.60),
**ÆLFRIC** comments that he has written about the deaths of all the apostles except
Matthias, "ðe ic ofacsian ne mihte" ("which I could not find"); see Faerber (2004 p
263), who cites this passage to explain the omission noted by Sisam (1953 p 164 note
2) and Zettel (1982 p 23). There are no Latin passions listed in *CANT* (280); see also
*BHL* 5695–719.

**Pseudo-Linus Martyrdom of Paul** [ANON.Pas.Paul./PS.LIN.]: *BHL* 6570; *CANT*
212; *NTA* 2.439; *RBMA* 230,4.
    ed.: Lipsius and Bonnet 1891–1903 1.23–44.

*MSS*    1. Oxford, St. John's College 28: HG 684.
       2. ? London, BL Cotton Nero E.i: HG 344.
       3. ? Salisbury, Cathedral Library 222 (olim Oxford, Bodleian Library Fell 1): HG
         623.
*Lists – Refs*    none.

Often attributed to Bishop Linus of Rome (d. 79), the immediate successor of St
Peter, as for example in the Oxford manuscript, this account of the saint's passion is
based on the final section of the *Acts of Paul*. Since Santos Otero (*NTA* 2.439) relates
this work to the **PSEUDO-LINUS MARTYRDOM OF PETER**, it can be dated to the fifth
century or perhaps later. After he brings Nero's cupbearer, Patroclus, back to life, Paul is
persecuted and finally beheaded by the emperor, but Paul again appears to him to
proclaim that he is not dead but lives with his God.

Zettel (1979 p 22) lists a "Passio S. Pauli apostoli" as item 68 in his reconstructed **COTTON-CORPUS LEGENDARY** (see Jackson and Lapidge 1996), and he identifies this text as similar to *BHL* 6570 and 6574, the version that occurs in the **PSEUDO-ABDIAS APOSTOLIC HISTORIES** (ed. Fabricius 1719 2.441–56); see also Webber (1992 p 156) and Jackson and Lapidge (1996 p 138).

The editors of **BEDE**'s **DE ORTHOGRAPHIA** (*CCSL* 123A.31 line 600) refer to chapter 8 line 14 of this work (cf. Lipsius and Bonnet 1891–1903 1.31 line 15), but the correspondence appears to be a single word.

**Actus Vercellenses** [ANON.Act.Verc./Act.Pt.]: *BHL* 6656; *CANT* 190.III; *NTA* 2.277–81 and 287–321; *RBMA* 235,1.

ed.: Lipsius and Bonnet 1891–1903 1.45–103.

*MSS – Refs*            none.

Named for the manuscript in which it survives (Vercelli, Biblioteca Capitolare CLVIII; sixth or seventh century), this work preserves much of the *Acts of Peter*, composed in Greek at the end of the second century; see *NTA* 2.277–83. It focuses primarily on Peter's confrontation with Simon Magus (chapters 7–29) and his martyrdom (chapters 30–41); the second part circulated also independently (*RBMA* 245,1).

Lapidge (in Lapidge and Rosier 1985 p 239 note 42) suggests that **ALDHELM** may have drawn on details from this work in the section on Peter in the **CARMINA ECCLESIASTICA** (ed. *MGH* AA 15).

**Pseudo-Linus Martyrdom of Peter** [ANON.Pas.Pt./PS.LIN.]: *ANT* p 427; *BHL* 6655; *CANT* 191; *NTA* 2.436–37.

ed.: Lipsius and Bonnet 1891–1903 1.1–22.

*MSS*        Oxford, St. John's College 28: HG 684.
*A-S Vers – Refs*        none.

Based on the *Acts of Peter* and probably influencing later accounts of the saint's death, this work seems to have been composed in the fifth century (*NTA* 2.437). Peter converts the four concubines of the Roman prefect Agrippa, who eventually has him crucified, at Peter's insistence, head downwards. A rubric in the Oxford manuscript (printed by Coxe 1852 2/6.10) asserts the work's authenticity and attributes it to Linus, bishop of Rome.

**Pseudo-Marcellus Martyrdom of Peter and Paul** [ANON.Pas.Pt.Paul./PS.
MARCEL.]: *BHL* 6659; *CANT* 193; *NTA* 2.440–42; *RBMA* 251,3.
   ed.: Lipsius and Bonnet 1891–1903 1.119–77.

*MSS – Lists*          none.
*A-S Vers*          1. *LS* 32 (Peter & Paul, B3.3.32).
            2. *ÆCHom* I, 26 (B1.1.28), *EETS* SS 17 lines 147–295.
            3. *HomU* 58 (Nap 16, B3.4.58), 98.5–101.5
*Quots/Cits – Refs*          none.

Although it contains some material not found in the Greek *Acts of Peter and Paul*
(ed. Lipsius and Bonnet 1891–1903 1.178–222), the Latin *Martyrdom* seems to
descend from this version, which offers an extended narrative uniting the missions of
the two apostles. Santos Otero (*NTA* 2.440) suggests the fourth century as a likely time
of composition. In it, Peter and Paul oppose Simon Magus before Nero and, after a
number of other exchanges, end his magic flight through their prayers. The two are
then martyred, Peter crucified head downward and Paul beheaded.
   Förster (1893 pp 185–93) notes that *Blickling Homily* 15 (*LS* 32; ed. Morris,
*EETS* OS 58, 63, 73) is a translation of this work. Förster (1892 pp 18–20) also points
out that ÆLFRIC uses it in the second half of his homily on the passion of Peter and
Paul (*ÆCHom* I, 26; ed. *EETS* SS 17.391–99 lines 147–295). Godden (*EETS* SS
18.216–21) details the relationship between the two texts. See too Faerber (2004),
who discusses Ælfric's sermon on Peter's Chair (*ÆLS*; B1.3.11; see **ACTA SANC-
TORUM, PETRONILLA ET FELICULA**). Bethurum (1957 p 132 note) identifies an
interpolation in **WULFSTAN OF YORK**'s *De temporibus Antichristi* as a translation
of part of this text; she does not print the passage, but it appears in *Napier* 16 (*HomU*
58; ed. Napier 1883 pp 98.5–101.5). Lionarons (1998 p 13) shows that it is independent of both the *Blickling* and Ælfrician versions.
   Cross (1972 pp 90–92 and 97–100) shows that Ælfric used this work to structure
his homily for Rogation Monday (*ÆCHom* II, 19; B1.2.24; ed. *EETS* SS 5.180–89);
see also Godden (*EETS* SS 18.519–29). Biggs and Hall (1996 pp 80–81) identify this
text as the source for a brief reference to the two magicians in Pharaoh's court, Jamnes
and Mambres, in Ælfric's "On Auguries" (*ÆLS*, Auguries, B1.3.18; ed. Skeat, *EETS*
OS 76 and 82). Cross (1979a p 170) notes that the pairing of Peter and Paul in
**CYNEWULF**'s *Fates of the Apostles* (A2.2; lines 11b–15; ed. Brooks 1961) may "hint"
at the use of this account. Cross and Hill (1982 p 92) offer it as an ultimate source for
question 34 in the Old English prose **SOLOMON AND SATURN** (*Sol I*, B5.1): "Tell me
what man was the first (to be) talking with a dog. I tell you, Saint Peter."
   A prayer to St Peter in the *Book of Cerne* (item 62, ed. Kuypers 1902 p 158 lines
10–15) corresponds to a passage from this text (173.3–8; see Kuypers p 233, Brown
1996 p 138, and **PRAYERBOOKS**).
   In addition to Lipsius's edition in Lipsius and Bonnet (1891–1903), the work is
also printed in Fábrega Grau (1953 2.283–93). For the knowledge of this work in
Ireland, see McNamara (1975 pp 99–101).

**Conflictio apostolorum Petri et Pauli cum Simone Mago et Passiones eorundem.**

Ogilvy (*BKE* p 72) takes this title from a list of books supposedly given by GREGORY THE GREAT to St. Augustine's Abbey, Canterbury. The list is recorded in the fifteenth-century *Historia monasterii S. Augustini Cantuariensis* by Thomas of Elmham (*BEH* 2158; *RS* 8.96–99), but Ogilvy offers no evidence that it reflects books from the Anglo-Saxon period.

**Martyrdom of Peter** [ANON.Pas.Pt.]: *BHL* 6664; *CANT* 195; *NTA* 2.437.
    ed.: Mombritius 1910 2.357–65.

*MSS*    1. ? London, BL Cotton Nero E.i: HG 344.
      2. ? Salisbury, Cathedral Library 222 (olim Oxford, Bodleian Library Fell 1): HG
        623.
*Lists – Refs*    none.

Zettel (1979 p 22) lists a "Passio S. Petri apostoli" as item 67 in his reconstructed COTTON-CORPUS LEGENDARY, and he identifies this text as similar to *BHL* 6664; see also Webber (1992 p 156) and Jackson and Lapidge (1996 p 138). Förster (1892 pp 18–21) links ÆLFRIC's Latin interjections opposing other traditions concerning Paul's and Peter's passion (CATHOLIC HOMILIES I, 26, B1.1.28; ed. Thorpe 1844–46 1.374 lines 25–27 [cf. *EETS* SS 17.393] and 1.382 lines 28–29 [cf. *EETS* SS 17.398]) to this text and to the MARTYRDOM OF PAUL. See also Zettel (1979 pp 177–78) and Godden (*EETS* SS 18.210).

In addition to Mombritius, a version of the work appears in the PSEUDO-ABDIAS APOSTOLIC HISTORIES (ed. Fabricius 1719 2.390–92 and 402–41).

**Pseudo-Marcellus Epistolae I et II ad fratres Nerei et Achillem:** *BHL* 6060. See ACTA SANCTORUM, NEREUS ET ACHILLEUS.

**Martyrdom of Philip** [ANON.Pas.Phil.]: *BHL* 6814; *CANT* 254; *NTA* 2.473; *RBMA* 254.
    ed.: Mombritius 1910 2.385.

*MSS*    1. Cambridge, Pembroke College 24: HG 130.
      2. London, BL Cotton Nero E.i: HG 344.
      3. Salisbury, Cathedral Library 221 (olim Oxford, Bodleian Library Fell 4):
        HG 635.
      4. Paris, Bibliothèque Nationale 10861: HG 898.

*Lists*        none.
*A-S Vers*      *ÆCHom* II, 17 (B1.2.21) 1–60.
*Quots/Cits*    1. Pas.Phil. 385.3–4: *Mart* (B19.ch) 73.5–7.
                2. Pas.Phil. 385.19–20: *Mart* (B19.ch) 73.7–8.
                3. Pas.Phil. 385.43: *Mart* (B19.ch) 73.9.
*Refs*         none.

In this brief *passio*, Philip converts the people of Scythia by driving out a dragon and resurrecting the people it has killed, and then travels to Asia. There is some confusion surrounding his death: in the version printed by Mombritius, he is martyred, while the one in the PSEUDO-ABDIAS APOSTOLIC HISTORIES (ed. Fabricius 1719 2.742) records only that he "perrexit ad Dominum." The presence of the text in the *Apostolic Histories* indicates that a Latin version existed in the sixth century; however, according to Santos Otero, it "shows no textual relationship of any kind with the Greek Acts of Philip" (*NTA* 2.473).

Godden (*EETS* SS 18.509) notes the presence of the *Martyrdom* in the Pembroke manuscript. Zettel (1979 p 19) identifies it as item 46 in his reconstructed COTTON-CORPUS LEGENDARY (see Jackson and Lapidge 1996): it appears in the London and Salisbury manuscripts; on the latter, see Webber (1992 pp 154–56). Godden (*EETS* SS 18.509) records that these manuscripts all follow the tradition in Fabricius concerning Philip's death.

Lapidge (in Lapidge and Rosier 1985 p 241 note 64) points out that in the section on Philip in ALDHELM's CARMINA ECCLESIASTICA (ed. *MGH* AA 15), Aldhelm departs from his main source (ISIDORE's DE ORTU ET OBITU PATRUM) in claiming that Philip preaches in Scythia, and offers the *Martyrdom* as a possible source. Cross (1979a pp 166–67) cites this work as a source for CYNEWULF's *Fates of the Apostles* (A2.2; lines 37b–41; ed. Brooks), mentioning the detail that Philip was crucified, which occurs in Mombritius.

Herzfeld (*EETS* OS 116.xxxviii) discusses this account as the source for details about Philip in the OLD ENGLISH MARTYROLOGY (B19.ch; ed. Kotzor 1981; see also Lapidge 2005). Cross (1979b pp 28–29) specifies that it is only the end of the entry (73.5–11) that corresponds to this source, and offers the three quotations listed above (his references are to Fabricius 1719, where the wording differs). Rauer (2000) considers the work (385.1–48) only a possible source for lines 5–11.

Förster (1892 p 22) notes that the material on Philip in ÆLFRIC's homily on Philip and James (*ÆCHom* II, 17; ed. Godden, *EETS* SS 5.169–73) is from this account. Godden (*EETS* SS 18.509), following Zettel (1979 pp 19 and 186–87) and focusing on the detail of the saint's peaceful death, comments that he "presumably found the legend in his copy of the Cotton-Corpus legendary."

**Martyrdom of Simon and Jude** [ANON.Pas.Sim.Iud.]: *BHL* 7749–51; *CANT* 284; *NTA* 2.481; see *RBMA* 255,14.
    ed.: Mombritius 1910 2.534–39.

*MSS – Lists*      none.
*A-S Vers*      *ÆCHom* II, 38 (B1.2.41).
*Quots/Cits*      Pas.Sim.Iud. 538.11: *Mart* (B19.ih) 240.9–11.
*Refs*      none.

Simon and Jude convert Persia by overcoming two magicians and performing other miracles. They are eventually martyred when they travel to the provinces to continue their missionary work. *BHL* distinguishes between versions with different endings: one in the PSEUDO-ABDIAS APOSTOLIC HISTORIES (ed. Fabricius 1719 2.608–36; *BHL* 7749; sixth century) and the other edited by Mombritius (*BHL* 7750). *BHL* 7751 refers to an appendix, found in Mombritius, that identifies Abdias as the author of ten books on the acts of the apostles.

Zettel (1979 p 28) includes the *Martyrdom* as item 121 in his reconstructed COTTON-CORPUS LEGENDARY (see Jackson and Lapidge 1996). It does not occur in either the Cotton or the Corpus manuscripts, but it is included in Oxford, Bodleian Library Bodley 354 (twelfth century), and in the table of contents in Salisbury, Cathedral Library 222 (olim Oxford, Bodleian Library Fell 1: HG 623; see Webber 1992 pp 156–57).

Herzfeld (*EETS* OS 116.xli) identifies the *Martyrdom* as relevant to the entry in the OLD ENGLISH MARTYROLOGY (B19.ih; ed. Kotzor 1981; see also Lapidge 2005). Cross (1979b pp 25–27) discusses "one identifying detail." Rauer (2000) lists it as a probable source for lines 6–11, and a possible source for an earlier passage (lines 2–5). Cross (1979a pp 169–70) considers it a source for CYNEWULF's *Fates of the Apostles* (A2.2; lines 75–84; ed. Brooks 1961).

Förster (1892 pp 24–25) notes that the *Martyrdom* is ÆLFRIC's source for his homily on Simon and Jude (*ÆCHom* II, 38; ed. Godden, *EETS* SS 5.280–87). Drawing on Zettel (1979 pp 28, 154–56 and 195–98), Godden (*EETS* SS 18.613) remarks that "Ælfric is generally closest to Mombritius of the printed versions," but that "in several respects" the Bodley manuscript is "closer to Ælfric than any single printed version."

**Martyrdom of Thomas** [ANON.Pas.Thom.]: *BHL* 8136; *RBMA* 259,8; see *NTA* 2.456.
      ed.: *TU* 122.3–42.

*MSS – Lists*      none.
*A-S Vers*      *ÆLS* (Thomas, B1.3.34; 13–424).
*Quots/Cits*      1. Pas.Thom. 10.4–6: ALDH.Pros.uirg. 255.20–23.
      2. Pas.Thom. 16.9–17.10: *Mart* (B19.hn) 265.6–10.
      3. Pas.Thom. 14.5–15.12: *Mart* (B19.hn) 265.10–15.
      4. Pas.Thom. 37.5–40.10: *Mart* (B19.hn) 265.15–266.2.
      5. Pas.Thom. 41.7–12: *Mart* (B19.hn) 266.7–14.
*Refs*      ? *ÆCHom* II, 39.2 (B1.2.43) 7–9.

The original *Acts of Thomas*, composed in Syriac but immediately translated into Greek, was apparently reworked to suit the views of orthodox and heretical groups, particularly the Manichees (*NTA* 2.323–24). Two Latin adaptations, the *Martyrdom* and the *De miraculis beati Thomae apostoli* (also printed by Zelzer, *TU* 122, but previously known from Fabricius 1719 2.687–736), have been largely stripped of their overt gnostic content (Zelzer, *TU* 122.xi–xxiii). Zelzer dates the two to the fourth century (p xxv).

Zettel (1979 p 33) lists this work as item 146 in his reconstructed **COTTON-CORPUS LEGENDARY** (see Jackson and Lapidge 1996). It does not occur in either the Cotton or the Corpus manuscript, but it is included in Oxford, Bodleian Library Bodley 354 (twelfth century), Hereford, Cathedral Library P.7.vi (twelfth century; see Bannister 1927 p 172) and in the table of contents in Salisbury, Cathedral Library 222 (olim Oxford, Bodleian Library Fell 1: HG 623; see Webber 1992 pp 156–57).

Wright (1993 p 246 note 143) identifies **ALDHELM**'s use of the *Martyrdom* in his prose **DE VIRGINITATE** (ed. *MGH* AA 15; see also Casiday 2003). Cross (1979a pp 167–69) concludes that **CYNEWULF**'s *Fates of the Apostles* (A2.2; lines 50–62; ed. Brooks 1961) probably draws on the *Martyrdom*. Herzfeld (*EETS* OS 116.240) identifies it as the source for the entry on Thomas in the **OLD ENGLISH MARTYROLOGY** (B19.hn; ed. Kotzor 1981; see also Lapidge 2005); Cross (1979b pp 21–23) agrees, and notes further that the *De miraculis* account does not include many relevant details. Rauer (2000) lists the four quotations above, as well as another (266.2–7), which draws on this (40.10–11) and another source.

As Loomis (1931 p 7) observes, **ÆLFRIC** adapts this work in his **LIVES OF SAINTS** (*ÆLS* Thomas; ed. Skeat, *EETS* OS 76 and 82), shortening and omitting some sections. Drawing on Zettel (1979 pp 145–46, 259–62, and 315), Jayatilaka (1997b) notes that "alternative readings closer to Ælfric are sometimes to be found in at least two manuscripts of the *Cotton-Corpus Legendary*"; her references in general are to Mombritius (1910 pp 606–14). Ælfric's possible reference to it in his "Apology" in his **CATHOLIC HOMILIES** II (*ÆCHom* II, 39.2; *EETS* SS 5.298) — "the Passion of Thomas we leave unwritten because it was long ago translated from Latin into English, in verse" — is further linked to this text by the reference to an exchange between the saint and a cupbearer, an account that **AUGUSTINE** condemns. Ælfric again mentions this incident at the beginning of the version in the *Lives of Saints*; on this problem, see Biggs (2005b).

There is some evidence that the Irish knew the original *Acts of Thomas*; see McNamara (1975 pp 118–19).

# APOCRYPHAL EPISTLES

This section considers three works in order of their probable dates of composition: the LETTERS OF CHRIST AND ABGAR, the EPISTLE OF PAUL TO THE LAODI-CEANS, and the SUNDAY LETTER. For the EPISTLE OF BARNABAS, see further below under MISCELLANEOUS. For the Pseudo-Marcellus *Epistolae I et II ad fratres Nerei et Achillem*, see the entry for NEREUS ET ACHILLEUS under ACTA SANCTORUM.

**Letters of Christ and Abgar** [ANON.Ep.Sal.]: *ANT* pp 538–42; *CANT* 88; *DACL* 1.87–97; *NTA* 1.492–99; *NTAP* 19; *RBMA* 147.
    ed.: *GCS* 9/1.89–97.

*MSS*     London, BL Royal 2.A.XX: HG 450.
*Lists*    none.
*A-S Vers*    *ÆLS* (Abdon & Sennes, B1.3.24) 81–188.
*Quots/Cits – Refs*    none.

Drijvers (*NTA* 1.496) argues that the "Abgar legend is a document of Christian propaganda which originated in a historical situation in Edessa at the end of the 3rd century." Central to the legend is an exchange of letters between Christ and King Abgar V Ukama of Edessa, in which Abgar asks Christ to cure him and offers to protect him from the Jews. In his reply, Christ declines, explaining that he must fulfill his mission, but promises to send a disciple. After Christ's Ascension, Addai (or Thaddaeus) carries out this work. In his HISTORIA ECCLESIASTICA I.13 (known through RUFINUS's Latin translation, ed. Mommsen, *GCS* 9), EUSEBIUS retells the legend, translating the letters. Other Church Fathers (e.g. AUGUSTINE, DE CONSENSU EVANGELISTARUM 11.16–18; ed. *CSEL* 43) noted that Christ left behind no collection of writings, which may have led to the letters being condemned in the GELASIAN DECREE (ed. Dobschütz, *TU* 38/4 lines 328–29).

The Royal manuscript, which contains only Christ's letter but with additions not found in the *Historia ecclesiastica*, is closely related to Irish prayer books; see *SEHI* 576 and Sims-Williams (1990 pp 275–327). Loomis (1931) notes that ÆLFRIC's source for his LIVES OF SAINTS (*EETS* OS 76 and 82) is Eusebius's *Historia ecclesiastica*. Jayatilaka (1996) details the borrowings. The text of the Royal manuscript has been printed in the appendix to Kuypers (1902 pp 205–06). An English translation of the relevant part of Eusebius's work is in *NTA* 1.497–99.

**Epistle of Paul to the Laodiceans** [ANON.Epist.Laod.]: *ANT* pp 543–46; *CANT* 305; *NTA* 2.42–46; *NTAP* 64; *RBMA* 233.
    ed.: Hall 2003 pp 82–83.

*MSS*        1.  London, BL Royal 1.E.VIII: HG 449.
             2.  ? Cambridge, Trinity College B.5.2 (148): HG 169.
*Lists – Quots/Cits*         none.
*Refs*        ? *ÆLet* 4 (Sigeweard, B1.8.4) 948.

    This short apocryphal letter is largely a tissue of quotations from the other Pauline epistles, composed presumably because the letter to the Laodiceans mentioned in Colossians 4.16 did not survive. Preserved only in Latin, it is found in many Bible manuscripts. In his catalogue, James (1900–04 1.186) asserts that the Cambridge manuscript "must have contained the Epistle to the Laodiceans," apparently basing his judgment on the explicit following the Epistle to the Hebrews at the end of the manuscript, which reads: "epistole Pauli numero xv$^{cim}$ expl." Hall (2003 pp 82–83) edits and translates the text from the Royal manuscript.
    In his *Letter to Sigeweard* (*ÆLet* 4, B1.8.4.3; ed. Crawford, *EETS* OS 160.57), ÆLFRIC attributes fifteen epistles to Paul, listing this work; see Hall (2003) and Biggs (2005a p 483). Lightfoot (1879 pp 282–84) provides a list of manuscripts including this epistle. It was known in Ireland, appearing in the *Book of Armagh*; see McNamara (1975 pp 103–04).


**Sunday Letter** [ANON.Epist.Sal.Dom.BN.12270]: *CANT* 311.7; *DACL* 3.1534–46 and 4.858–994; *NTAP* 20; *RBMA* 148,3.
    ed.: Delehaye 1899 pp 181–84.

*MSS – Lists*        none.
*A-S Vers*        1.  *HomM* 6 (KerOthoB 10, B3.5.6).
             2.  *HomU* 36 (Nap 45, B3.4.36).
             3.  *HomU* 54 (Priebsch, B3.4.54).
*Quots/Cits – Refs*        none.

    The *Sunday Letter* (*Epistula e caelo missa de seruando dominica*, also known as the *Heavenly Letter* and the *Carta Dominica*) was perhaps composed in Greek in the sixth century (*RBMA* 148), although McNally (*CCSL* 108B. 175), recalling that it is first referred to in a letter of Licinianus, bishop of Carthagena, at the end of the sixth century, suggests that its "most probable place of origin is the West, probably Africa, Spain or Rome, since the association of the letter with Jerusalem and Bethlehem seems to represent a later tradition; and, it is less likely that the author, if he were Oriental, would conceive the letter as dropped by the Lord in Old Rome, the center of Occidental Christianity." It became so widely disseminated in the West that it was condemned by a Lateran Synod in 745 and in **CHARLEMAGNE**'s *Admonitio* *generalis* (789); see Delehaye (1899) and Wright (1993 p 221). Whitelock (1982 pp 50–51) notes that "there is no evidence that it was known in England until Pehtred spread knowledge of it"; she places **PEHTRED** in the first half of the ninth century, "living in a diocese under the authority of the metropolitan church of York, but not in the diocese of York or Lindisfarne" (see also Wright 1993 p 45 note 184). The letter purports to be from Christ, and to be written variously in his own blood, with a golden rod, or dictated to an angel, and to have fallen on one of the principal altars of Christendom — often Rome, Jerusalem, or Bethlehem. The work survives in a number of Latin manuscripts (that have been only generally divided into recensions), but has yet to be identified in manuscripts known in England during the Anglo-Saxon period.

The Old English versions, however, can be divided into three groups that are related to different recensions of the known Latin tradition. One is covered here, the others in the following entries. *Napier* 45 (*HomU* 36; ed. Napier 1883 pp 226–32) and another version (*HomU* 54; ed. Priebsch 1899 pp 135–38) are generally agreed to represent the first Latin recension, which survives in Paris, Bibliothèque Nationale lat. 12270 (ed. Delehaye 1899) and Vienna, Österreichische Nationalbibliothek lat. 1355 (ed. Priebsch 1899 pp 130–34); see Whitelock (1982 p 54) and Lees (1985 p 132). The Paris manuscript is recognized as particularly close to *HomU* 54; see Priebsch (1936 p 10), Whitelock (1982 p 62 note 95), and Lees (1985 pp 133–34). Apparently a homily destroyed in the fire of 1731 (*HomM* 6, KerOthoB 10) belonged to this group; see Whitelock (1982 p 54 note 51).

Related to the *Sunday Letter* is a tradition of SUNDAY LISTS (MISCELLANEOUS; see Lees 1985 pp 136–43). Five Old English homilies — *Napier* 43 (*HomU* 35.1, B3.4.35.1), *Napier* 44 (*HomU* 35.2, B3.4.35.2), *Napier* 45, *Napier* 57 (*HomU* 46, B3.4.46; ed. Napier 1883 pp 291–99) and "Be þam drihtenlican sunnandæg folces lar" (*HomU* 53, NapSunEpist; ed. Napier 1901 pp 357–62) — which draw on a *Sunday Letter* have *Sunday Lists* inserted into the texts. Although there are three fifteenth-century Latin manuscripts in the British Library that combine the two works (Lees 1985 pp 135–36), none have been identified from our period. Whitelock (1982 p 60) argues that they were joined in the Latin text used by Pehtred and by the author of the Irish *Cáin Domnaig* (see the third entry on the *Sunday Letter*, below).

In addition to the Latin texts mentioned in this and the following entries, see also editions by Priebsch (1901 pp 400–06; London, BL Royal 8.F.VI), Röhricht (1890 pp 440–42; Hamburg, Bibliothek der Hansestadt, S. Petri Kirche 30b), and Rivière (1906 pp 602–05; Toulouse, Bibliothèque Publique 208). For the Old English homilies, see also Jost (1950 pp 221–36) and Faerber (2001). An overview of the subject can be found in Deletant (1977).

Clare A. Lees

**Sunday Letter** [ANON.Epist.Sal.Dom.clm.9550]: *CANT* 311.6.
    ed.: Delehaye 1899 pp 179–81.

*MSS – Lists*          none.
*A-S Vers*          1. *HomU* 46 (Nap 57, B3.4.46).
        2. *HomU* 53 (NapSunEpis, B3.4.53).
*Quots/Cits – Refs*          none.

The second group of Old English homilies that translate this apocryphon includes *Napier* 57 (*HomU* 46; ed. Napier 1883 pp 289–91) and "Be þam drihtenlican sunnandæg folces lar" (*HomU* 53, NapSunEpist; ed. Napier 1901 pp 357–62). Whitelock (1982 p 55) states that these are "independent translations of a text with similarities with [Munich, Bayerische Staatsbibliothek] clm 9550."

**Sunday Letter** [ANON.Epist.Sal.Dom.perd.].
        ed.: lost.

*MSS – Lists*          none.
*A-S Vers*          1. *HomU* 35.1 (Nap 43, B3.4.35.1).
        2. *HomU* 35.2 (Nap 44, B3.4.35.2).
*Quots/Cits*          none.
*Refs*          ECGRED.Epist. 21–22.

The third group of Old English homilies that translate this apocryphon includes *Napier* 43 (*HomU* 35.1; ed. Napier 1883 pp 205–15) and *Napier* 44 (Nap 35.2; ed. Napier 1883 pp 215–26). Whitelock (1982 p 51) has discussed these homilies in detail, arguing that they "are variant versions of a lost homily" that in turn was based on the book by **PEHTRED** mentioned in **ECGRED**'s **LETTER TO WULFSIGE** (ed. Whitelock 1982 pp 48–49; see also Wright 1993 p 45 note 184 and Faerber 2001). This letter makes it clear that the book contained a version of the *Sunday Letter*. Whitelock (1982 pp 52–58) also compares these two Old English homilies with the Irish *Cáin Domnaig* (on the Irish tradition, see McNamara 1975 pp 60–63 and Wright 1993 pp 221–22), and both the Old English and Old Irish texts with Munich, Bayerische Staatsbibliothek clm 9550 (pp 58–59). She notes that a fragmentary *Sunday Letter* in the **CATECHESIS CELTICA** (**HIBERNO-LATIN BIBLICAL COMMENTARIES**; see Wright 1990a pp 117–18) is closer to both vernacular versions for the section it preserves (Whitelock 1982 pp 59–60).

**Sunday Letter** [ANON.Epist.Sal.Dom.Tarragona].
        ed.: Priebsch 1936 pp 35–37.

*MSS – Quots/Cits*          none.
*Refs*          ? BONIF.Epist. 59, 115.13–28.

Printed among the letters of **BONIFACE** are the acts of the Lateran Synod, convened by Pope Zacharias on 25 October 745 to examine the teachings of Clement, an Irish bishop, and Aldebert, a Frankish bishop, both of whom had been denounced by Boniface. One of the charges against Aldebert was that he used a letter which he claimed "to be from Jesus and to have fallen from heaven" (*MGH* ES 115.10–11; see Russell 1964 pp 238–40). The opening of the letter was read and recorded. Priebsch (1936 pp 4–5) notes that this opening is similar to that printed from the transcription of a now-lost manuscript in the Cathedral Library of Tarragona by Petrus de Marca, archbishop of Paris (d. 1164). McNally (*CCSL* 108B.176) comments that "on the basis of this meager evidence, it is impossible either to date [this version], establish its provenance or determine its exact relation to the universal tradition of the *Carta Dominica*."

# APOCRYPHAL APOCALYPSES

Apocalyptic literature, which deals with the end of the present world and the beginning of the next, appears in Jewish communities around 200 B.C. *ODCC* (p 83) identifies Daniel as the first of these works, although similar "tendencies can be seen in the prophetic writings." An important theme throughout the New Testament (e.g. Matthew 24–25, Mark 13, Luke 21, 1 Corinthians 15, and 1 Thessalonians 4), the tradition finds expression in the final book of the Bible. For introductions to the genre, see *ANT* pp 591–92, *NTA* 2.542–91, and Collins (1988). The six works included here are arranged alphabetically by the name with which they are associated. Three apocryphal Jewish apocalypses are included above under OLD TESTAMENT APOCRYPHA: JUBILEES, 1 ENOCH, and 4 EZRA; see also the SIBYLLINE ORACLES and PSEUDO-METHODIUS REVELATIONS. For the APOCRYPHA PRISCILLIANISTICA, the SEVEN HEAVENS APOCRYPHON, the FIFTEEN SIGNS BEFORE JUDGMENT, and the THREE UTTERANCES APOCRYPHON, see below under MISCELLANEOUS.

**Shepherd of Hermas** [ANON.Past.Herm.L[1]]: *CPG* 1052; *DACL* 6.2265–90; *GCS* 86–87; *RBMA* 267; see also *KVS* HER; *NTA* 2.592–602; *ODCC* 764–65.
   ed.: Hilgenfeld 1873.

*MSS*   Cambridge, Corpus Christi College 265: HG 73.
*Lists – A-S Vers*   none.
*Quots/Cits*   see below.
*Refs*   ? BEDA.Retract.Act. 12.15.

The *Shepherd of Hermas* (*Pastor Hermae*) was composed in Greek at Rome in the second century, or perhaps as early as the end of the first century A.D. The *NTA* describes the work as an "Apocalypse in its form and style, but not in its contents, since it includes no disclosures of the eschatological future or of the world beyond" (2.593); see also Bauckham (1974 pp 29–30), Hellholm (1980), and Osiek (1986). Hermas, who describes himself as a freed Christian slave who became a merchant and who later suffered persecution, is identified as the brother of the bishop of Rome in the *Muratorian Canon* and other sources, but scholars are not agreed on how much of the work can be attributed to Hermas himself.
   The *Shepherd* is traditionally divided into five Visions, twelve Mandates, and ten Similitudes, and is thought to have been combined from two originally independent

books (Visions I–IV, and Visions V–Similitudes VIII, supplemented by Similitudes IX–X; see *NTA* 2.593–95 and Barnard 1968 p 32), or according to Giet (1963) three different works (Visions I–IV, Similitude IX, and the Mandates and Similitudes I–VIII). Leutzsch (in Körtner and Leutzsch 1988 pp 130–32), however, defends the integrity of the text.

In Visions I–IV, Hermas encounters the Church in the form of an old woman who gradually becomes more youthful. She instructs him concerning sin and penance (I) and gives him a book (II) that provides for a single repentance after baptism. Hermas also sees a tower (III) and a beast (IV), which the old woman identifies as the Church and a future persecution respectively. In Vision V the angel of repentance appears to Hermas in the form of the Shepherd, who then expounds Christian ethics and prophecy in the Mandates, followed by allegorical parables in the Similitudes.

The *Shepherd* was regarded as Scripture in the early Greek Church (*ODCC* p 764). JEROME, in DE VIRIS ILLUSTRIBUS, says that it was virtually unknown in the West (*PL* 23.626), but the *Shepherd* is cited or mentioned by various early Latin authors (see De Gephardt and Harnack 1877 pp lxi–lxx; *DS* 7.332–33; Courcelle 1969 pp 91, 94–95, and 228), not always favorably, although a favorable judgment by ORIGEN was repeated by SEDULIUS SCOTTUS (see De Gephardt and Harnack 1877 pp lxiv–lxv note 1). Dronke (1981 pp 37–38) argues that St Patrick knew the work.

Two Latin versions have survived: the Vulgata (L$^1$, dating from the second century, surviving in more than two dozen manuscripts and fragments) and the Palatina (L$^2$, dating from the fourth or fifth century, surviving in two fifteenth-century manuscripts and in the Düsseldorf fragments; see the following entry). For lists of the Latin manuscripts see Dekkers (1994). The Vulgata includes the end of the book, lacking in the Greek manuscripts. On the relationship between the Latin and Greek versions see Carlini (1983). On the Latin versions see Mazzini and Lorenzini (1981). On the Palatina version see also Mazzini (1980). I have not been able to confirm Ogilvy's statement (*BKE* p 157) that St. Gall, Stiftsbibliothek 151, pt 3 "may go back to an English exemplar."

The brief extract concerning marriage (from Mandate IV.1) in the Cambridge manuscript corresponds to the COLLECTIO CANONUM HIBERNENSIS 46.15 (ed. Wasserschleben 1885 pp 188–89; see Bateson 1895 p 720); the *Hibernensis* also contains Mandate IV.2 in the Vulgata version, and extracts from Mandate IV in the Palatina version occur in related canonical collections, including Orléans, Bibliothèque Municipale 221 (193) and Paris, Bibliothèque Nationale lat. 3182 (see Carlini 1985).

Commenting on the reference to guardian angels in Acts 12.15 in his RETRACTATIO IN ACTUS APOSTOLORUM, BEDE states "quod unusquisque nostrum habeat angelos et in libro Pastoris et in multis sanctae scripturae locis inuenitur" (*CCSL* 121.159). The reference is probably to Mandate VI, as Laistner indicates in the apparatus of his edition, rather than to Vision V, as Laistner (1933 p 83) had earlier suggested. Laistner (1933 p 83) states that "it was undoubtedly [the Vulgata version] to which Bede had access," but the Düsseldorf manuscript suggests that if Bede did know the work at first hand, it might well have been in the Palatina version. According to Jenkins (1935 p 182), however, "we may doubt if he knew the book except at second hand," since he does not refer to it on the significance of the stones of the Temple in

DE TEMPLO. Ogilvy thinks it "likely" that Bede knew the work first hand, in view of the Düsseldorf fragments, which Lowe considers to have been written probably in the north of England. But the passage to which Bede refers on the guardian angels was cited or paraphrased in several patristic works, including Origen's DE PRINCIPIS III.ii.4 (in RUFINUS's translation; *PG* 11.309 and *GCS* 22.251) with attribution to "Pastoris liber" (cf. Daniélou 1976 pp 80–81), and CASSIAN, CONLATIONES VIII.xvii.2 (*CSEL* 13.233) with attribution to "liber Pastoris" and in reference to Acts 12.15 (see Courcelle 1969 p 228). De Gebhardt and Harnack (1877 p lxvii and note 4) had already suggested that Bede's reference, as well as one in the *Visio Wettini*, was taken over from Cassian. (A passage in London, BL Cotton Nero A.ii fol 35 [*CLA* 2.186; beyond the part listed in HG] is from Jerome's translation of Origen, *Homiliae in Lucam* [*PL* 26.243; see *BHM* 4A.21], which in turn paraphrases the *Shepherd*).

The same passage on the guardian angels has been cited by Menner (1941 p 143) as an early example of the conception of the good and bad angels appearing in the poetic SOLOMON AND SATURN (*MSol*, A13; ed. Menner 1941 lines 472–501) with reference to similar descriptions in *Vercelli Homily* 4 (*HomU* 9, B3.4.9; ed. Scragg, *EETS* OS 300 lines 337–42) and *Guthlac A* (*GuthA*, A3.2; ed. Roberts 1979 lines 114b–35). See also Sims-Williams (1990 p 268) and Wright (1993 p 260).

The Greek text is edited by Leutzsch in Körtner and Leutzsch (1998 pp 107–497); see also Whittaker (*GCS* 48). For English translations see Crombie (1885) and Snyder (1968); for a French translation by Joly see *SChr* 53. For a concordance of Latin words (with their respective Greek equivalents) in both the Vulgata and Palatina versions, see Urbán (1999 pp 694–718).

Charles D. Wright

**Shepherd of Hermas** [ANON.Past.Herm.L²]: *CPG* 1052; *DACL* 6.2265–90; *GCS* 86–87; *RBMA* 267; see also *KVS* HER; *NTA* 2.592–602; *ODCC* pp 764–65.
   ed.: Vezzoni 1994.

*MSS*  Düsseldorf, Landes- und Stadtbibliothek K 1: B 215 + K 2: C 118 + K 15: 009 + K 19: Z 8/8 + M. Th.u.Sch.29a (Ink.) Bd. 4 (pastedowns): HG 819.
*Lists – A-S Vers*  none.
*Quots/Cits*  see below.
*Refs*  ? BEDA.Retract.Act. 12.15.

As noted in the previous entry, the *Shepherd* survives in two Latin versions. This second version, the Palatina, dates from the fourth or fifth century and survives in two fifteenth-century manuscripts and the Düsseldorf fragments, which Lowe assigns probably to the north of England (*CLA* 8.1187). The fragments were first identified by Coens (1956 pp 90–91); Zechiel-Eckes (2003 pp 30–31) registers the new shelf-marks (see also pp 27–28, 47, 60–61, and 65–66). Vezzoni (1987) gives a semi-diplomatic edition of Mandates VIII, IX, and the beginning of X as transmitted in the fragment K

2: C 118 (*olim* C 118), consisting of two folios and a small strip of the first leaf's conjugate. The fragment's variant readings are incorporated in the apparatus of Vezzoni's 1994 critical edition (260.1–261.15; 261.16–33; and 263.1–264.32).

Most of the Düsseldorf fragments were recovered from books belonging to the abbey of Beyenburg near Werden. According to Zechiel-Eckes (2002), they may be the remains of a manuscript brought to Werden from York in about 772/73 by Liudger, **ALCUIN**'s Frisian pupil, though Barker-Benfield (1991 p 53 and note 43) regards the arguments for Werden provenance "weaker than most" and Bullough (2004 p 260) states that "this attractive notion has no worthwhile evidence to support it. . . ."

On **BEDE**'s reference to the *Shepherd*, see the previous entry.

Charles D. Wright

**Apocalypse of John** [ANON.Apoc.Ioh.]: *ANT* p 684; *BHG* 921–22h; *CANT* 331; *RBMA* 268.
    ed.: Tischendorf 1866 pp 70–93.

In this apocalypse, Christ answers John's questions, providing a detailed account of the end of the world: the reign of Antichrist, the death of all the living, the resurrection, the saving of sacred objects, the cleansing of the earth, the coming of Christ, the opening of the seven seals, the judgment, the punishment of the damned, and the reward of the saved. Focusing on the verse that describes the protection of icons, Whealey (2002) challenges Court's (2000 pp 25–29) dating of the text to the late-fourth century, and argues instead for the "eighth or ninth century when icons were being contested among Greek-speaking Christians" (p 535); she considers the Islamic conquest of the Middle East as also influencing the text. In addition to the Greek manuscripts edited by Tischendorf (1866), it has been found in several other languages (see *CANT* 331), but not in Latin. For this reason, and since there is considerable overlap between the Bible and the apocryphal traditions (and within the traditions themselves), Grau's (1908) use of it to offer parallels for *Christ III* (*ChristC*, A3.1; ed. Cook 1909) must be treated with caution (see Biggs 1986 p 2).

English translations appear in Walker (1870 pp 493–503) and Court (2000 pp 33–47). On the Irish evidence, see McNamara (2003b pp 87–91).

**Apocalypse of the Virgin** [ANON.Apoc.Mariae]: *ANT* pp 686–87; see *RBMA* 273.
    ed.: Wenger 1955 pp 258–59.

*MSS – A-S Vers*          none.
*Quots/Cits*          see below.
*Refs*      none.

Bauckham (1992 pp 854–56) suggests that the Greek *Apocalypse of the Virgin* and the additions to narratives of the Assumption of the Virgin in Latin (TRANSITUS) probably descend independently from the APOCALYPSE OF PAUL. With the Latin, he groups texts in Ethiopic, Irish, and Syriac, dating this apocalypse to around the fifth century; see also Mimouni (1993).

One detail, Mary's role in aiding condemned souls, in two Old English homilies — *Vercelli Homily* 15 (*HomU* 6, B3.4.6; ed. Scragg, *EETS* OS 300) and a sermon for Easter Day that survives in two versions (*NicD*, B8.5.3.2; ed. Hulme 1903–04 pp 610–14; and *NicE*; see the GOSPEL OF NICODEMUS) — may go back to this work: it has come to be known as "Delivering the Damned." In the *Apocalypse*, Mary is taken to hell with the apostles after her death so that they can view its torments. They plead with Christ, and he eventually grants a respite for the suffering souls. In the Anglo-Saxon texts, Mary, Michael, and Peter plead for the damned after the Judgment, and each is granted a third of the condemned souls. For further details, see Clayton (1986c), Hill (1992), Cutforth (1993), and Karkov (2003).

ÆLFRIC was presumably familiar with this vernacular version, and objected that neither Mary nor any other saint could save those condemned by Christ (*ÆCHom* II, 44, B1.2.48; lines 184–95; ed. Godden, *EETS* SS 5.327–34; see also Godden, *EETS* SS 18.660, and Hill 1992).

For the knowledge of this text in Ireland, see Donaghue (1942 p 9).

Mary Clayton

**Apocalypse of Paul** [ANON.Apoc.Pauli]: *ANT* 616–44; *BHL* 6580–82; *CANT* 325; *NTA* 2.712–48; *RBMA* 275–76.
    ed.: Silverstein and Hilhorst 1997 pp 66–167.

*MSS – Lists*       none.
*A-S Vers*        *HomM* 1 (B3.5.1).
*Quots/Cits*      none.
*Refs*       1. ALDH.Pros.uirg. 256.7–14.
         2. *ÆCHom* II, 22 (B1.2.26) 14–16.

Commonly known in the West as the *Visio sancti Pauli* (Jiroušková 2006 p 5 proposes restricting this title to the Latin redactions), this apocryphon was probably composed in Greek in the mid-third century. It survives in three long Latin versions found in seven manuscripts, all printed by Silverstein and Hilhorst (1997); see also Hilhorst (2003). Silverstein and Hilhorst's edition makes it clear that there are significant differences within (except for version 3, which is represented by only one manuscript) and between these groups. Although it lacks some details found in other manuscripts, Paris, Bibliothèque Nationale Nouv.acq.lat. 1631 (ed. James 1893 pp 11–42) contains the fullest account of the vision, and represents the version translated from the Greek between the mid-fifth and the opening decades of the sixth century (Silverstein and Hilhorst p 12; see also Biggs 2000). This text begins with the discovery of the record of the vision in the foundations of the house where Paul once had lived, and then shifts to Paul's account of his experience after he has been "caught up to the third heaven" (2 Corinthians 12.2). He hears creation's complaints to God against men's sins and then describes how angels report to God each day about men's activities. An angel takes him to see the souls of the sinners and the just, and shows him their deaths and judgments. Paul then visits paradise and hell. In answer to his prayers, Christ grants the damned respite from their punishment on Sundays. Paul again visits paradise, and the vision ends abruptly with him speaking to Elias.

Although Jiroušková (2006 pp 29–35) has recently proposed a new way of grouping the Latin texts that descend from the longer versions, previous scholars, particularly Silverstein (1935, 1959, and 1976), divided them into eleven redactions; on redaction XI see the following entry. According to Silverstein (1959 p 212), redaction IV "has special currency in England (perhaps even its origin there)"; the known manuscripts of this redaction, however, are later than our period (see Silverstein 1935 pp 220–21 for a list of manuscripts, and compare the descriptions in Jiroušková 2006 pp 37–139). Wright (1993 pp 106–07) notes that the redactions as a group "eliminate much of the Long Latin text, including the episode of the going-out of the souls and the entire vision of heaven, focusing instead on Paul's guided tour of hell, which they embellish with lurid interpolations." He identifies "reflexes of three interpolated motifs" — "the Hanging Sinner, the Men with Tongues of Iron and the Dragon Parthemon" — in *Blickling Homily* 16 on the Dedication of Saint Michael's Church (*LS* 25, B3.3.25; ed. Morris, *EETS* OS 58, 63, 73.196–211) and in *Vercelli Homily* 9 (*HomS* 4, B3.2.4; ed. Scragg, *EETS* OS 300.158–83) to "suggest that a redaction circulated in England in some form in the tenth century" (1993 p 107).

An eighth-century booklist from Fulda in an Anglo-Latin script lists an "apocalipsis postuli sancti Pauli" (see Lapidge 2006 p 152), which Schrimpf (1992 p 6) suggests is likely to refer either to this apocryphon or to a manuscript from Fulda containing the last book of the Bible and sermons on it by **CAESARIUS OF ARLES**.

The *Apocalypse* was popular in Anglo-Saxon England as an accessible and instructive guide to the fate of the soul at the moment of death. One clear indication of its popularity is the vigor with which it was condemned by two of the most articulate voices of the period: **ALDHELM** (prose **DE VIRGINITATE**, ed. *MGH* AA 15), writing around the turn of the eighth century, spurns the work by categorizing it with "other absurdities of the apocrypha"; and **ÆLFRIC** (*EETS* SS 5.190; see Kabir 2001a pp 14–48), writing three centuries later, repudiates it as "a false composition." Yet the influence of the *Apocalypse* continued to be felt not only through the work itself but also through three accounts of visions that drew on it: the life of Fursey (see **ACTA SANCTORUM, FURSEUS**; retold by **BEDE** in his **HISTORIA ECCLESIASTICA** III.xix, ed. Colgrave and Mynors 1969), Bede's discussion of Dryhthelm (*Historia ecclesiastica* V.xii), and **BONIFACE**'s letter to Eadburga concerning a monk of Wenlock (ed. *MGH* ES 1.7–15; see Sims-Williams 1990 pp 243–72), which in turn was translated into Old English in the tenth or eleventh century (*Let* 1, B6.1; ed. Sisam 1953 pp 199–224).

Only the first part of the *Apocalypse* was actually translated into Old English, existing in a unique copy, *HomM* 1 (ed. Healey 1978 pp 63–73). Luiselli Fadda (1974) has concluded that the translation follows a Long Latin Version, and Healey (1978) has argued that none of the extant Long Latin Versions is its source. Matter found in the Old English but lacking in the Long Latin and yet confirmed as original by the Russian and Syriac versions establishes in a positive way the existence of another Latin recension, the source of the Old English.

A number of Old English texts are indebted to the *Apocalypse* for significant motifs as well as for several minor themes. The incident of the going-out of souls can be found in the Old English version of Bede's *Historia ecclesiastica* (*Bede* 5, B9.6.7; ed. *EETS* OS 95–96.436–42), *Guthlac A* (*GuthA*, A3.2; ed. Roberts 1979 lines 1–29), and three versions of the THREE UTTERANCES APOCRYPHON (see below under MISCELLANEOUS): *HomM* 5 (B3.5.5; ed. Willard 1935a pp 39–57 [partial]; re-edited by Luiselli Fadda 1977 pp 8–21), *HomS* 5 (B3.2.5; ed. Willard 1935a pp 38–56 [partial]; re-edited by Teresi 2002 pp 226–29), and *HomS* 31 (B3.2.31; ed. Willard 1935a pp 38–54; re-edited by Bazire and Cross 1982 pp 121–23). Acker (1986) has analyzed this motif in *Blickling Homily* 4 (*HomS* 14, B3.2.14; ed. Morris, *EETS* OS 58, 63, 73.39–53 and 195). The contending of angels and devils for souls, a motif also present in the SHEPHERD OF HERMAS and the *Three Utterances Apocryphon*, is noted by Menner (1941 p 143) in *Solomon and Saturn II* lines 477–88 (*MSol*, A13; SOLOMON AND SATURN) and is discussed with reference to *Vercelli Homily* 4 (*HomU* 9, B3.4.9; ed. Scragg, *EETS* OS 300.90–104) and *Napier* 46 (*HomU* 37, B3.4.37; ed. Napier 1883 pp 232–42) by Wright (1993 pp 260–61) and Anlezark (2003 pp 130–31).

The address of the soul to the body can be found in another anonymous homily printed by Willard (*HomM* 8, B3.5.8; ed. Willard 1935b pp 963–65 [partial]), an anonymous homily in two parts edited by Healey (*HomM* 14.1, B3.5.14.1 and *HomM* 14.2, B3.5.14.2; ed. Healey 1973 pp 294–96 and 324–40), *Assmann* 14 (*HomS* 6, B3.2.6; ed. *BaP* 3.164–69), *Vercelli Homily* 4, *Napier* 29 (*HomU* 26, B3.4.26; ed. Napier 1883 pp 134–43), the "Macarius Homily" (*HomU* 55, ed. Thorpe 1840 2.394–400), and the Old English poems *Soul and Body I* and *II* (*Soul I* and *II*, A2.3 and 3.19; ed. *ASPR* 2 and 3). On this tradition, see Di Sciacca (2006).

The respite of the damned, which is the climax of Paul's journey to hell in the *Apocalypse*, appears domesticated in *Guthlac A* (*GuthA*, A3.2; ed. Roberts 1979 lines 205–14), *HomM* 8, *HomM* 14.2, *Napier* 43 (*HomU* 35.1, B3.4.35.1; ed. Napier 1883 pp 205–15), *Napier* 44 (*HomU* 35.2, B3.4.35.2; ed. Napier 1883 pp 215–26), *HomU* 55, and *Soul and Body I* and *II*.

The correspondence of punishment to sin, which conveys a straightforward justice in the *Apocalypse*, is appropriated by Old English writers in *Blickling Homily* 4, the homily for Wednesday in Rogationtide (*HomS* 42, B3.2.42; ed. Bazire and Cross 1982 pp 62–64), *Napier* 46, the translation of Boniface's letter to Eadburga (*Let* 1, B6.1; ed. Sisam 1953 pp 199–224), and *Blickling Homily* 16. On *Vercelli Homily* 9, see Wright (1993 pp 113–16).

Minor influences of the *Apocalypse* may be seen in the detail of men with tongues of iron (see Wright 1993 pp 145–56) in *Vercelli Homily* 9, *Napier* 43, and one of the Old English versions of the *Apocalypse of Thomas* (*HomU* 12.2, B3.4.12.2; ed. Willard

1935a pp 4–6). Moreover, as Hill (1969a) has suggested, the *Apocalypse* is a possible source for the northwest direction of hell in *Genesis B* (*GenB*, A1.1; ed. *ASPR* 1 line 275), and, as Cross and Hill (1982 p 120) note, the location of hell in the west in the Old English prose *Solomon and Saturn* (*Sol I*, B5.1; SOLOMON AND SATURN) and *Adrian and Ritheus* (*Ad*, B5.2); Cross and Hill (1982 p 119) also cite it as a possible ultimate source for the identification in *Solomon and Saturn* of the four rivers in paradise with milk, honey, wine, and oil.

Finally, Wright (1993 pp 122–36) has reviewed the vexed question of the relationship of the hell scene in the *Apocalypse* with the hell scene in *Blickling Homily* 16 and with the description of Grendel's mere in BEOWULF (*Beo*, A4.1; ed. Klaeber 1950 lines 1367–76). Considering all of the redactions, he concludes that the Anglo-Saxon homilist drew on a lost version of the *Visio*, perhaps used by the poet; in any case, he argues that the poet must have known the apocryphon in some form. Anlezark (2003 pp 131–32) relates this discussion to the fall of the angels in *Solomon and Saturn* II (*MSol*, A13; ed. Menner 1941 lines 441–66). Despite its censure by Aldhelm and Ælfric, Anglo-Saxon homilists and poets drew upon the *Apocalypse* to articulate the direct relationship between human deeds and the fate of the soul.

For studies of the Old English texts, see Healey (1978 pp 96–98). The work was also known to the Irish; see McNamara (1975 pp 108–09 and 2003b pp 80–87) and Wright (1993 pp 109–13). A new edition of the Armenian version is *CCSA* 3.

A. diPaolo Healey

**Apocalypse of Paul** [ANON.Apoc.Pauli.Pal.lat.220]: *CANT* 325.
   ed.: Jiroušková 2006 pp 918–21.

*MSS*      ? Rome, Vatican City, Biblioteca Apostolica Vaticana Pal.lat. 220.
*Lists – Quots/Cits*      none.
*Refs*      ? ALDH.Pros.uirg. 256.7–14.

The Vatican manuscript, in an Anglo-Saxon hand of the ninth century, has also been published by Dwyer (1988 pp 125–29). See also the discussion by Wright (1990c and 2003 p 39) and Jiroušková (2006 pp 16–17 and 142–43). This redaction is known in most of the scholarship as redaction XI. On the possibility that ALDHELM refers specifically to this version in his prose DE VIRGINITATE (ed. Gwara, *CCSL* 124–24A), see Kabir (2001a pp 16 and 55) and Biggs (2003 pp 16–17). Wright (1993) has shown the significance of this redaction for *Blickling Homily* 16 and BEOWULF; see the main entry above. See also that entry for a possible mention of the apocryphon in an eighth-century booklist from Fulda.

**Apocalypse of Peter** [ANON.Apoc.Petri]: *ANT* 593–615; *CANT* 317; *NTA* 2. 620–38.
    ed.: *ANT* pp 600–12.

*MSS – Refs*      none.

This *Apocalypse*, known in antiquity, survives primarily in Ethiopic and Greek (fragmentary) versions. No Latin texts have been identified. In it, Christ reveals to his disciples details of the Second Coming and specifies punishments that await particular sinners. Wright (1993 pp 130–31) cites it twice as perhaps the ultimate source (via a version of the APOCALYPSE OF PAUL) for details in *Blickling Homily* 16 (*LS* 25, MichaelMor, B3.3.25; ed. Morris, *EETS* OS 58, 63, 73). See also Luiselli Fadda (1977 pp 40–41).

**Apocalypse of Thomas** [ANON.Apoc.Thom.]: *ANT* 645–51; *CANT* 326; *CPL* 796a; *NTA* 2.748–52; *RBMA* 280.
    ed.: Förster 1955 pp 27–33.

*MSS*      1. ? Rome, Vatican City, Biblioteca Apostolica Vaticana Pal.lat. 220.
         2. ? Würzburg, Universitätsbibliothek M.p.th.f. 28.
*Lists*      none.
*A-S Vers*      1. *HomS* 26 (*BlHom* 7, B3.2.26).
         2. *HomS* 33 (B3.2.33).
         3. *HomS* 44 (B3.2.44).
         4. *HomU* 6 (*VercHom* 15, B3.4.6).
         5. *HomU* 12.1 (Först, B3.4.12.1).
         6. *HomU* 12.2 (Willard, B3.4.12.2).
*Quots/Cits – Refs*      none.

This *Apocalypse*, probably composed in Latin, purports to be Christ's revelation to Thomas concerning the end of the world, listing signs that will occur on each of the seven days preceding Judgment. It is condemned in the so-called GELASIAN DECREE (ed. Dobschütz, *TU* 38/4 line 293).

The *Apocalypse* survives in three forms. A shorter, non-interpolated version is "likely to have originated prior to the fifth century" and "seems to have found favor in Priscillianist circles" (*ANT* p 645). A longer one adds a historical-prophetic introduction that refers enigmatically to events of the first half of the fifth century. Finally, there are other abbreviated texts that contain only the list of signs. Wright (2003 pp 27–30) notes that "there is a remarkable degree of variation even within the manuscripts of each version" and that the textual tradition "has never been adequately sorted out." The edition designated above is a composite text; for an interpolated version, see Wilhelm (1907 pp 40*–42*). Wright (2003), who edits six new Latin texts (one first noted by Swan 1998), demonstrates the importance of considering all the known versions in order to understand the Anglo-Saxon evidence.

Wright (2003 pp 31–32) identifies the text in the Würzburg manuscript, first noted by Bischoff, as "a substantially complete interpolated text," though it does omit the political "prophecies" referring to events of the fifth century. He finds no evidence to support the traditional connection of this manuscript with Burghard, an Anglo-Saxon associate of **BONIFACE**, but he notes "insular features in the letter-forms and particularly in the ornamentation" (pp 31–32) and recalls Lowe's claim that it was "written in a German centre where Anglo-Saxon influence was still alive, presumably in Bavaria" (*CLA* 9.1408). Citing Bischoff, Wright also notes that Pal.lat. 220, an interpolated version previously known but not yet published, "was written in Anglo-Saxon script in the Middle or Upper Rhine region in the early ninth century" (p 39). He also discusses Rome, Vatican City, Biblioteca Apostolica Vaticana Reg.lat. 49, a late-tenth-century Breton manuscript that contains an abbreviated version (p 37).

Förster (1955) notes that two of the Old English versions, *Vercelli Homily* 15 (*HomU* 6, B3.4.6; ed. Scragg, *EETS* OS 300.253–61) and the one found in Cambridge, Corpus Christ College 41 (*HomU* 12.1; ed. Förster 1955 pp 17–27), draw material from the interpolation. Wright (2003 p 43) contests Förster's claim that *Blickling Homily* 7 (*HomS* 26; ed. Morris, *EETS* OS 58, 63, 73) has "a few general statements" from this source. Wright, however, argues that the absence of interpolated material in this and two other homilies, one for Rogationtide (*HomS* 33; ed. Förster 1913 pp 128–37) and a second for Wednesday in Rogationtide (*HomS* 44; ed. Bazire and Cross 1982 pp 47–54), does not mean that the original non-interpolated version circulated in Anglo-Saxon England, but rather that "these homilists chose to focus on the signs of the seven days, which occur in *both* versions" or that "their Latin sources were abbreviated texts that had already removed the characteristic interpolation" (p 43). While he does not provide a full analysis of the sources of the Old English versions, Wright offers examples to show that all the Latin texts must be considered. In a forthcoming paper on *Vercelli Homily* 15, Wright notes one reading from the non-interpolated version, but gives reasons why he still does not think such a version was available to the homilist.

The difficulty in identifying exclusive echoes of either the *Apocalypse* or the *Fifteen Signs* in poetic texts arises because the signs often have some basis in biblical passages such as Matthew 24.30. For example, *Christ III* (*ChristC*, A3.1; ed. Cook 1909; see Biggs 1986), often dated to the ninth century, does not list signs for the days preceding Judgment, but it contains in its description of the destruction of the world details found in these traditions. See, however, the suggestion by Cross (1982 p 105 note 10) that the *Apocalypse* may be the ultimate source for the phrase "mare siccabitur" in **PSEUDO-AUGUSTINE** SERMO **251**, and Wright (2003 pp 40–41 note 78). Probably deriving from the *Apocalypse* is the tradition of the FIFTEEN SIGNS BEFORE JUDGMENT (discussed below under MISCELLANEOUS). For further information on the Irish evidence, see McNamara (1975 pp 119–21 and 2003b pp 92–97). On the Old English tradition, see also Faerber (1993).

Frederick M. Biggs and Charles D. Wright

# MISCELLANEOUS

Gathered here in alphabetical order are ten texts, or more loosely traditions, which appear related to the apocrypha and are sometimes referred to as apocryphal. The APOCRYPHA PRISCILLIANISTICA is itself a collection of various texts, including the SEVEN HEAVENS APOCRYPHON. Also eschatological in nature are the FIFTEEN SIGNS BEFORE JUDGMENT (related to the APOCALYPSE OF THOMAS) and the THREE UTTERANCES APOCRYPHON, known in Anglo-Saxon England in three versions. Two other miscellaneous texts are loosely related to the life of Christ: the TRINUBIUM ANNAE recounts the three marriages of the mother of the Virgin Mary, and the HISTORY OF THE HOLY ROOD-TREE provides an elaborate history of the wood from which the Cross was made. Three texts, the BREVIARIUM APOSTOLORUM, NOMINA LOCORUM IN QUO APOSTOLI REQUIESCUNT, and NOTITIA DE LOCIS APOSTOLO-RUM, concern the apostles as a group; and one non-canonical epistle, the EPISTLE OF BARNABAS, is included here in part because of the way it was used in Anglo-Saxon England. Finally, the SUNDAY LISTS, which become associated with the SUNDAY LETTER, incorporate apocryphal traditions into their accounts of sacred events that happened on Sundays. As a group, these works often show the dissemination of "new" apocryphal traditions during the Anglo-Saxon period.

**Apocrypha Priscillianistica** [ANON.Apoc.Pris.]: *BCLL* 1252; *CPL* 790–95; *KVS* AN Bruyne; *RBMA* 283.
    ed.: De Bruyne 1907.

*MSS*      1. London, BL Royal 5.E.XIII: HG 459.
        2. Salisbury, Cathedral Library 9: HG 699.
        3. ? Munich, Bayerische Staatsbibliothek clm 19410.
*Lists – A-S Vers*    none.
*Quots/Cits*    HomS 44 (B3.2.44) 51.91–96: see below.
*Refs*    none.

The *Apocrypha Priscillianistica* consist of six texts published by De Bruyne (1907) from Karlsruhe, Badische Landesbibliothek Aug. CCLIV (end of the eighth century, from Novara; see *CLA* 8.1100 and Cau 1971–74 pp 29–32), the first six items in a larger compilation headed in the manuscript "incipit collectario de diversis senten-tiis." The Royal manuscript includes the beginning of De Bruyne's item 6 (*Liber*

73

*"canon in ebreica" Hieronimi presbiteri, CPL* 795; see also *BHM* 403 and Bischoff 1976 p 159 note 126) in an expanded version, before breaking off; on the manuscript, see Warner and Gilson (1921 1.116), Petitmengin (1993 pp 622–26), Hall (1996 pp 48–49), and Ambrose (2005 pp 108–14). The Salisbury and Munich manuscripts include variant texts of item 4 (*Homilia de die iudicii, CPL* 793), on which see Wright (1993 p 226, crediting the discovery to J. E. Cross). On the Salisbury manuscript see generally Schenkl (1891–1908 no. 3608), Webber (1992 pp 148–49), and Hall (1994 pp 136–37). The Munich manuscript, written at Passau during the episcopacy of Hartwig (840 x 866), contains several items that suggest indirect connections to Anglo-Saxon England, including a sylloge of Roman inscriptions attributed to **MILRED OF WORCESTER**, the poem SANCTE SATOR attributed to **THEODORE OF CANTERBURY**, and a futhorc of Anglian type; see Wright (1993 pp 63–65), Brunhölzl (2000), and Gretsch and Gneuss (2005), who argue that some of the Old High German glosses to *Sancte sator* in the manuscript must derive from Old English glosses. Wright (1993 p 65 note 82) points out that substantial portions of the *Apocrypha Priscillianistica* (including part of item 4, but not the Judgment passage) also occur in Einsiedeln, Stiftsbibliothek 199 (*CLA* 7.875). Item 2 is an epitome of the so-called SEVEN HEAVENS APOCRYPHON. Item 3 includes parallels with the APOCALYPSE OF THOMAS (see Bihlmeyer 1911). The Karlsruhe manuscript also contains a text of the THREE UTTERANCES APOCRYPHON (see Wack and Wright 1991).

De Bruyne's theory of Priscillianist origins for these pieces has since been abandoned (see Vollmann 1965 p 48), but James (1918–19 p 16) remarked that they "appear to be from a Celtic workshop," an opinion supported by many other scholars; for details, see Wright (1987 pp 135–36) and Frede (*KVS* p 124). Wright (1993 pp 64–66) outlines the parallels with Irish traditions, including the *Seven Heavens Apocryphon*, extracts from **HIBERNO-LATIN BIBLICAL COMMENTARIES** (first remarked by Dumville 1973 p 327), and other themes and enumerations paralleled in Hiberno-Latin compilations, including the LIBER DE NUMERIS, the FLORILEGIUM FRISINGENSE, the CATECHESIS CELTICA, and the homilies IN NOMINE DEI SUMMI.

Wright (1990b; see also Wright 1993 pp 225–26) shows that a Judgment theme in item 4 — in which Christ demands a pledge for each man's thoughts, words, and deeds, and each responds that he has nothing to pledge but his soul — is the ultimate source for a closely similar passage in *HomS* 44 (B3.2.44; ed. Bazire and Cross 1982 pp 47–54 lines 91–96), where the Old English term *wedd* corresponds to the Latin *area* (= *arrha*). A similar idea occurs in several other Old English homilies. Luiselli Fadda (1977 p 101) printed part of the theme from item 4 opposite a passage from a homily for Rogationtide (*HomS* 32, B3.2.32; ed. Bazire and Cross 1982 pp 131–35), but here there are no close verbal parallels with the Latin, and only one other homily, *In Sabbato sancto* (*HomS* 25, B3.2.25; ed. Ruth Evans 1981 p 142 lines 351–53) uses the distinctive term *wedd*. Wright points out, however, that **CYNEWULF**'s *Elene* (*El*, A2.6; ed. *ASPR* 2; lines 1281b–86a) echoes the theme with the phrase *wed gesyllan* and the "thought, word, deed" triad. For an echo of this tradition in an Old Frisian legal text, see Hill (1998).

Charles D. Wright

**Breviarium apostolorum** [ANON.Breu.apos.]: *BHL* 652; *RBMA* 191,1.
  ed.: Mohlberg 1981 pp 260–61.

*MSS*    none.
*Lists*    ? see APOCRYPHAL ACTS (above).
*A-S Vers – Refs*    none.

The *Breviarium* lists thirteen apostles (including both Paul and Matthias, but excluding Judas Iscariot) and provides in most cases a brief biography, the feast day, and an etymology for the name of each. The first manuscript witness of the work is in the two supplementary quires of the *Gelasian Sacramentary* (Rome, Vatican City, Biblioteca Apostolica Vaticana Reg.lat. 316) preserved in Paris (Bibliothèque Nationale lat. 7193; see Lowe 1925–26 pp 357–73), a manuscript that dates to the eighth century. As noted by de Gaiffier (1963), the work also appears in Rome, Vatican City, Biblioteca Apostolica Vaticana Pal. lat. 235, but beyond the folios accepted by HG 910.

The possibility that the *Breviarium* is a source for **CYNEWULF**'s *Fates of the Apostles* (*Fates*, A2.2; ed. Brooks 1961) has been discussed since Sarrazin (1889), but the problem has remained unresolved because there is much overlap among the possible sources, and no single source has been identified for the entire poem; see, in particular, Cross (1979a passim). Lapidge (in Lapidge and Rosier 1985 p 42) asserts that section 4 of **ALDHELM**'s **CARMINA ECCLESIASTICA** ("On the Altars of the Twelve Apostles"; ed. *MGH* AA 15) belongs to a tradition that includes this work.

Schermann's edition (1907 pp 207–11) notes readings from six manuscripts. It is translated in Allen and Calder (1976 pp 37–39).

**Delivering the Damned**: see APOCALYPSE OF THE VIRGIN.

**Epistle of Barnabas** [ANON.Ep.Barn.]: *CPG* 1050; *KVS* p 199; *ODCC* p 160.
  ed.: Heer 1908 pp 2–89.

*MSS – Refs*    none.

Although usually considered among the works of the *Apostolic Fathers* (*ODCC* p 91; see also *NTA* 2.33), the *Epistle of Barnabas* is mentioned here because the single motif that requires its inclusion — the claim in *Adrian and Ritheus* (*Ad*, B5.2; ed. Cross and Hill 1982 p 148) that "Belda the fish in the sea" is "sometimes female and sometimes male" — strongly resembles a number of the naturalistic, sapiential, and etiological motifs in the prose SOLOMON AND SATURN (*Sol I*, B5.1) which appear to rest ultimately on apocryphal traditions. Some support for including the *Epistle of Barnabas* among the apocrypha is provided by its appearance in the fourth-century

*Codex Sinaiticus* and by **CLEMENT OF ALEXANDRIA**'s attribution of the letter to Barnabas, companion of Paul in the Acts of the Apostles (especially 13–15). The letter itself attacks Jewish practice concerning, for example, sacrifice, fasting, and circumcision, and seeks to explain Christian belief. It was probably written near the end of the first century A.D. by a Christian living in Alexandria. In addition to the copy in the *Codex Sinaiticus*, the *Epistle* survives in a number of Greek manuscripts and fragments and in a single Latin version that breaks off at the end of chapter 17.

In discussing the Belda passage in *Adrian and Ritheus*, Cross and Hill (1982 p 148) note that *Epistle* 10.7 forbids the eating of the *belua* "quia haec bestia alternis annis mutat naturam et fit modo masculus, modo femina" (Heer 1908 p 61; "because that animal in alternate years changes its sex and is at one time male and at another time female"). See further their explanations of other problems arising from this question.

**Fifteen Signs before Judgment** [ANON.Quindecim.signis].
    ed.: Bayless and Lapidge 1998 p 178.

*MSS – Lists*      none.
*A-S Vers*      *Notes* 22 (Warn, B24.22).
*Quots/Cits – Refs*      none.

The *Fifteen Signs before Judgment* was perhaps inspired by the listing of signs that will occur on each of the seven days preceding Judgment in the **APOCALYPSE OF THOMAS**. Heist (1952) specifically argues that the early Middle Irish poem *Saltair na Rann* provides the transition; however, this thesis seems questionable in light of more recent work on the **PSEUDO-BEDE COLLECTANEA BEDAE**, in which a Latin version of the work appears. Lapidge (in Bayless and Lapidge 1998 p 12) concludes that "the majority of its localizable contents originated either in Ireland or England, or in an Irish foundation on the Continent, and that the majority of its datable contents are most plausibly assigned to the middle decades of the eighth century"; see also Lendinara (2003 pp 98–101). On the Irish evidence, see also McNamara (1975 pp 128–38 and 2003b pp 92–97).

An Old English translation (*Notes* 22, B24.22; ed. Warner, *EETS* OS 152.89–91) appears in the twelfth-century manuscript London, BL Cotton Vespasian D.xiv.

The work has been cited, particularly by Hill (1972b; see also 1969b and 1971), as a possible source for *Christ III* (*ChristC*, A3.1; ed. Cook 1909; see also Biggs 1986). As with the *Apocalypse of Thomas*, the difficulty is establishing exclusive relationships between the two texts.

**History of the Holy-Rood Tree** [ANON.Hist.ligno.crucis].
  ed.: *EETS* OS 103.41–53 and 57–63.

*MSS – Lists*        none.
*A-S Vers*        *LS* 5 (InventCrossNap, B3.3.5).
*Quots/Cits – Refs*        none.

Incorporating at its end a brief version of the INVENTIO SANCTAE CRUCIS (see ACTA SANCTORUM, IESUS CHRISTUS), this legend provides an elaborate history involving numerous miracles of the Cross. Three rods discovered by Moses are passed to David, who places them in a well so they grow into a single tree. Solomon tries but fails to use its wood in building the Temple, where it remains until it is used at the time of the Crucifixion.

Napier (*EETS* OS 103) prints the Latin text from two manuscripts, one of the twelfth, the other of the fourteenth century; the earlier manuscript breaks off near the end, but Napier plausibly suggests that it probably once had a conclusion "identical with" that in the later one (p 53). He also edits a vernacular version from Oxford, Bodleian Library Bodley 343 (*LS* 5), a twelfth-century manuscript. Ker (1940 pp 84–85) discovered an Old English fragment (in an eleventh-century hand) that corresponds to two passages from Napier's vernacular text, confirming that the work was known in Anglo-Saxon England.

The relationship of this legend to those that describe the Cross as having originated in paradise has been discussed by Quinn (1962). It is to the latter tradition that Kaske (1967 pp 64–67) refers in interpreting *Riddle 60* (A3.31.2; ed. *ASPR* 3) and the *Husband's Message* (A3.32; ed. *ASPR* 3). On legends of the Cross in Anglo-Saxon England, see also Stevens (1977; with a new preface by Thomas D. Hill).

**Nomina locorum in quo apostoli requiescunt** [ANON.Nom.apost.]: *BHL* 651d.
  ed.: *SS* 140.195–97.

*MSS*        Durham, Cathedral Library A.IV.19: HG 223.
*Lists – Refs*        none.

As the title indicates, this text lists the resting-places of the apostles, including John the Baptist and Stephen. It occurs in the *Durham Ritual* (ed. Lindelöf, *SS* 140.195–97), where it is accompanied by an interlinear gloss in Old English (*DurRitGlCom*; C13.1).

**Notitia de locis apostolorum** [ANON.Notit.apost.]: *BHL* 648.
  ed.: Schermann 1907 pp 212–13.

*MSS – Refs*        none.

Printed in the introductory material to the MARTYROLOGIUM HIERONYMIA-
NUM (see **MARTYROLOGIES**) in the *PL* (30.435–37), the *Notitia* lists the feasts of
twelve apostles, in most cases a place with which they are associated, and in some cases
additional biographical details.

Brooks (1961 p xxx) comments that the order of apostles in **CYNEWULF**'s *Fates
of the Apostles* (A2.2) is closest to that found in this work; see also Cross (1979a).
Thacker (2000 p 277) suggests that it "represents insular tradition." The text appears
in the *AS* (Nov, vol 2 pars posterior, p 2), from which Allen and Calder (1976 p 37)
translate.

**Seven Heavens Apocryphon** [ANON.Septem.cael.].

The so-called *Seven Heavens Apocryphon* describes (in broken and confused
fashion) the journey and purgation of the soul through the heavens, assigning names to
each heaven as well as to the doors of each. For a survey of the motif in early Jewish and
Christian apocalypses, see Collins (1995). The apocryphon survives in a Latin epitome
in Karlsruhe, Badische Landesbibliothek Aug. CCLIV (see **APOCRYPHA PRISCILLIA-
NISTICA**) and in variant forms in three Irish texts: the *Vision of Adomnán*, the *Evernew
Tongue*, and an excerpt in the *Liber Flavus Fergusiorum* (ed. Mac Niocaill 1956). The
relationships among these texts have been studied by James (1918–19, with suggested
emendations for the Latin fragment in the *Apocrypha Priscillianistica*), Seymour (1923,
with a translation of the Latin from the *Apocrypha Priscillianistica*, pp 22–23),
Seymour (1927 and 1930 pp 112–20), Dando (1972), Dumville (1977–78),
Stevenson (1982), Bauckham (1993), and Carey (2003). For lists of the names of the
seven heavens in Hiberno-Latin texts, see Cross (1986 pp 78–79 and 90–91) and C.
D. Wright and R. Wright (2004 p 87 note 14). The list in London, BL Royal 8.C.III
(HG 475) is "apparently taken from a version of the *Reference Bible*" (see **HIBERNO-
LATIN BIBLICAL COMMENTARIES**, no. 1, as well as Wright 1990a and 1993
p 219).

The apocryphon appears in one of the Old English versions of the **APOCALYPSE
OF THOMAS** (*HomU* 12.2, B3.4.12.2; ed. Willard 1935a pp 4–6). Willard (1935a pp
1–30) provides a detailed examination of the relationship between the homily and the
other versions known at the time (see also Wright 1993 pp 218–21). He finds a use of
it in an Easter Day homily in Cambridge, Corpus Christi College 162 (*HomS* 27; ed.
Lees 1986 lines 35–38; see her discussion p 132): in the beginning God creates seven
heavens, the seventh as a seat for the Trinity (1935a p 23 note 113); see also Wright
(1993 p 265), who discusses an allusion to "the heaven of the Holy Trinity" in *Vercelli
Homily* 4 (*HomU* 9, B3.4.9; ed. Scragg, *EETS* OS 300.90–104). In addition, Willard

discusses a passage in a homily for the Third Sunday after Epiphany, "Be Heofon-warum and be Helwarum" (*HomS* 5, B3.2.5; ed. Teresi 2002 pp 226–29; partially edited by Willard 1935a pp 38–56), on the descent of the soul through twelve dragons and twelve circles of hell (see pp 24–28), which he shows is closely related to the Old English and Latin versions of the apocryphon; on this motif see Kabir (2001b), Carey (2003), and Rowley (2003). Kabir (2001a pp 290–91) suggests that the motif is alluded to in *Napier* 29 (*HomU* 26, B3.4.26; ed. Napier 1881 p 141 lines 23–25), and that the homily's description of devils stabbing a sinner as his soul tries to exit the body (lines 4–11) is also influenced by the *Seven Heavens Apocryphon*. Wright (1993 pp 220–21) discusses another detail from this homily "not printed or discussed by Willard, but which probably also derives from the Gnostic sources of the *Seven Heavens Apocryphon*: the fire of hell . . . is nine times hotter than the fire of Judgement."

Charles D. Wright

**Sunday Lists** [ANON.Dies.dom.]: *DACL* 4.985–86; see also DIES DOMINICA (HIBERNO-LATIN BIBLICAL COMMENTARIES, Wright 1990a no. 4).

*Sunday Lists* enumerate sacred events that happened on Sundays to increase veneration of the day. Tveitane (1966 p 127) proposed that they "developed from a shorter form, agreeing with biblical tradition, towards a much longer, apocryphal version, which appears together with and within the Sunday Letter" (see SUNDAY LETTER). Lees (1985) divides them into "short lists with scriptural identification of the day" (including examples from PSEUDO-ALCUIN, HRABANUS MAURUS, ISIDORE, and POPE LEO I), "lists in councils," "expanded lists" (including PSEUDO-AUGUSTINE, SERMO APP. 167; the *Bobbio Missal*; and Cambridge, Pembroke College 25 [see HOMILIARIES, HOMILIARY OF SAINT-PÈRE DE CHARTRES]), and "Insular lists including those in 'Sunday Letters.'"

In her fourth category, Lees places three texts edited by McNally (*CCSL* 108B.181–86; see Bischoff 1976 no. 39; McNamara 1975 p 63, no. 52C; Kelly 1988 pp 548–49; *BCLL* 903–05; and, in addition to the references below, *RBMA* 10060,1 [Recension I] and 11562,1 [Recension III]) in a collection of Hiberno-Latin writings. One, Recension II (ed. *CCSL* 108B.183–84), survives in Rome, Vatican City, Biblioteca Apostolica Vaticana Pal.lat. 220, a ninth-century manuscript written in an Anglo-Saxon hand (see Wright 1993 p 111 and 2003 p 39); Wright (1990a) calls attention to two other copies of this recension, unknown to McNally: Karlsruhe, Badische Landesbibliothek Aug. CCLV, fol 8 (ninth century; for the incipit and explicit, see *RBMA* 9419 [not cross-referenced at *RBMA* 11560,1]) and St. Gall, Stiftsbibliothek 682, pp 330–34. Six other texts in this category are Old English homilies that use both the *Sunday Letter* and *Sunday List*: *Napier* 43 (*HomU* 35.1; ed. Napier 1883 pp 205–15), *Napier* 44 (*HomU* 35.2; ed. Napier 1883 pp 215–26), *Napier* 45 (*HomU* 36; ed. Napier 1883 pp 226–32), *Napier* 57 (*HomU* 46; ed. Napier 1883 pp 289–91), "Be þam drihtenlican sunnandæg folces lar" (*HomU* 53; ed. Napier

1901 pp 357–62), and an Easter Day homily in Cambridge, Corpus Christi College 162 (*HomS* 27; ed. Lees 1986 pp 117–23). Lees also includes a list from London, Lambeth Palace 487 (ed. *EETS* OS 29/34.139–45), but the manuscript is not in HG.

The relationships among these texts have not yet been fully established. Whitelock (1982 pp 62–64) suggests that *HomU* 35.1, *HomU* 35.2, *HomU* 46, and *HomU* 53 as well as the Irish *Cáin Domnaig* all used "the same, or a similar, list." Lees (1985 p 149) states that *HomS* 27 "must be described as a variant of the 'Sunday List' tradition." She concludes her study by noting that "the order of the items within individual lists can be dictated by personal idiosyncracy."


**Three Utterances Apocryphon** [ANON.Exitu.anim.].

The *Three Utterances Apocryphon*, which describes the contest of angels and devils for souls as they leave the body and the exclamations of the souls as they are led to heaven or to hell, is one of the eschatological themes found in Old English homilies that appear to have been transmitted by the Irish; see Willard (1935a p 145) and Wright (1993 pp 215–18). An Old Irish version was edited by Marstrander (1911). A Latin version was published by Dudley (1911 pp 164–65) from an eleventh-century manuscript, Paris, Bibliothèque Nationale lat. 2628, and republished by Willard (1935a pp 38–54). Other Latin texts have been edited by Willard (1937b pp 150–57), Grégoire (1966 pp 224–25; he identified five more manuscripts), McNally (1979 pp 134–36; from two manuscripts, one of which, Rome, Vatican City, Biblioteca Apostolica Vaticana Pal.lat. 220, is treated in an entry below), and García Larragueta (1984 pp 139–46). Wright (1993 pp 216–17), who has identified thirty-nine manuscripts, notes that "many of the earliest show Insular palaeographical symptoms," suggesting that "Irish and Anglo-Saxon missions played an important role in the early transmission of the sermon on the Continent." See also C. D. Wright and R. Wright (2004 p 84). Willard (1937b) distinguished two main recensions of the Latin sermon: the more common one that begins "Primum quidem decet nos audire iustitiam, deinde intellegere," and a variant recension that begins, "Et cum anima uniuscuiusque migraverit de suo corpore, duo hostes in obviam veniunt." A third, abbreviated recension was identified by Wack and Wright (1991 pp 189–90) from Munich, Bayerische Staatsbibliothek clm 28135, treated in an entry below.

Willard (1935a pp 38–57) published partial editions of three Old English versions of the apocryphon. One, from Oxford, Bodleian Library Hatton 114 (*HomS* 31, B3.2.31) has been re-edited by Bazire and Cross (1982 pp 121–23). The second, titled "Be Heofonwarum and be Helwarum" (*HomS* 5, B3.2.5; ed. Teresi 2002 pp 226–29; partially edited by Willard 1935a pp 38–56), is from London, BL Cotton Faustina A.ix and Cambridge, Corpus Christi College 302; this homily is unusual in transferring the scene to the Last Judgment. On the third, from Oxford, Bodleian Library Junius 85/86, see the entry below. Wright (1993 p 217) states that the Hatton and Faustina/Corpus homilies "are closest to the previously edited versions of the Latin sermon, though both show significant divergences and are clearly not translated directly from any known Latin text." Teresi (2000 pp 104–06) designates this form of the exemplum as "tradition A," which "portrays two bands of angels, one good and bright and one evil and black, fighting for the possession of a soul whose fate has not yet been determined," whereas the Junius version (based on the abbreviated recension in Munich clm 28135, treated in a separate entry) belongs to "tradition B," in which "the soul's destiny has already been determined and it shows in its colour when it comes out of the body, to be met by the appropriate band only" (p 105).

In **BEDE**'s account of the vision of the thegn of King Coenred of the Mercians (**HISTORIA ECCLESIASTICA** V.xiii), a demon claims his sinful soul with the words "noster est iste," which Colgrave and Mynors (1969 p 500 note 1, citing Willard 1935a pp 95ff.) suggest is a "reminiscence" of the cry of the devils and angels in the *Three Utterances Apocryphon* ("noster est ille vir/homo"). See also Wright (2001 p 348) and Sims-Williams (1990 p 255), who considers this "perhaps an echo" of the *Apocryphon*, though he also notes the cry "noster est" in a **PSEUDO-AUGUSTINE** sermon, **AD FRATRES IN EREMO 69**, and in related soul-and-body sermons (ed. Dudley 1909 p 228).

Willard (1935a pp 74–76) has also noted the influence of the *Three Utterances Apocryphon* in conjunction with the **APOCALYPSE OF PAUL** in *Napier* 46 (*HomU* 37, B3.4.37; ed. Napier 1883 pp 232–42, at 235.6–21 and 236.17–237.10). Teresi (2002 pp 222–23 note 45) notes that the *Three Utterances* text in *HomS* 5 (ed. Teresi p 227 lines 20–21) refers to Paul weeping for the souls. On the relationships of the Old English and Latin homiletic version, see also Di Sciacca (2002 pp 241–43 and note 58), who suggests some further echoes of the *Three Utterances* in *Vercelli Homily* 4 (*HomU* 9, B3.4.9; ed. Scragg, *EETS* OS 300) and also in the parallel accounts of the going-out of souls in *Napier* 29 (*HomU* 26, B3.4.26; ed. Napier 1883 pp 134–43) and the "Macarius Homily" (*HomU* 55, B3.4.55; ed. Thorpe 1840 2.394–400).

Roberts (1979 pp 24–25 and 29; and 1988 pp 6 and 9) suggests that the *Three Utterances* may have influenced the depiction of the soul's journey in *Guthlac A* lines 1–29 and 781ff. and that the demons' gentle treatment of Guthlac after his journey to the gates of hell (lines 699 and 732) may echo the angels' gentle treatment of the good soul in the *Three Utterances*; she reprints part of Dudley's Latin text in an appendix, p 230.

Charles D. Wright

**Three Utterances Apocryphon** [ANON.Exitu.anim.pal.lat.220].
   ed.: McNally 1979 pp 134–36.

*MSS*     ? Rome, Vatican City, Biblioteca Apostolica Vaticana Pal.lat. 220.
*Lists – Refs*     none.

   The Vatican manuscript was written in an Anglo-Saxon hand of the early-ninth century (*CLA* 9.1408 and Wright 2003 p 39). The *Three Utterances Apocryphon* (in the recension "Primum quidem decet nos audire iustitiam, deinde intellegere") is the first of seven sermons rubricated *In nomine Dei summi*; see **HIBERNO-LATIN BIBLI-CAL COMMENTARIES** (Wright 1990a no. 47). For a recent discussion of these sermons, see O'Loughlin (2001, with reference to the *Three Utterances* at pp 36–37). O'Loughlin (1998) has translated all these homilies (for the *Three Utterances*, see pp 101–05). Teresi (2000 pp 105–06) characterizes this text of the *Three Utterances* as "the closest Latin version" to *HomS* 31 (B3.2.31) and *HomS* 5 (B3.2.5), for which see the main entry above.

Charles D. Wright

**Three Utterances Apocryphon** [ANON.Exitu.anim.clm.6433].
  ed.: unedited.

*MSS*     ? Munich, Bayerische Staatsbibliothek clm 6433.
*Lists – Refs*     none.

A copy of the Latin recension "Primum quidem decet nos audire iustitiam, deinde intellegere" appears in the Munich manuscript, which contains the *Florilegium Frisingense* (ed. *CCSL* 108D), written by Peregrinus, an Anglo-Saxon, in Freising at the end of the eighth century and now preserved in Munich (*CLA* 9.1283; Bischoff 1960 pp 61–63 and 73–75; and Wright 1993 p 56). See also **HIBERNO-LATIN BIBLICAL COMMENTARIES** (Wright 1990a no. 40).

Charles. D. Wright

**Three Utterances Apocryphon** [ANON.Exitu.anim.clm.28135].
  ed.: Wack and Wright 1991 pp 189–90.

*MSS – Lists*     none.
*A-S Vers*     *HomM* 5 (Willard; B3.5.5).
*Quots/Cits – Refs*     none.

An abbreviated version of the *Three Utterances Apocryphon* in Oxford, Bodleian Library Junius 85/86 (*HomM* 5) was edited by Willard (1935a pp 39–57) and re-edited by Luiselli Fadda (1977 pp 8–21). Wack and Wright (1991) establish that its source is a distinctive abbreviated redaction that begins "Anima hominis peccatoris cum exigerit de corpore," found in a ninth-century manuscript, Munich, Bayerische Staatsbibliothek clm 28135 (see **HIBERNO-LATIN BIBLICAL COMMEN-TARIES**; Wright 1990a no. 49), which also includes a text of the longer version "Primum quidem decet nos. . . ." The abbreviated recension (in both the Latin and the Old English) omits the initial struggle between the devils and angels and incorporates unique variants within the utterances of both the damned and saved. Teresi (2000 p 105) designates this form of the exemplum as "tradition B," in contrast to tradition A, for which see the main entry, above. Kabir (2001a pp 51–52) comments on another distinctive feature, the mention of paradise as the interim destination of the good soul.

Willard (1935b p 980 note 77) points out that in *Vercelli Homily* 4 (*HomU* 9, B3.4.9; ed. Scragg, *EETS* OS 300.90–104 lines 120–23) the angels bless the good soul after it is conducted before God's throne with the same Psalm verses (64.5–6, "Beatus quem eligisti . . .") that the angels use to praise the good soul in the *Three Utterances.* Wright (1993 pp 264–65) compares the phrasing of *Vercelli* 4 with the version in *HomM* 5 (as edited by Luiselli Fadda) and its Latin source in clm 28135. In his note on the passage in *Vercelli* 4, Scragg (*EETS* OS 300.106) also mentions the similar phrasing with the passage in *HomM* 5 and says that "the sentence is so far from the wording of the psalm that I suspect a common Old English source for the two instances." Lendinara (1993 pp 310–11) has discussed the Old English translations of the word *tabernaculis* from Psalm 64.5 in the Old English *Three Utterances* homilies.

On clm 28135 see also C. D. Wright and R. Wright (2004 p 83).

Charles D. Wright

**Trinubium Annae** [ANON.Trinub.An.]: *BHL* 505zl.
   ed.: Hall 2002 p 115.

*MSS*    Cambridge, St. John's College 35: HG 147.
*Lists*    none.
*A-S Vers*    *HomU* 56 (Warner 43, B3.4.56).
*Quots/Cits – Refs*    none.

**HAYMO OF AUXERRE**'s HISTORIAE SACRAE EPITOME (*PL* 118.823–24) provides the earliest known detailed account of Anne's three marriages — to Joachim, Cleophas, and Salome — and of the three Marys born from these unions: Mary the mother of Jesus; Mary Cleophas, who married Alpheus and bore James the Less and Joseph; and Mary, who married Zebedee and bore John the Evangelist and James the Great. For references to expressions of similar ideas elsewhere in Carolingian sermons, see Pope (*EETS* OS 259.218–19) and Hall (2002 pp 108–09). The legend became popular because it contributed to the story of Anne and explained both the references to Christ's brothers and the identities of the Marys at the Crucifixion.

The Cambridge manuscript contains the earliest known independently circulating version of the story. Hall (2002 p 113) suggests that it was written at Bury St. Edmunds "at the end of the eleventh or beginning of the twelfth century." Gransden (2004 p 642) adds that it may have been copied from a continental archetype brought there by Abbot Baldwin (d. 1097). As Hall (2002 pp 131–33) has shown, it represents the textual tradition of the Old English translation that is appended to a sermon, known as *Warner* 43 (*HomU* 56; ed. *EETS* OS 152.139), on the Assumption of the Virgin authored by **RALPH D'ESCURES**, bishop of Rochester and later archbishop of Canterbury (1114–22) in a twelfth-century manuscript (London, BL Cotton Vespasian D.xiv; HG 392). Against this evidence for the late arrival of this material in England must be weighed ÆLFRIC's references, noted by Pope (*EETS* OS 259.217–20), to John the Evangelist as Christ's "mother's sister's son." Indeed, Biggs (forthcoming) argues that since Ælfric elsewhere stresses that Anne and Joachim lived according to the Old Law, a detail found in both the Latin and Old English versions of the *Trinubium Annae* discussed here, he may have known this tradition or perhaps even have played a role in promoting its independent circulation.

Frederick M. Biggs and Thomas N. Hall

# BIBLIOGRAPHY

Acerbi, Antonio. 1996. "Gli apocrifi tra auctoritas e veritas." In *La Bibbia nel Medioevo*, ed. Giuseppe Cremascoli and Claudio Leonardi, 109–39. Collana 'La Bibbia nella storia' 16. Bologna.

Acker, Paul. 1986. "The Going-Out of the Soul in Blickling Homily IV." *English Language Notes* 23/4: 1–3.

Aerts, Willem J., and George A. A. Kortekaas, eds. 1998. *Die Apokalypse des Pseudo-Methodius: Die ältesten griechischen und lateinischen Übersetzungen*. 2 vols. Corpus Scriptorum Christianorum Orientalium 569–70, Subsidia 97–98. Louvain.

Alexander, Paul J. 1985. *The Byzantine Apocalyptic Tradition*. Ed. Dorothy deF. Abrahamse. Berkeley, Calif.

Allen, Michael J. B., and Daniel G. Calder. 1976. *Sources and Analogues of Old English Poetry: The Major Latin Texts in Translation*. Cambridge.

Allen, Thomas P. 1968. "A Critical Edition of the Old English Gospel of Nicodemus." Ph.D. diss., Rice University.

Ambrose, Shannon. 2005. "The *Collectio Canonum Hibernensis* and the Literature of the Anglo-Saxon Benedictine Reform." *Viator* 36: 107–18.

Anderson, Gary A. 1998. "Adam and Eve in the 'Life of Adam and Eve.'" In *Biblical Figures outside the Bible*, ed. Michael E. Stone and Theodore A. Bergen, 7–32. Harrisburg, Pa.

———. 2000. "The Punishment of Adam and Eve in the *Life of Adam and Eve*." In Anderson, Stone, and Tromp 2000 pp 57–81.

Anderson, Gary A., and Michael E. Stone. 1999. *A Synopsis of the Books of Adam and Eve*. 2nd revised ed. Society of Biblical Literature, Early Judaism and Its Literature 17. Atlanta, Ga.

Anderson, Gary A., Michael Stone, and Johannes Tromp. 2000. *Literature on Adam and Eve*. Studia in Veteris Testamenti Pseudepigrapha 15. Leiden.

Anlezark, Daniel. 2002. "Sceaf, Japheth and the Origins of the Anglo-Saxons." *Anglo-Saxon England* 31: 13–46.

———. 2003. "The Fall of the Angels in *Solomon and Saturn II*." In Powell and Scragg 2003 pp 121–33.

Atherton, M. 1996. "The Sources of the ANON (OE) Vercelli Homily 6 (Cameron B.3.4.10)." *Fontes Anglo-Saxonici: World Wide Web Register*, http://fontes.english.ox.ac.uk/, accessed May 2005.

Baesecke, Georg. 1933. *Der Vocabularius Sti. Galli in der angelsächsischen Mission*. Halle.

Bannister, Arthur Thomas. 1927. *A Descriptive Catalogue of the Manuscripts in the Hereford Cathedral Library.* Hereford.

Barker-Benfield, B. C. 1991. "The Werden 'Heptateuch.'" *Anglo-Saxon England* 20: 43–64.

Barnard, L. W. 1968. "The Shepherd of Hermas in Recent Study." *Heythrop Journal* 9: 29–36.

Bateson, Mary. 1895. "A Worcester Cathedral Book of Ecclesiastical Collections, Made *c.* 1000 A.D." *English Historical Review* 10: 712–31.

Bauckham, R. J. 1974. "The Great Tribulation in the Shepherd of Hermas." *Journal of Theological Studies* n.s. 25: 27–40.

Bauckham, Richard. 1992. "Virgin, Apocalypses of the." In *The Anchor Bible Dictionary*, ed. David Noel Freedman, 6.854–56. 6 vols. New York.

———. 1993. "The Apocalypse of the Seven Heavens: The Latin Versions." *Apocrypha* 4: 141–73.

Baumler, Ellen B. 1985. *Andrew in the City of the Cannibals: A Comparative Study of the Latin, Greek, and Old English Texts.* Ph.D. diss., University of Kansas.

Bayless, Martha, and Michael Lapidge, eds. 1998. *Collectanea Pseudo-Bedae.* Scriptores Latini Hiberniae 14. Dublin.

Bazire, Joyce, and James E. Cross, eds. 1982. *Eleven Old English Rogationtide Homilies.* Toronto.

Bensly, Robert L., and M. R. James, eds. 1895. *The Fourth Book of Ezra.* Texts and Studies 3/2. Cambridge.

Bergren, Theodore A. 1998. *Sixth Ezra: The Text and Origin.* New York.

Bethurum, Dorothy, ed. 1957. *The Homilies of Wulfstan.* Oxford. Reprinted with corrections 1971.

*Bibliotheca Phillippica, N.S.: Medieval MSS, Part I. Catalogue of Thirty-Nine Manuscripts of the 9th–16th Century.* 1965. London.

Biggs, Frederick M. 1986. *The Sources of Christ III: A Revision of Cook's Notes.* Old English Newsletter Subsidia 12. Binghamton, N.Y.

———. 1988. "The Passion of Andreas: *Andreas* 1398–1491." *Studies in Philology* 85: 413–27.

———. 1989–90. "The Fourfold Division of Souls: The Old English 'Christ III' and the Insular Homiletic Tradition." *Traditio* 45: 69–85.

———. 2000. Review of Silverstein and Hilhorst 1997. *Journal of Medieval Latin* 10: 433–35.

———. 2002. "Vercelli Homily 6 and the Apocryphal *Gospel of Pseudo-Matthew*." *Notes and Queries* n.s. 49: 176–78.

———. 2003. "An Introduction and Overview of Recent Work." In Powell and Scragg 2003 pp 1–25.

———. 2005a. "Ælfric's Andrew and the Apocrypha." *Journal of English and Germanic Philology* 104: 475–96.

———. 2005b. "Ælfric's Comments about the *Passio Thomae*." *Notes and Queries* n.s. 52: 5–8.

———. forthcoming. "Ælfric and the Apocrypha of Anna and Joachim."

Biggs, Frederick M., and Thomas N. Hall. 1996. "Traditions concerning Jamnes and Mambres in Anglo-Saxon England." *Anglo-Saxon England* 25: 69–89.

Biggs, Frederick M., Thomas D. Hill, and Paul E. Szarmach, eds., with the assistance of Karen Hammond. 1990. *Sources of Anglo-Saxon Literary Culture: A Trial Version.* Medieval & Renaissance Texts & Studies 74. Binghamton, N.Y.

Bihlmeyer, D. P. 1911. "Un texte non interpolé de l'Apocalypse de Thomas." *Revue Bénédictine* 28: 270–82.

Birch, Walter deG., ed. 1892. *Liber Vitae: Register and Martyrology of New Minster and Hyde Abbey Winchester.* Hampshire Record Society. London.

Bischoff, Bernhard. 1951. "Die lateinischen Übersetzungen und Bearbeitungen aus den Oracula Sibyllina." In *Mélanges Joseph De Ghellinck, S. J.*, 121–47. Museum Lessianum, Section Historique 13. Gembloux. Reprinted in Bischoff 1966–81 1.150–71.

———. 1960. *Die südostdeutschen Schreibschulen und Bibliotheken in der Karolingerzeit. I: Die Bayerischen Diözesen.* Wiesbaden.

———. 1965–68. "Die Handschrift." In *Der Stuttgarter Bilderpsalter: Bibl. fol. 23, Würtembergische Landesbibliothek, Stuttgart,* 2.15–30. 2 vols. Stuttgart.

———. 1966–81. *Mittelalterliche Studien: Ausgewählte Aufsätze zur Schriftkunde und Literaturgeschichte.* 3 vols. Stuttgart.

———. 1976. "Turning-Points in the History of Latin Exegesis in the Early Irish Church: A.D. 650–800." Trans. Colm O'Grady in McNamara 1976 pp 74–160. From "Wendepunkte in der Geschichte der lateinischen Exegese im Frühmittelalter," in Bischoff 1966–81 1.205–73.

Bischoff, Bernhard, and Michael Lapidge. 1994. *Biblical Commentaries from the Canterbury School of Theodore and Hadrian.* Cambridge Studies in Anglo-Saxon England 10. Cambridge.

Black, Matthew, ed. 1985. *The Book of Enoch or I Enoch: A New English Edition with Commentary and Textual Notes.* Studia in Veteris Testamenti Pseudepigrapha 7. Leiden.

Blatt, Franz, ed. 1930. *Die lateinischen Bearbeitungen der Acta Andreae et Matthiae apud Anthropophagos.* Beihefte zur Zeitschrift für die neutestamentliche Wissenschaft und die Kunde der älteren Kirche 12. Giessen.

Boenig, Robert. 1991. *The Acts of Andrew in the Country of the Cannibals: Translations from the Greek, Latin, and Old English.* Garland Library of Medieval Literature, Series B, 70. New York.

Böttrich, Christfried. 1995. *Adam als Mikrokosmos. Eine Untersuchung zum slavischen Henochbuch.* Judentum und Umwelt 59. Frankfurt am Main.

———. 2001. "The Melchizedek Story of *2 (Slavonic) Enoch*: A Reaction to A. Orlov." *Journal for the Study of Judaism in the Persian, Hellenistic and Roman Period* 32: 445–70.

Bonnet, Max. 1895. "La Passion de S. Barthélemy en quelle langue a-t-elle été écrite?" *Analecta Bollandiana* 14: 353–66.

Bouterwek, Karl W. 1856. "Das Beowulflied: Eine Vorlesung." *Germania* 1: 385–418.

Bovon, François. 2003. "Canonical and Apocryphal Acts of Apostles." *Journal of Early Christian Studies* 11: 165–94.

Bovon, François, and Pierre Geoltrain, eds. 1997. *Écrits apocryphes chrétiens*. Vol. 1. Ligugé.

Bovon, François, Ann Graham Brock, and Christopher R. Matthews, eds. 1999. *The Apocryphal Acts of the Apostles*. Harvard Divinity School Studies. Cambridge, Mass.

Bovon, François, Michel van Esbroeck, et al., eds. 1981. *Les actes apocryphes des Apôtres: Christianisme et monde païen*. Publications de la Faculté de Théologie de l'Université de Genève 4. Paris.

Brooks, Kenneth R., ed. 1961. *Andreas and the Fates of the Apostles*. Oxford.

Brown, Michelle P. 1996. *The Book of Cerne: Prayer, Patronage and Power in Ninth-Century England*. London.

Brunhölzl, Franz. 2000. *Studien zum geistigen Leben in Passau im achten und neunten Jahrhundert*. Abhandlungen der Marburger Gelehrten Gesellschaft 26. Munich.

Budge, E. A. Wallis, ed. and trans. 1913. *Coptic Apocrypha in the Dialect of Upper Egypt*. London.

————, ed. and trans. 1927. *The Book of the Cave of Treasures: A History of the Patriarchs and the Kings Their Successors from the Creation to the Crucifixion of Christ. Translated from the Syriac Text of the British Museum MS. Add. 25875*. London.

Bullough, Donald A. 2004. *Alcuin: Achievement and Reputation. Being Part of the Ford Lectures Delivered in Oxford in Hilary Term 1980*. Education and Society in the Middle Ages and Renaissance 16. Leiden and Boston.

Bulst, W. 1938. "Eine Anglo-lateinische Übersetzung aus dem Griechischen um 700." *Zeitschrift für deutsches Altertum* 75: 105–11.

Burlin, Robert B. 1968. *The Old English Advent: A Typological Commentary*. Yale Studies in English 168. New Haven, Conn.

Campbell, Jackson J. 1982. "To Hell and Back: Latin Tradition and Literary Use of the 'Descensus ad Inferos' in Old English." *Viator* 13: 107–58.

Canal-Sánchez, Jose M. 1968. "Antiguas versiónes latinas del Protoevangelio de Santiago." *Ephemerides Mariologicae* 18: 431–73.

Carey, John. 2003. "The Seven Heavens and the Twelve Dragons in Insular Apocalyptic." In McNamara 2003a pp 121–36.

Carlini, Antonio. 1983. "La tradizione manoscritta del Pastor di Hermas." In *Papyrus Erzherzog Rainer (P. Rainer Cent.): Festschrift zum 100-jährigen Bestehen der Papyrussammlung der Österreichischen Nationalbibliothek*. Vol. 1: *Textband*, 97–100. Vienna.

————. 1985. "Due estratti del *Pastore* di Erma nella versione palatina in *Par. Lat.* 3182." *Studi classici e orientali* 35: 311–12.

Casiday, Augustine. 2003. "Thomas Didymus from India to England." *Quaestio Insularis: Selected Proceedings of the Cambridge Colloquium in Anglo-Saxon, Norse and Celtic* 4: 70–81.

————. 2004. "St Aldhelm on Apocrypha." *Journal of Theological Studies* n.s. 55: 147–57.

Cassidy, Frederic G., and Richard N. Ringler, eds. 1971. *Bright's Old English Grammar and Reader*. New York.

Cau, E. 1971–74. "Scrittura e cultura a Novara (secoli VIII–IX)." *Ricerche Medievali* 6–9: 1–87.

Cerbelaud, Dominique. 1984. "Le nom d'Adam et les points cardinaux: Recherches sur un thème patristique." *Vigiliae Christianae* 38: 285–301.

Ceriani, A. M., ed. 1861. *Fragmenta latina Evangelii S. Lucae, Parvae Genesis et Assumptionis Mosis, Baruch, Threni et Epistola Jeremiae versionis syriacae Pauli Telensis cum notis et initio prolegomenon in integram ejusdem versionis editionem.* Monumenta sacra et profana 1/1. Milan.

Charles, R. H., ed. 1895. *The Ethiopic Version of the Hebrew Book of Jubilees.* Anecdota Oxoniensia, Semitic Series 8. Oxford.

———. 1897. *The Assumption of Moses, Translated from the Latin Sixth Century MS, the Unemended Text of Which is Published herewith, together with the Text in Its Restored and Critically Emended Form, Edited with Introduction, Notes, and Indices.* London.

———. 1902. *The Book of Jubilees or the Little Genesis, Translated from the Editor's Ethiopic Text, and Edited with Introduction, Notes, and Indices.* London.

———. 1912. *The Book of Enoch, or I Enoch, Translated from the Editor's Ethiopic Text, and Edited with the Introduction, Notes, and Indexes of the First Edition wholly Recast, Enlarged, and Rewritten.* Oxford.

Charlesworth, James H. 1988. "Research on the New Testament Apocrypha and Pseudepigrapha." *ANRW* II 25/5.3919–68.

Cherchi, Paulo. 1984. "A Legend from St. Bartholomew's Gospel in the Twelfth-Century." *Revue Biblique* 91: 212–18.

Clayton, Mary. 1986a. "Ælfric and the Nativity of the Blessed Virgin Mary." *Anglia* 104: 286–315.

———. 1986b. "Blickling Homily XIII Reconsidered." *Leeds Studies in English* 17: 25–40.

———. 1986c. "Delivering the Damned: A Motif in Old English Homiletic Prose." *Medium Ævum* 55: 92–102.

———. 1990a. *The Cult of the Virgin Mary in Anglo-Saxon England.* Cambridge Studies in Anglo-Saxon England 2. Cambridge.

———. 1990b. "The Sources of Ælfric, Assmann 3 (Homily for the Nativity of the Blessed Virgin Mary; Cameron B.1.5.8)." *Fontes Anglo-Saxonici: World Wide Web Register,* http://fontes.english.ox.ac.uk/, accessed May 2005.

———. 1998. *The Apocryphal Gospels of Mary in Anglo-Saxon England.* Cambridge Studies in Anglo-Saxon England 26. Cambridge.

———. 1999. "The *Transitus Mariae*: The Tradition and Its Origins." *Apocrypha* 10: 74–98.

———. 2000. "The Sources of the ANON (OE) Euangelium Pseudo-Matthaei (Cameron B.3.3.18)." *Fontes Anglo-Saxonici: World Wide Web Register,* http://fontes.english.ox.ac.uk/, accessed May 2005.

Clayton, Mary, and Hugh Magennis. 1994. *The Old English Lives of St Margaret.* Cambridge Studies in Anglo-Saxon England 9. Cambridge.

Clubb, Merrel Dare, ed. 1925. *Christ and Satan: An Old English Poem.* Yale Studies in English 70. New Haven, Conn.

Coatsworth, Elizabeth. 2003. "The Book of Enoch and Anglo-Saxon Art." In Powell and Scragg 2003 pp 135–50.

Cockayne, Thomas O. 1861. *Narratiuncula Anglice conscriptæ*. London.

———. 1864–66. *Leechdoms, Wortcunning and Starcraft of Early England*. 3 vols. *RS* 35. London. Reprinted Wiesbaden, 1965.

Coens, Maurice. 1956. "Aux origines de la céphalophorie: un fragment retrouvé d'une ancienne Passion de S. Juste, martyr de Beauvais." *Analecta Bollandiana* 74: 86–114.

Cohn, Leopold. 1898. "An Apocryphal Work Ascribed to Philo of Alexandria." *Jewish Quarterly Review* 10: 277–332.

Cole, Andrew. 2001. "Jewish Apocrypha and Christian Epistemologies of the Fall: The *Dialogi* of Gregory the Great and the Old Saxon *Genesis*." In *Rome and the North: The Early Reception of Gregory the Great in Germanic Europe*, ed. Rolf H. Bremmer Jr, Kees Dekker, and David F. Johnson, 157–88. Paris.

Colgrave, Bertram, and R. A. B. Mynors, eds. 1969. *Bede's Ecclesiastical History of the English People*. Oxford.

Collett, Katherine Ann Smith. 1981. "The Gospel of Nicodemus in Anglo-Saxon England." Ph.D. diss., University of Pennsylvania.

Collins, Adela Yarbro. 1988. "Early Christian Apocalyptic Literature." *ANRW* II 25/6.4665–711.

———. 1995. "The Seven Heavens in Jewish and Christian Apocalypses." In *Death, Ecstasy, and Other Worldly Journeys*, ed. John J. Collins and Michael Fishbane, 59–93. Albany, N.Y.

Cook, Albert S., ed. 1909. *The Christ of Cynewulf: A Poem in Three Parts, The Advent, The Ascension, and the Last Judgment*. 2nd ed. Boston. Reprinted with a new Preface by John C. Pope, Hamden, Conn., 1964.

Cothenet, Edouard. 1988. "Le Protévangile de Jacques: origine, genre et signification d'un premier midrash chrétien sur la Nativité de Marie." *ANRW* II 25/6.4253–69.

Courcelle, Pierre. 1969. *Late Latin Writers and Their Greek Sources*. Trans. H. Wedeck. Cambridge, Mass.

Court, John M. 2000. *The Book of Revelation and the Johannine Apocalyptic Tradition*. Sheffield.

Coxe, H. O. 1852. *Catalogus codicum mss. qui in Collegiis aulisque Oxoniensibus hodie adservantur*. 2 vols. Oxford.

Crawford, Samuel J. 1923. "The Late Old English Notes of MS. (British Museum) Cotton Claudius B.iv." *Anglia* 47: 124–35.

———. 1927. *The Gospel of Nicodemus*. The Awle Ryale Series. Edinburgh.

Crombie, F., trans. 1885. "The Shepherd of Hermas." In *The Ante-Nicene Fathers: The Writings of the Fathers down to A.D. 325*, Vol. 2: *The Fathers of the Second Century: Hermas, Tatian, Athenagoras, Theophilus, and Clement of Alexandria (entire)*, ed. Alexander Roberts and James Donaldson, 9–55. Reprinted Peabody, Mass., 1995.

Cross, J. E. 1963. *Ælfric and the Mediaeval Homiliary: Objection and Contribution*. Scripta Minora Regiae Societatis Humaniorum Litterarum Lundensis 4. Lund.

———— 1972. "The Literate Anglo-Saxon: On Sources and Disseminations." *Proceedings of the British Academy* 58: 67–100.

————. 1979a. "Cynewulf's Traditions about the Apostles in *Fates of the Apostles*." *Anglo-Saxon England* 8: 163–75.

————. 1979b. "The Apostles in the *Old English Martyrology*." *Mediaevalia* 5: 15–59.

————. 1982. "A Doomsday Passage in an Old English Sermon for Lent." *Anglia* 100: 103–08.

————. 1985a. "On the Library of the Old English Martyrologist." In Lapidge and Gneuss 1985 pp 227–49.

————. 1985b. "The Use of Patristic Homilies in the Old English Martyrology." *Anglo-Saxon England* 14: 107–28.

————. 1986. "Towards the Identification of Old English Literary Ideas — Old Workings and New Seams." In Szarmach 1986 pp 77–101.

————. 1987a. *Cambridge Pembroke College MS 25: A Carolingian Sermonary Used by Anglo-Saxon Preachers*. King's College London Medieval Studies 1. London.

————. 1987b. "The Insular Connections of a Sermon for Holy Innocents." In *Medieval Literature and Antiquities: Studies in Honour of Basil Cottle*, ed. Myra Stokes and T. L. Burton, 57–70. Cambridge.

Cross, J. E., ed. with contributions by Denis Brearley, Julia Crick, Thomas N. Hall, and Andy Orchard. 1996. *Two Old English Apocrypha and Their Manuscript Source: The Gospel of Nichodemus and the Avenging of the Saviour*. Cambridge Studies in Anglo-Saxon England 19. Cambridge.

Cross, J. E., and Julia Crick. 1996 "The Manuscript: Saint-Omer, Bibliothèque Municipale, 202." In Cross 1996 pp 10–35.

Cross, J. E., and Thomas D. Hill, eds. and trans. 1982. *The Prose Solomon and Saturn and Adrian and Ritheus*. McMaster Old English Studies and Texts 1. Toronto.

Crotty, Genevieve. 1939. "The Exeter *Harrowing of Hell*: A Re-Interpretation." *PMLA* 54: 349–58.

Cutforth, Sarah. 1993. "Delivering the Damned in Old English Homilies: An Additional Note." *Notes and Queries* n.s. 40: 435–37.

D'Alverny, Marie-Thérèse. 1976. "L'homme comme symbole: le microcosme." In *Simboli e simbologia nell'alto Medioevo, 3–9 aprile 1975*, Settimane di studio del Centro italiano di studi sull'alto Medioevo 23, 1.123–83. 2 vols. Spoleto.

Dando, Marcel. 1972. "Les Gnostiques d'Egypte, les Priscillianistes d'Espagne et l'église primitive d'Irlande." *Cahiers d'Études Cathares* 23: 3–34.

Daniélou, Jean. 1976. *The Angels and Their Mission*. Trans. David Heimann. Westminster, Md.

De Bruyne, Donatien. 1907. "Fragments retrouvés d'apocryphes priscillianistes." *Revue Bénédictine* 24: 318–35.

de Gaiffier, Baudouin. 1963. "Le Breviarium Apostolorum (BHL. 652). Tradition manuscrite et oeuvres apparentées." *Analecta Bollandiana* 81: 89–116.

De Gebhardt, O., and A. Harnack, eds. 1877. *Patrum Apostolicorum Opera*. Vol. 3. Leipzig.

Dekkers, E. 1994. "Les traductions latines du *Pasteur* d'Hermas." *Euphrosyne* 22: 13–26.

Delehaye, H. 1899. "Note sur la légende de la lettre du Christ tombée du ciel." *Académie Royale de Belgique: Bulletin de la classe des lettres.* Reprinted in *Mélanges d'hagiographie grecque et latine,* Subsidia Hagiographica 42 (Brussels, 1966), pp 150–78.

Deletant, Dennis. 1977. "The Sunday Legend." *Revue des Études Sud-est Européennes* 15: 431–51.

Deshman, Robert. 1977. "The Leofric Missal and Tenth-Century English Art." *Anglo-Saxon England* 6: 145–73.

de Smedt, C., J. de Backer, F. van Ortroy, and J. van den Gheyn. 1889. "Catalogus codicum hagiographicorum bibliothecae civitatis Carnotensis." *Analecta Bollandiana* 8: 86–208.

de Strycker, Émile. 1961. *La forme la plus ancienne du Protévangile de Jacques: recherches sur le papyrus Bodmer 5 avec une édition critique du texte grec et une traduction annotée.* Subsidia Hagiographia 33. Brussels.

D'Evelyn, Charlotte. 1918. "The Middle English Metrical Version of the *Revelations* of Methodius; With a Study of the Influence of Methodius in Middle-English Writings." *PMLA* 33: 135–203.

Di Sciacca, Claudia. 2002. "Due note a tre omelie anglosassoni sul tema dell'anima e il corpo." In *Antichità gemaniche, 2.parte: 2 Seminario avanzato in filologia germanica,* ed. Vittoria Dolcetti Corazza and Renato Gendre, 223–50. Bibliotheca germanica 12. Alessandria.

———. 2006. "The *Ubi Sunt* Motif and the Soul-and-Body Legend in Old English Homilies: Sources and Relationships." *Journal of English and Germanic Philology* 105: 365–87.

Doane, A. N., ed. 1978. *Genesis A: A New Edition.* Madison, Wis.

———, ed. 1991. *The Saxon Genesis: An Edition of the West Saxon Genesis B and the Old Saxon Vatican Genesis.* Madison, Wis.

Dobschütz, Ernst von. 1899. *Christusbilder: Untersuchungen zur christlichen Legende.* *TU* 18. Leipzig.

———, ed. 1912. *Das Decretum Gelasianum de libris recipiendis et non recipiendis. TU* 38/4. Leipzig.

Donaghue, Charles, ed. 1942. *The Testament of Mary: The Gaelic Version of the Dormitio Mariae together with an Irish Latin Version.* Fordham University Studies, Language Series 1. New York.

Dronke, Peter. 1981. "St Patrick's Reading." *Cambridge Medieval Celtic Studies* 1: 21–38.

Dubois, Jacques, and Geneviève Renaud, eds. 1976. *Édition pratique des martyrologes de Bède, de l'anonyme lyonnais et de Florus.* Paris.

Duchesne, L., ed. 1955. *Liber Pontificalis.* 2nd ed. 2 vols. Paris.

Dudley, Louise. 1909. "An Early Homily on the 'Body and Soul' Theme." *Journal of English and Germanic Philology* 8: 225–53.

———. 1911. *The Egyptian Elements in the Legend of the Body and Soul.* Bryn Mawr College Monographs 8. Baltimore, Md.

Dumville, David N. 1972. "Liturgical Drama and Panegyric Responsory from the Eighth Century? A Re-examination of the Origin and Contents of the Ninth-

Century Section of the Book of Cerne." *Journal of Theological Studies* n.s. 23: 374–406.

———. 1973. "Biblical Apocrypha and the Early Irish: A Preliminary Investigation." *Proceedings of the Royal Irish Academy* 73C: 299–338.

———. 1977–78. "Towards an Interpretation of *Fís Adamnán*." *Studia Celtica* 12–13: 62–77.

Dwyer, M. E. 1988. "An Unstudied Redaction of the *Visio Pauli*." *Manuscripta* 32: 121–38.

Earl, James W. 1980. "The Typological Structure of *Andreas*." In *Old English Literature in Context: Ten Essays*, ed. John D. Niles, 66–89. Cambridge.

Eis, Gerhard. 1935. *Beiträge zur mittelhochdeutschen Legende und Mystik: Untersuchungen und Texte*. Germanische Studien 161. Berlin.

Emerson, Oliver F. 1906. "Legends of Cain, Especially in Old and Middle English." *PMLA* 21: 831–929.

Evans, J. M. 1968. *Paradise Lost and the Genesis Tradition*. Oxford.

Evans, Ruth. 1981. "An Anonymous Old English Homily for Holy Saturday." *Leeds Studies in English* n.s. 12: 129–53.

Fábrega Grau, Angel, ed. 1953. *Pasionario hispánico (siglos VII–XI)*. 2 vols. Monumenta Hispaniae sacra: Serie litúrgica 6. Madrid.

Fabricius, J. A. 1719. *Codex apocryphus Novi Testamenti*. 2nd ed. 3 vols in 2. Hamburg.

Faerber, Robert. 1993. "L'*Apocalypse de Thomas* en vieil-anglais." *Apocrypha* 4: 125–39.

———. 1999. "La tradition littéraire de la dormition et de l'assomption de Marie en anglais ancien." *Apocrypha* 10: 99–138.

———. 2001. "La *Lettre du Christ tombée du ciel* en anglais ancien: les sermons Napier 43–44." *Apocrypha* 12: 173–209.

———. 2004. "Les *Acta apocrypha apostolorum* dans le corpus homilétique vieil-anglais. Ælfric: *De passione apostolorum Petri et Pauli* et *Cathedra Petri*." *Apocrypha* 15: 259–94.

———. 2005. "Les *Acta apocrypha apostolorum* dans le corpus homilétique vieil-anglais: *Acta Andreae*." *Apocrypha* 16: 199–227.

Fassler, Margot. 2000. "Mary's Nativity, Fulbert of Chartres, and the *Stirps Jesse*: Liturgical Innovation circa 1000 and Its Afterlife." *Speculum* 75: 389–434.

Finnegan, Robert Emmett, ed. 1977. *Christ and Satan: A Critical Edition*. Waterloo, Ontario.

Flamion, J. 1911. *Les Actes apocryphes de l'Apôtre André: Les Actes d'André et de Mathias, de Pierre et d'André et les textes apparentés*. Recueil de Travaux 33. Louvain.

Förster, Max. 1892. *Über die Quellen von Ælfric's Homiliae Catholicae. I. Legenden.* Berlin.

———. 1893. "Zu den Blickling Homilies." *Archiv für das Studium der neueren Sprachen und Literaturen* 91: 179–206.

———. 1902. "Das lateinisch-altenglische Fragment der Apokryphe von Jamnes und Mambres." *Archiv für das Studium der neueren Sprachen und Literaturen* 108: 15–28.

———. 1906. "Altenglische Predigtquellen. I." *Archiv für das Studium der neueren Sprachen und Literaturen* 116: 301–14.

————. 1907–08. "Adams Erschaffung und Namengebung: ein lateinisches Fragment des s.g. slawischen Henoch." *Archiv für Religionswissenschaft* 11: 477–529.

————. 1908. "Beiträge zur mittelalterlichen Volkskunde. II." *Archiv für das Studium der neueren Sprachen und Literaturen* 120: 296–305.

————. 1910. "Das älteste mittellateinische Gesprächbuchlein." *Romanische Forschungen* 27: 342–48.

————. 1913. "Der Vercelli-Codex CXVII nebst Abdruck einiger altenglischer Homilien der Handschrift." In *Festschrift für Lorenz Morsbach dargebracht von Freunden und Schüllern*, ed. Ferdinand Holthausen and Heinrich Spies, 21–179. Studien zur englischen Philologie 50. Halle a.S.

————. 1955. "A New Version of the Apocalypse of Thomas in Old English." *Anglia* 73: 6–36.

Friis-Jensen, Karsten, and James M. W. Willoughby, eds. 2001. *Peterborough Abbey.* Corpus of British Medieval Library Catalogues 8. London.

García Larragueta, Santos Augustín. 1984. *Las Glosas Emilianenses: Edición y Estudio.* Biblioteca de Temas Riojanos 54. Logroño.

Geffcken, J., ed. 1902. *Die Oracula Sibyllina. GCS* 8. Leipzig.

Giet, Stanislas. 1963. *Hermas et les Pasteurs.* Paris.

Gneuss, Helmut. 1981. "A Preliminary List of Manuscripts Written or Owned in England up to 1100." *Anglo-Saxon England* 9: 1–60.

Godman, Peter, ed. 1982. *Alcuin: The Bishops, Kings, and Saints of York.* Oxford.

Gollancz, Israel. 1927. *The Caedmon Manuscript of Anglo-Saxon Biblical Poetry: Junius XI in the Bodleian Library.* Oxford.

Goodwin, C. W., ed. and trans. 1851. *The Anglo-Saxon Legends of St. Andrew and St. Veronica.* Cambridge.

Gransden, Antonia. 2004. "The Cult of St Mary at Beodericesworth and then in Bury St Edmunds Abbey to c. 1150." *Journal of Ecclesiastical History* 55: 627–53.

Grant, Raymond J. S., ed. 1982. *Three Homilies from Cambridge, Corpus Christi College 41: The Assumption, St Michael and the Passion.* Ottawa.

Grattan, J. H. G., and Charles Singer. 1952. *Anglo-Saxon Magic and Medicine Illustrated Specially from the Semi-Pagan Text 'Lacnunga'.* Publications of the Wellcome Historical Medical Museum n.s. 3. London.

Grau, Gustav. 1908. *Quellen und Verwandtschaften der älteren germanischen Darstellungen des jüngsten Gerichtes.* Studien zur englischen Philologie 31. Halle.

Grégoire, Réginald. 1966. *Les homéliaires du moyen âge: Inventaire et analyse de manuscrits.* Rerum Ecclesiasticarum Documenta, Series Maior, Fontes 6. Rome.

Gretsch, Mechthild, and Helmut Gneuss. 2005. "Anglo-Saxon Glosses to a Theodorean Poem?" In *Latin Learning and English Lore: Studies in Anglo-Saxon Literature for Michael Lapidge*, ed. Katherine O'Brien O'Keeffe and Andy Orchard, 1.9–46. 2 vols. Toronto.

Groos, Arthur. 1983. "The 'Elder Angel' in *Guthlac A*." *Anglia* 101: 141–46.

Haibach-Reinisch, Monika, ed. 1962. *Ein neuer 'Transitus Mariae' des Pseudo-Melito: text-kritische Ausgabe und Darlegung der Bedeutung dieser ursprünglicheren Fassung für Apokryphenforschung und lateinische und deutsche Dichtung des Mittelalters.* Bibliotheca assumptionis B. Virginis Mariae 5. Rome.

Hall, Thomas N. 1988. "The Ages of Christ and Mary in the Hyde Register and in Old English Literature." *Notes and Queries* n.s. 35: 4–11.

———. 1989–90. "The Reversal of the Jordan in Vercelli Homily 16 and in Old English Literature." *Traditio* 45: 53–86.

———. 1994. Review of Webber 1992. *Analytical and Enumerative Bibliography* n.s. 8: 133–40.

———. 1996. "The *Euangelium Nichodemi* and *Vindicta Saluatoris* in Anglo-Saxon England." In Cross 1996 pp 36–81.

———. 2002. "The Earliest Anglo-Latin Text of the *Trinubium Annae* (*BHL* 505zl)." In *Via Crucis: Essays on Early Medieval Sources and Ideas in Memory of J. E. Cross*, ed. Thomas N. Hall with assistance from Thomas D. Hill and Charles D. Wright, 104–37. Medieval European Studies 1. Morgantown, W.V.

———. 2003. "Ælfric and the Epistle to the Laodicians." In Powell and Scragg 2003 pp 65–83.

Handley, Rima. 1974. "British Museum Ms. Cotton Vespasian D. xiv." *Notes and Queries* n.s. 21: 243–50.

Hanna, Ralph. 2002. *A Descriptive Catalogue of the Western Manuscripts of St John's College, Oxford.* Oxford.

Hawkes, Jane. 1995. "The Wirksworth Slab: An Iconography of *humilitas.*" *Peritia* 9: 246–77.

Healey, Antonette diPaolo. 1973. "The Vision of St. Paul." Ph.D. diss., University of Toronto.

———, ed. 1978. *The Old English Vision of St. Paul.* Speculum Anniversary Monographs 2. Cambridge, Mass.

———. 1985. "Anglo-Saxon Use of the Apocryphal Gospel." In *The Anglo-Saxons: Synthesis and Achievement*, ed. J. Douglas Woods and David A. E. Pelteret, 93–104. Waterloo, Ontario.

Heer, Joseph. M. 1908. *Die Versio Latina des Barnabasbriefes und ihr Verhältnis zur altlateinischen Bibel.* Freiburg im Breisgau.

Heimann, Adelheid. 1966. "Three Illustrations from the Bury St. Edmund Psalter and Their Prototypes." *Journal of the Warburg and Courtauld Institutes* 29: 39–46.

Heist, William W. 1952. *The Fifteen Signs before Doomsday.* East Lansing, Mich.

Hellholm, David. 1980. *Das Visionenbuch des Hermas als Apocalypse: formgeschichtliche und texttheoretische Studien zu einer literarischen Gattung.* Vol. 1. Coniectanea Biblica, New Testament Series 13/1. Lund.

Henderson, George. 1986. "The Imagery of St Guthlac of Croyland." In *England in the Thirteenth Century: Proceedings of the 1984 Harlaxton Symposium*, ed. W. M. Ormrod, 76–94. Dover, N.H.

Hilgenfeld, A., ed. 1873. *Hermae Pastor.* Leipzig.

Hilhorst, A., and Pieter J. Lalleman. 2000. "The Acts of Andrew and Matthias: Is It Part of the Original Acts of Andrew?" In *The Apocryphal Acts of Andrew*, ed. Jan N. Bremmer, 1–14. Studies on the Apocryphal Acts of the Apostles 5. Leuven.

Hilhorst, Anthony. 2003. "The Apocalypse of Paul: Earlier History and Later Influence." In McNamara 2003a pp 61–74.

Hill, Thomas D. 1968. "Figural Narrative in *Andreas*: The Conversion of the Merme-
    donians." *Neuphilologische Mitteilungen* 70: 261–73.
———. 1969a. "Some Remarks on 'The Site of Lucifer's Throne.'" *Anglia* 87: 303–
    11.
———. 1969b. "Notes on the Eschatology of the Old English *Christ III*." *Neuphilo-
    logische Mitteilungen* 70: 672–79.
———. 1971. "Further Notes on the Eschatology of the Old English *Christ III*."
    *Neuphilologische Mitteilungen* 72: 691–98.
———. 1972a. "Cosmic Stasis and the Birth of Christ: The Old English *Descent into
    Hell*, Lines 99–106." *Journal of English and Germanic Philology* 71: 382–89.
———. 1972b. "The Old World, the Levelling of the Earth, and the Burning of the
    Sea: Three Eschatological Images in the Old English 'Christ III.'" *Notes and
    Queries* n.s. 19: 323–25.
———. 1974. "Raguel and Ragnel: Notes on the Literary Genealogy of a Devil."
    *Names* 22: 145–49.
———. 1977a. "The *Æcerbot* Charm and Its Christian User." *Anglo-Saxon England* 6:
    213–21.
———. 1977b. "A Liturgical Source for *Christ I* 164–213 (Advent Lyric VII)."
    *Medium Ævum* 46: 12–15.
———. 1977c. "The Fall of Satan in the Old English *Christ and Satan*." *Journal of
    English and Germanic Philology* 76: 315–25.
———. 1979. "The Middle Way: *Idel-wuldor* and *Egesa* in the Old English *Guthlac
    A*." *Review of English Studies* n.s. 30: 182–87.
———. 1986. "Literary History and Old English Poetry: The Case of *Christ I, II*, and
    *III*." In Szarmach 1986 pp 3–22.
———. 1987. "The Myth of the Ark-Born Son of Noe and the West-Saxon Royal
    Genealogical Tables." *Harvard Theological Review* 80: 379–83.
———. 1992. "Delivering the Damned in Old English Anonymous Homilies and
    Jón Arason's *Ljómur*." *Medium Ævum* 61: 75–82.
———. 1998. "Two Notes on the Old Frisian 'Fia-Eth.'" In *Approaches to Old Frisian
    Philology*, ed. Rolf H. Bremmer, Thomas S. B. Johnston, and Oebele Vries, 169–
    78. Amsterdamer Beiträge zur älteren Germanistik 49. Amsterdam.
Hofmann, Norbert J. 2000. *Die Assumptio Mosis: Studien zur Rezeption massgültiger
    Überlieferung*. Supplements to the Journal for the Study of Judaism 67. Leiden.
Hulme, William H. 1898. "The Old English Version of the Gospel of Nicodemus."
    *PMLA* 13: 457–542.
———. 1903–04. "The Old English Gospel of Nicodemus." *Modern Philology* 1:
    579–614.
Izydorczyk, Zbigniew. 1993. *Manuscripts of the Evangelium Nicodemi: A Census*. Sub-
    sidia Mediaevalia 21. Toronto.
———, ed. 1997. *The Medieval Gospel of Nicodemus: Texts, Intertexts, and Contexts in
    Western Europe*. Medieval & Renaissance Texts & Studies 158. Tempe, Ariz.
Izydorczyk, Zbigniew, and Jean-Daniel Dubois. 1997. "Nicodemus's Gospel before
    and beyond the Medieval West." In Izydorczyk 1997 pp 21–41.

Jackson, Peter, and Michael Lapidge. 1996. "The Contents of the Cotton-Corpus Legendary." In Szarmach 1996 pp 131–46.

James, Montague Rhodes. 1893. *Apocrypha Anecdota: A Collection of Thirteen Apocryphal Books and Fragments now first Edited from Manuscripts.* Texts and Studies 2/3. Cambridge.

———. 1900–04. *The Western Manuscripts in the Library of Trinity College, Cambridge: A Descriptive Catalogue.* 4 vols. Cambridge.

———. 1901. "A Fragment of the 'Penitence of Jannes and Jambres.'" *Journal of Theological Studies* 2: 572–77.

———. 1906. "Notes on Apocrypha." *Journal of Theological Studies* 7: 562–68.

———. 1909–10. "Names of Angels in Anglo-Saxon and Other Documents." *Journal of Theological Studies* 11: 569–71.

———. 1911–12. *A Descriptive Catalogue of the Manuscripts in the Library of Corpus Christi College Cambridge.* 2 vols. Cambridge.

———. 1914. "The Apocryphal Ezekiel." *Journal of Theological Studies* 15: 236–43.

———. 1918–19. "Irish Apocrypha." *Journal of Theological Studies* 20: 9–16.

———. 1924. *The Apocryphal New Testament: Being the Apocryphal Gospels, Acts, Epistles, and Apocalypses with Other Narratives and Fragments.* Oxford.

Jayatilaka, R. 1996. "The Sources of Ælfric, *Lives of Saints* 24 (SS Abdon and Sennes; Cameron B.1.3.24)." *Fontes Anglo-Saxonici: World Wide Web Register*, http://fontes.english.ox.ac.uk/, accessed April 2005.

———. 1997a. "The Sources of Ælfric, *Lives of Saints* 15 (St Mark, the Evangelist; Cameron B.1.3.16)." *Fontes Anglo-Saxonici: World Wide Web Register*, http://fontes.english.ox.ac.uk/, accessed January 2002.

———. 1997b. "The Sources of Ælfric, *Lives of Saints* 36 (Passion of St Thomas the Apostle; Cameron B.1.3.34)." *Fontes Anglo-Saxonici: World Wide Web Register*, http://fontes.english.ox.ac.uk/, accessed 14 January 2002.

Jenkins, Claude. 1935. "Bede as Exegete and Theologian." In *Bede: His Life, Times, and Writings: Essays in Commemoration of the Twelfth Centenary of His Death*, ed. A. Hamilton Thompson, 152–200. Oxford. Reprinted New York, 1966.

Jiroušková, Lenka. 2006. *Die Visio Pauli: Wege und Wandlungen einer orientalischen Apokryphe im lateinischen Mittelalter unter Einschluss der alttschechischen und deutschsprachigen Textzeugen.* Mittellateinische Studien und Texte 34. Leiden.

Jolly, Karen Louise. 1996. *Popular Religion in Late Saxon England: Elf Charms in Context.* Chapel Hill, N.C.

Joly, R., ed. 1958. *Hermas: Le Pasteur. SChr* 53. Paris.

Jordan, Louis. 1986. "Demonic Elements in Anglo-Saxon Iconography." In Szarmach 1986 pp 281–317.

Jost, Karl. 1950. *Wulfstanstudien.* Schweizer anglistische Arbeiten 23. Bern.

Kabir, Ananya Jahanara. 2001a. *Paradise, Death and Doomsday in Anglo-Saxon Literature.* Cambridge Studies in Anglo-Saxon England 32. Cambridge.

———. 2001b. "From Twelve Devouring Dragons to the *Develes Ers*: The Medieval History of an Apocryphal Punitive Motif." *Archiv für das Studium der neueren Sprachen und Literaturen* 238: 280–98.

Kaestli, Jean-Daniel. 1981. "Les principales orientations de la recherche sur les Actes Apocryphes des Apôtres." In Bovon, van Esbroeck, et al. 1981 pp 49–67.

———. 1988. "Où en est l'étude de l'"Évangile de Barthélemy'?" *Revue Biblique* 95: 5–33.

———. 1996. "Le *Protévangile de Jacques* en latin: état de la question et perspectives nouvelles." *Revue d'Histoire des Textes* 26: 41–102.

———, trans. 1997. "Questions de Barthélemy." In Bovon and Geoltrain 1997 pp 256–305.

Kaestli, Jean-Daniel, and Pierre Cherix, trans. 1997. "Livre de la Résurrection de Jésus-Christ par l'Apôtre Barthélemy." In Bovon and Geoltrain 1997 pp 307–56.

Karkov, Catherine E. 2001. *Text and Picture in Anglo-Saxon England: Narrative Strategies in the Junius 11 Manuscript.* Cambridge Studies in Anglo-Saxon England 31. Cambridge.

———. 2003. "Judgment and Salvation in the New Minster Liber Vitae." In Powell and Scragg 2003 pp 151–63.

Kaske, R. E. 1967. "A Poem of the Cross in the Exeter Book: 'Riddle 60' and 'The Husband's Message.'" *Traditio* 23: 41–71.

———. 1971. "*Beowulf* and the Book of Enoch." *Speculum* 46: 421–31.

Kelly, Joseph F. 1988. "A Catalogue of Early Medieval Hiberno-Latin Biblical Commentaries (I)." *Traditio* 44: 537–71.

Ker, N. R. 1940. "An Eleventh-Century Old English Legend of the Cross before Christ." *Medium Ævum* 9: 84–85.

———. 1964. *Medieval Libraries of Great Britain: A List of Surviving Books.* 2nd ed. Royal Historical Society Guides and Handbooks 3. London.

Ker, W. P., and A. S. Napier, eds. 1901. *An English Miscellany Presented to Dr. Furnivall.* Oxford.

Kim, H. C., ed. 1973. *The Gospel of Nicodemus: Gesta Salvatoris.* Toronto Medieval Latin Texts 2. Toronto.

Kisch, Guido, ed. 1949. *Pseudo-Philo's Liber Antiquitatum Biblicarum.* Notre Dame, Ind.

Kitzinger, Ernst. 1956. "The Coffin-Reliquary." In *The Relics of Saint Cuthbert: Studies by Various Authors Collected and Edited with an Historical Introduction,* ed. C. F. Battiscombe, 202–304. Oxford.

Klaeber, Frederick, ed. 1950. *Beowulf and the Fight at Finnsburg.* 3rd ed. Lexington, Mass.

Klijn, A. F. J. 1983. *Der lateinische Text der Apokalypse des Esra. Mit einem Index grammaticus von G. Mussies.* TU 131. Berlin.

Knibb, Michael A. 1978. *The Ethiopic Book of Enoch: A New Edition in the Light of the Aramaic Dead Sea Fragments.* 2 vols. Oxford.

Körtner, Ulrich H. J., and Martin Leutzsch, eds. and trans. 1988. *Papiasfragmente. Hirt des Hermas.* Schriften des Urchristentums 3. Darmstadt.

Kotzor, Günter, ed. 1981. *Das altenglische Martyrologium.* 2 vols. Bayerische Akademie der Wissenschaften, philosophisch-historische Klasse, Abhandlungen, n.F. 88. Munich.

Kuypers, A. B., ed. 1902. *The Prayer Book of Aedelueld the Bishop, Commonly Called the Book of Cerne*. Cambridge.

Laistner, M. L. W. 1933. "Bede as a Classical and a Patristic Scholar." *Transactions of the Royal Historical Society* 4th ser. 16: 69–94.

Lapidge, Michael. 1988. *Abbreviations for Sources and Specification of Standard Editions for Sources*. Binghamton N.Y.

———. 2005. "Acca of Hexham and the Origin of the *Old English Martyrology*." *Analecta Bollandiana* 123: 29–78.

———. 2006. *The Anglo-Saxon Library*. Oxford.

Lapidge, Michael, and Helmut Gneuss, eds. 1985. *Learning and Literature in Anglo-Saxon England: Studies Presented to Peter Clemoes on the Occasion of His Sixty-Fifth Birthday*. Cambridge.

Lapidge, Michael, and James Rosier, trans. 1985. *Aldhelm: The Poetic Works*. Cambridge.

Laureys, Marc, and Daniel Verhelst. 1988. "Pseudo-Methodius, *Revelationes*: Textgeschichte und kritische Edition. Ein Leuven-Groninger Forschungsprojekt." In *The Use and Abuse of Eschatology in the Middle Ages*, ed. Werner Verbeke, Daniel Verhelst, and Andries Welkenhuysen, 112–36. Leuven.

Lazius, W. 1551. *Abdiae episcopi Babyloniae Historia certaminis apostolorum*. Basel.

Lees, Clare A. 1985. "The 'Sunday Letter' and the 'Sunday Lists.'" *Anglo-Saxon England* 14: 129–51.

———. 1986. "Theme and Echo in an Anonymous Old English Homily for Easter." *Traditio* 42: 115–42.

Lendinara, Patrizia. 1993. "The Old English Renderings of Latin *tabernaculum* and *tentorium*." In *Anglo-Saxonica: Beiträge zur Vor- und Frühgeschichte der englischen Sprache und zur altenglischen Literatur. Festschrift für Hans Schabram zum 65. Geburtstag*, ed. Klaus R. Grinda and Claus-Dieter Wetzel, 289–325. Munich.

———. 2003. "The *Versus Sibyllae de die iudicii* in Anglo-Saxon England." In Powell and Scragg 2003 pp 85–101.

Lightfoot, J. B., ed. 1879. *Saint Paul's Epistles to the Colossians and to Philemon: A Revised Text*. Reprinted Grand Rapids, Mich., 1959.

Lindsay, W. M., ed. 1911. *Isidori Hispalensis Episcopi Etymologiarum sive Originum libri xx*. 2 vols. Oxford.

Lindström, Bengt. 2005. Review of Cross 1996. *Studia Neophilologica* 77: 116–20.

Lionarons, Joyce Tally. 1998. "Another Old English Text of the *Passio Petri et Pauli*." *Notes and Queries* n.s. 45: 12–14.

Lipsius, R. A., and M. Bonnet, eds. 1891–1903. *Acta Apostolorum Apocrypha*. 2 vols. Leipzig.

Lolos, Anastasios, ed. 1976. *Die Apokalypse des Ps. Methodios*. Beiträge zur klassischen Philologie 83. Meisenheim am Glan.

Longenecker, Bruce W. 1995. *2 Esdras*. Sheffield.

Loomis, Grant. 1931. "Further Sources of Ælfric's *Lives of the Saints* and His Translations from the Old Testament." *Harvard Studies and Notes in Philology and Literature* 13: 1–8.

Lopez Ferreiro, Antonia. 1898–1911. *Historia de la Santa A. M. Iglesia de Santiago de Compostela*. 11 vols. Santiago.

Love, R. C. 2000a. "The Sources of Bede, *Martyrologium*." *Fontes Anglo-Saxonici: World Wide Web Register*, http://fontes.english.ox.ac.uk/, accessed January 2002.

———. 2000b. "The Sources of Bede, *Explanatio Apocalypsis*." *Fontes Anglo-Saxonici: World Wide Web Register*, http://fontes.english.ox.ac.uk/, accessed January 2002.

Lowe, E. A. 1925–26. "The Vatican MS of the Gelasian Sacramentary and Its Supplement at Paris." *Journal of Theological Studies* 27: 357–73.

Luiselli Fadda, Anna Maria. 1972. "'De descensu Christi ad inferos': una inedita omelia anglosassone." *Studi Medievali* 3rd ser. 13: 989–1011.

———. 1974. "Una inedita traduzione anglosassone della *Visio Pauli* (MS Junius 85, ff 3r–11v)." *Studi Medievali* 3rd ser. 15: 482–95.

———, ed. 1977. *Nuove omelie anglosassoni della rinascenza benedettina*. Filologia germanica, Testi e Studi 1. Florence.

Lusini, G. 2001. "Nouvelles recherches sur le texte du Pasteur d'Hermas." *Apocrypha* 12: 79–97.

MacDonald, Dennis R., ed. 1986a. *The Apocryphal Acts of Apostles*. Semeia 38. Decatur, Ga.

———. 1986b. "The *Acts of Andrew and Matthias* and the *Acts of Andrew*." In MacDonald 1986a pp 9–26 and 35–39.

———, ed. 1990. *The Acts of Andrew and the Acts of Andrew and Matthias in the City of the Cannibals*. Texts and Translations 33, Christian Apocrypha Series 1. Atlanta, Ga.

Mac Niocaill, Gearoid. 1956. "Na Seacht Neamha." *Éigse* 8: 239–41.

Marchand, James W. 1991. "The *Partridge*? An Old English Multiquote." *Neophilologus* 75: 603–11.

Marocco, G. 1950. "Nuovi documenti sull'Assunzione del Medio Evo latino: due 'transitus' dai codici 59 et 105 di Ivrea." *Marianum* 12: 449–52.

Marstrander, Carl. 1911. "The Two Deaths." *Ériu* 5: 120–25.

Marx, C. W. 1997. "The *Gospel of Nicodemus* in Old English and Middle English." In Izydorczyk 1997 pp 207–59.

Matter, E. Ann. 1982. "The 'Revelatio Esdrae' in Latin and English Traditions." *Revue Bénédictine* 92: 376–92.

Mazzini, Innocenzo. 1980. "Il codice Urbinate 486 e la versione Palatina del Pastore de Erma." *Prometheus* 6: 181–89.

Mazzini, Innocenzo, and E. Lorenzini. 1981. "Il Pastore di Erma: due versioni latine o due antologie di versioni?" *Civiltà classica e cristiana* 2: 45–86.

McNally, R. E. 1957. *Der irische Liber de Numeris: eine Quellenanalyse des pseudo-isidorischen Liber de numeris*. Inaugural-Dissertation, Munich.

———. 1979. "'In Nomine Dei Summi': Seven Hiberno-Latin Sermons." *Traditio* 35: 121–43.

McNamara, Martin. 1975. *The Apocrypha in the Irish Church*. Dublin.

———, ed. 1976. *Biblical Studies: The Medieval Irish Contribution*. Proceedings of the Irish Biblical Association 1. Dublin.

————. 1986. *Glossa in Psalmos. The Hiberno-Latin Gloss on the Psalms of Codex Palatinus Latinus 68.* Studi e Testi 310. Vatican City.

————. 2002. "Apocryphal Infancy Narratives: European and Irish Transmission." In *Ireland and Europe in the Early Middle Ages: Texts and Transmission,* ed. Próinséas Ní Chatháin and Michael Richter, 123–46. Dublin.

————, ed. 2003a. *Apocalyptic and Eschatalogical Heritage: The Middle Eastern and Celtic Realms.* Dublin.

————. 2003b. "Apocalyptic and Eschatalogical Texts in Irish Literature: Oriental Connections?" In McNamara 2003a pp 75–97.

Mearns, James. 1914. *The Canticles of the Christian Church Eastern and Western in Early and Medieval Times.* Cambridge.

Mellinkoff, Ruth. 1979. "Cain's Monstrous Progeny in *Beowulf:* Part I Noachic Tradition." *Anglo-Saxon England* 8: 143–62.

————. 1981. "Cain's Monstrous Progeny in *Beowulf:* Part II Postdiluvian Survival." *Anglo-Saxon England* 9: 183–97.

Menner, Robert J., ed. 1941. *The Poetical Dialogues of Solomon and Saturn.* MLA Monograph 13. New York.

Mercati, Giovani. 1901. "Anecdota apocrypha latina. Una 'Visio' ed una 'Revelatio' d'Escra con un decreto di Clemente Romano. B. Una 'Revalatio Esdrae de qualitatibus anni.'" In *Nota di Letteratura Biblica e Cristiana Antica,* 74–80. Studi e Testi 5. Vatican City.

Meyer, Wilhelm. ed. 1878. "Vita Adae et Evae." *Abhandlungen der königlich bayerischen Akademie der Wissenschaften, philosophisch-philologische Klasse* 14/3.185–250. Munich.

Milik, J. T., ed. 1976. *The Books of Enoch: Aramaic Fragments of Qumrân Cave 4.* With the collaboration of Matthew Black. Oxford.

Mimouni, Simon Claude. 1993. "Les *Apocalypses de la Vierge*: état de la question." *Apocrypha* 4: 101–12.

————. 1995. *Dormition et Assomption de Marie: Histoire des traditions anciennes.* Théologie historique 98. Paris.

Mohlberg, Leo Cunibert, ed. 1981. *Liber Sacramentorum Romanae Aeclesiae ordinis anni circuli: Cod. Vat. Reg. lat. 316, Paris Bibl. Nat. 7193, 41/56 (Sacramentarium Gelasianum).* 3rd ed. improved and enlarged by Leo Eizenhöfer. Rome.

Mombritius, B., ed. 1910. *Sanctuarium seu Vitae Sanctorum.* 2nd ed. 2 vols. Paris.

Mommsen, Theodor, ed. 1903–09. *Die Kirchengeschichte: Die Lateinische Übersetzung des Rufinus.* 3 vols. Bd. 2 of *Eusebius Werke,* ed. Eduard Schwartz. *GCS* 9. Leipzig.

Morey, James H. 1990. "Adam and Judas in the Old English *Christ and Satan.*" *Studies in Philology* 87: 397–409.

Moricca, Umberto. 1921 and 1922. "Un nuovo testo dell'evangelo di Bartolomeo." *Revue Biblique* 30: 481–516 and 31: 20–30.

Morrell, Minnie Cate. 1965. *A Manual of Old English Biblical Materials.* Knoxville, Tenn.

Mozley, J. H. 1929. "The Vitae Adae." *Journal of Theological Studies* 30: 121–49.

Mueller, James R. 1994. *The Five Fragments of the Apocryphon of Ezekiel: A Critical Study.* Journal for the Study of the Pseudepigrapha (and Related Literature), Supplement Series 5. Sheffield.

Munier, Charles. 1994. "La chronique Pseudo-hiéronymienne de Sélestat: un schéma de catéchèse baptismale?" *Revue Bénédictine* 104: 106–22.

Murdoch, Brian O. 1976. *The Irish Adam and Eve Story from Saltair na Rann.* 2 vols. Dublin.

———. 2003. *The Medieval Popular Bible: Expansions of Genesis in the Middle Ages.* Cambridge.

Napier, A. S., ed. 1883. *Wulfstan. Sammlung der ihm zugeschriebenen Homilien nebst Untersuchungen über ihre Echtheit. I. Text und Varianten.* Sammlung englischer Denkmäler 4. Berlin. Reprinted with an appendix by Klaus Ostheeren, Dublin, 1967.

———. 1889. "Altenglische Kleinigkeiten." *Anglia* 11: 1–10.

———. 1901. "Contributions to Old English Literature. I. An Old English Homily on the Observance of Sunday." In Ker and Napier 1901 pp 355–62.

Nausea, F. 1531. *Anonymi Philalethi Eusebiani in vitas, miracula passionesque apostolorum rhapsodiae.* Cologne.

O'Brien O'Keeffe, Katherine. 1991. "The Geographic List of *Solomon and Saturn II.*" *Anglo-Saxon England* 20: 123–41.

O'Ceallaigh, G. C. 1963. "Dating the Commentaries of Nicodemus." *Harvard Theological Review* 61: 21–58.

O'Leary, Aideen M. 2003. "Apostolic *Passiones* in Early Anglo-Saxon England." In Powell and Scragg 2003 pp 103–19.

O'Loughlin, Thomas. 1998. "The Celtic Homily: Creeds and Eschatology." *Milltown Studies* 41: 99–115.

———. 2001. "Irish Preaching before the End of the Ninth Century: Assessing the Extent of Our Evidence." In *Irish Preaching 700–1700*, ed. Alan J. Fletcher and Raymond Gillespie, 18–39. Dublin.

O'Neill, Patrick P. 1997. "The 'Solomon and Saturn' Dialogues." *Anglo-Saxon England* 26: 139–65.

Orchard, Andy. 1994. *The Poetic Art of Aldhelm.* Cambridge Studies in Anglo-Saxon England 8. Cambridge.

———. 1995. *Pride and Prodigies: Studies in the Monsters of the 'Beowulf' Manuscript.* Cambridge. Revised paperback ed., Toronto, 2003.

Orlov, Andrei A. 2003. "On the Polemical Nature of *2 (Slavonic) Enoch*: A Reply to C. Böttrich." *Journal for the Study of Judaism in the Persian, Hellenistic and Roman Period* 34: 274–303.

Osiek, Carolyn. 1986. "The Genre and Function of the Shepherd of Hermas." *Semeia* 36: 113–21.

Ott, J. H. 1892. *Über die Quellen der Heiligenleben in Ælfrics Lives of Saints I.* Diss., Halle-Wittenberg. Halle a.S.

Pächt, Otto. 1961. "A Cycle of English Frescoes in Spain." *Burlington Magazine* 103: 166–75.

Peltola, Niilo. 1972. "Grendel's Descent from Cain Reconsidered." *Neuphilologische Mitteilungen* 73: 284–91.

Petitmengin, Pierre. 1993. "La compilation 'De uindictis magnis magnorum peccatorum': Exemples d'anthropophagie tirés des sièges de Jérusalem et de Samarie." In *Philologia sacra: Biblische und patristische Studien für Hermann J. Frede und Walter Thiele zu ihrem siebzigsten Geburtstag,* ed. Roger Gryson, 2.622–38. 2 vols. Vetus Latina: Aus der Geschichte der lateinischen Bibel 24/2. Freiburg.

Pettorelli, Jean-Pierre. 1998. "La Vie latine d'Adam et Ève." *Archivum Latinitatis Medii Aevi* 56: 5–104.

———. 1999a. "La Vie latine d'Adam et Ève: Analyse de la tradition manuscrite." *Apocrypha* 10: 220–320.

———. 1999b. "Vie latine d'Adam et Ève: La recension de Paris, BNF, lat. 3832." *Archivum Latinitatis Medii Aevi* 57: 5–52.

———. 2002. "Deux témoins latins singuliers de la *Vie d'Adam et Ève*: Paris, BNF, lat. 3832 & Milan, B. Ambrosiana, O 35 Sup." *Journal for the Study of Judaism in the Persian, Hellenistic and Roman Period* 23: 1–27.

Philippart, Guy. 1977. *Les légendiers latins et autres manuscrits hagiographiques.* Typologie des sources du moyen âge occidental 24–25. Turnhout.

———. 1989. "Les fragments palimpsestes de l'Évangile de Nicodème dans le *Vindobonensis* 563 (V^e s.?)." *Analecta Bollandiana* 107: 171–88.

Pietersma, Albert, ed. 1994. *The Apocryphon of Jannes and Jambres the Magicians. P. Chester Beatty XVI (with New Editions of Papyrus Vindobonensis Greek inv. 29456 + 29828 and British Library Cotton Tiberius B.v f.87).* Religions in the Graeco-Roman World 119. Leiden.

Plummer, Charles, ed. 1896. *Venerabilis Baedae Opera Historica.* 2 vols. Oxford.

Powell, Kathryn, and Donald Scragg, eds. 2003. *Apocryphal Texts and Traditions in Anglo-Saxon England.* Publications of the Manchester Centre for Anglo-Saxon Studies 2. Cambridge.

Prescott, A. 1987. "The Structure of English Pre-Conquest Benedictionals." *British Library Journal* 13: 118–58.

Priebsch, Robert. 1899. "The Chief Sources of Some Anglo-Saxon Homilies." *Otia Merseiana* 1: 129–47.

———. 1901. "John Audelay's Poem on the Observance of Sunday and Its Source." In Ker and Napier 1901 pp 397–407.

———. 1936. *Letter from Heaven.* Oxford.

Prieur, Jean-Marc. 1986. "Response." In MacDonald 1986a pp 27–33.

Prinz, Otto. 1985. "Eine frühe abendländische Aktualisierung der lateinischen Übersetzung des Pseudo-Methodios." *Deutsches Archiv für Erforschung des Mittelalters* 41: 1–23.

Proud, Joana. 2001. "The Sources of the ANON (OE) Life of St James the Greater (Cameron B.3.3.11)." *Fontes Anglo-Saxonici: World Wide Web Register,* http://fontes.english.ox.ac.uk/, accessed January 2002.

Quentin, Henri. 1908. *Les martyrologes historiques du Moyen Âge: Étude sur la formation du Martyrologe Romain.* Paris. Reprinted Aalen, 1969.

Quinn, Esther Casier. 1962. *The Quest of Seth for the Oil of Life.* Chicago.

Rauer, Christine. 2000. "The Sources of the ANON OE Martyrology (Cameron B.19)." *Fontes Anglo-Saxonici: World Wide Web Register*, http//fontes.english.ox. ac.uk/, accessed May 2005.

————. 2003. "The Sources of the *Old English Martyrology*." *Anglo-Saxon England* 32: 89–109.

Rehm, Bernhard, ed. 1994. *Die Pseudoklementinen*. Vol 2: *Rekognitionen in Rufins Übersetzung*. 2nd ed. by Georg Strecker. *GCS* 51. Berlin.

Reinink, G. J., ed. 1993. *Die syrische Apokalypse des Pseudo-Methodius*. 2 vols. Corpus Scriptorum Christianorum Orientalium 540–41, Scriptores Syri 220–21. Louvain.

————. 1996. "Pseudo-Methodius and the Pseudo-Ephremian 'Sermo de Fine Mundi.'" In *Media Latinitas: A Collection of Essays to Mark the Occasion of the Retirement of L. J. Engels*, ed. R. I. A. Nip, H. van Dijk, E. M. C. van Houts, C. H. Kneepkens, and G. A. A. Kortekaas, 317–21. Instrumenta Patristica 28. Turnhout.

Reinsch, Robert. 1879. *Die Pseudo-Evangelien von Jesu und Maria's Kindheit in der romanischen und germanischen Literatur*. Halle.

Remly, Lynn L. 1974. "Salome in England: A Note on 'Vercelli Homily X,' 165–74 (Pseudo-Wulfstan XLIX, 257; 9–18)." *Vetera Christianorum* 11: 121–23.

Revard, Stella P. 2005. "From Metanoia to Apocalypse: *Paradise Lost* and the Apocryphal *Lives of Adam and Eve*." *Journal of English and Germanic Philology* 104: 80–102.

Reynolds, Roger. 1983. "Unity and Diversity in Carolingian Canon Law Collections: The Case of the Collectio Hibernensis and Its Derivatives." In *Carolingian Essays: Andrew W. Mellon Lectures in Early Christian Studies*, ed. Ute-Renate Blumenthal, 99–135. Washington, D.C.

Ri, Su-Min, ed. 1987. *La caverne des trésors: Les deux recensions syriaques*. Corpus Scriptorum Christianorum Orientalium 486–87, Scriptores Syri 207–08. Louvain.

Rivière, Ernest M. 1906. "La Lettre du Christ tombée du ciel." *Revue des Questions Historiques* n.s. 35: 600–05.

Roberts, Jane, ed. 1979. *The Guthlac Poems of the Exeter Book*. Oxford.

————. 1988. "*Guthlac A*: Sources and Source Hunting." In *Medieval English Studies Presented to George Kane*, ed. Edward Donald Kennedy, Ronald Waldron, and Joseph S. Wittig, 1–18. Woodbridge.

Röhricht, Reinhold. 1890. "Ein 'Brief Christi.'" *Zeitschrift für Kirchengeschichte* 11: 436–42.

Rosser, Susan. 2000. "The Sources of Cynewulf, *Fates of the Apostles* (Cameron A.2.2)." *Fontes Anglo-Saxonici: World Wide Web Register*, http://fontes.english.ox.ac.uk/, accessed June 2005.

Rowley, Sharon M. 2003. "'A wese\n/dan nacodnisse and þa ecan þistru': Language and Mortality in the Homily for Doomsday in Cambridge, Corpus Christi College MS 41." *English Studies* 84: 493–510.

Russell, Jeffrey B. 1964. "Saint Boniface and the Eccentrics." *Church History* 33: 235–47.

Sackur, Ernst, ed. 1898. *Sibyllinische Texte und Forschungen: Pseudomethodius, Adso und die Tiburtinische Sibylle*. Halle a.S. Reprinted Turin, 1963.

Santos Otero, Aurelio de, ed. and trans. 1999. *Los evangelios apócrifos: Colección de textos griegos y latinos, versión crítica, estudios introductorios y comentarios*. 10th ed. Biblioteca de autores Cristianos 148. Madrid.

Sarrazin, Gregor. 1889. "Die *Fata Apostolorum* und die Dichter Kynewulf." *Anglia* 12: 375–87.

Saxl, Fritz. 1943. "The Ruthwell Cross." *Journal of the Warburg and Courtauld Institutes* 6: 1–19. Reprinted in *England and the Mediterranean Tradition: Studies in Art, History, and Literature*, 1–19. London, 1945.

Schaar, Claes. 1949. *Critical Studies in the Cynewulf Group*. Lund Studies in English 17. Lund. Reprinted New York, 1967.

Schenkl, Heinrich. 1891–1908. *Bibliotheca Patrum Latinorum Britannica*. 3 vols in 1. Vienna. Reprinted Hildesheim, 1969.

Schermann, T. 1907. *Prophetarum vitae fabulosae, indices apostolorum discipulorumque Domini Dorotheo, Epiphanio, Hippolyto aliisque vindicata*. Leipzig.

Schmetterer, Viktor. 1981. *Drei altenglische religiöse Texte aus der Handschrift Cotton Vespasianus D XIV*. Dissertationen der Universität Wien 150. Vienna.

Schneider, H. 1960. "Der Vulgata-Text der *Oratio Manasse*." *Biblische Zeitschrift* n.s. 4: 277–82.

Schönbach, Anton. 1876. Review of Tischendorf 1876. *Anzeiger* 2: 149–212.

Schrimpf, Gangolf, with Josef Leinweiber and Thomas Martin. 1992. *Mittelalterliche Bücherverzeichnisse des Klosters Fulda und andere Beiträge zur Geschichte der Bibliothek des Klosters Fulda im Mittelalter*. Fuldaer Studien 4. Frankfurt am Main.

Seymour, St. John D. 1923. "The Seven Heavens in Irish Literature." *Zeitschrift für celtische Philologie* 14: 18–30.

———. 1927. "The Vision of Adamnan." *Proceedings of the Royal Irish Academy* 37C: 304–12.

———. 1930. *Irish Visions of the Other-World*. London.

Silverstein, Theodore. 1935. *The Visio Sancti Pauli: The History of the Apocalypse in Latin, together with Nine Texts*. Studies and Documents 4. London.

———. 1959. "The Vision of St. Paul: New Links and Patterns in the Western Tradition." *Archives d'histoire doctrinale et littéraire du moyen âge* 34: 199–248.

———. 1976. "The Graz and Zurich Apocalypse of Saint Paul: An Independent Medieval Witness to the Greek." In *Medieval Learning and Literature: Essays Presented to Richard William Hunt*, ed. J. J. G. Alexander and M. T. Gibson, 166–80. Oxford.

Silverstein, Theodore, and Anthony Hilhorst, eds. 1997. *Apocalypse of Paul: A New Critical Edition of Three Long Latin Versions*. Cahiers d'Orientalisme 21. Geneva.

Sims-Williams, Patrick. 1990. *Religion and Literature in Western England 600–800*. Cambridge Studies in Anglo-Saxon England 3. Cambridge.

Sisam, Kenneth. 1953. *Studies in the History of Old English Literature*. Oxford.

Snyder, Graydon F., trans. 1968. *The Shepherd of Hermas*. The Apostolic Fathers 6. Camden, N.J.

Stevens, William O. 1977. *The Cross in the Life and Literature of the Anglo-Saxons*. With a new Preface by Thomas D. Hill. Yale Studies in English 22. Hamden, Conn.

Stevenson, Jane. 1982. "Ascent through the Heavens, from Egypt to Ireland." *Cambridge Medieval Celtic Studies* 4: 21–35.

Stone, Michael E. 1982. "The Metamorphosis of Ezra: Jewish Apocalypse and Medieval Vision." *Journal of Theological Studies* 33: 1–18.

———. 1990. *Fourth Ezra: A Commentary on the Book of Fourth Ezra*. Hermeneia—A Critical and Historical Commentary on the Bible. Minneapolis, Minn.

———. 1992. *A History of the Literature of Adam and Eve*. Society of Biblical Literature, Early Judaism and Its Literature 3. Atlanta, Ga.

Stoneman, William P. 1984. "The Latin and Old English Notes in the Old English Illustrated Hexateuch (BL Cotton Claudius B.iv)." Unpublished paper delivered at the 19th International Congress on Medieval Studies at Kalamazoo, May 10–13, 1984, Session 43, "Symposium on the Sources of Anglo-Saxon Culture: Literary Sources II."

Stork, Nancy, ed. 1990. *Through a Gloss Darkly: Aldhelm's Riddles in the British Library MS. Royal 12.C.xxiii*. Studies and Texts 98. Toronto.

Storms, Godfrid. 1948. *Anglo-Saxon Magic*. The Hague.

Swan, Mary. 1998. "The Apocalypse of Thomas in Old English." *Leeds Studies in English* n.s. 29: 333–46.

Swanton, Michael, ed. 1996. *The Dream of the Rood*. New ed. Exeter Medieval Texts and Studies. Exeter.

Szarmach, Paul E., ed. 1986. *Sources of Anglo-Saxon Culture*. Studies in Medieval Culture 20. Kalamazoo, Mich.

———, ed. 1996. *Holy Men and Holy Women: Old English Prose Saints' Lives and Their Contexts*. Albany, N.Y.

Szittya, Penn. 1973. "The Living Stone and the Patriarchs: Typological Imagery in *Andreas*, Lines 706–810." *Journal of English and Germanic Philology* 72: 167–74.

Talamo Atenolfi, Giuseppe, ed. 1958. *I Testi medioevali degli Atti di S. Matteo l'evangelista*. Rome.

Temple, Elżbieta. 1976. *Anglo-Saxon Manuscripts 900–1066*. A Survey of Manuscripts Illuminated in the British Isles 2. London.

Teresi, Loredana. 2000. "Mnemonic Transmission of Old English Texts in the Post-Conquest Period." In *Rewriting Old English in the Twelfth Century*, ed. Mary Swan and Elaine M. Treharne, 98–116. Cambridge Studies in Anglo-Saxon England 30. Cambridge.

———. 2002. "*Be Heofonwarum 7 be Helwarum*: A Complete Edition." In *Early Medieval English Texts and Interpretations: Studies Presented to Donald G. Scragg*, ed. Elaine Treharne and Susan Rosser, 211–44. Medieval and Renaissance Texts and Studies 252. Tempe, Ariz.

Thacker, Alan. 2000. "In Search of Saints: The English Church and the Cult of Roman Apostles and Martyrs in the Seventh and Eighth Centuries." In *Early Medieval Rome and the Christian West: Essays in Honour of Donald A. Bullough*, ed. Julia M. H. Smith, 247–77. The Medieval Mediterranean 28. Leiden.

Thomson, R. M. 2001. *A Descriptive Catalogue of the Medieval Manuscripts in Worcester Cathedral Library*. Cambridge.

Thorpe, Benjamin, ed. 1840. *Ancient Laws and Institutes of England*. 2 vols. Great Britain Public Records Commission 28. London.

——, ed. 1844–46. *The Homilies of the Anglo-Saxon Church. The First Part, containing The Sermones Catholici, or Homilies of Ælfric*. 2 vols. London.

Tischendorf, Constantin von, ed. 1851. *Acta Apostolorum Apocrypha*. Leipzig.

——, ed. 1866. *Apocalypses Apocryphae*. Leipzig.

——, ed. 1876. *Evangelia Apocrypha*. 2nd ed. Leipzig.

Tristram, Hildegard L. C., ed. 1970. *Vier altenglische Predigten aus der hererodoxen Tradition*. Freiburg im Breisgau.

——. 1975. "Der 'homo octipartitus' in der irischen und altenglischen Literatur." *Zeitschrift für celtische Philologie* 34: 119–53.

Tromp, Johannes. 1993. *The Assumption of Moses: A Critical Edition with Commentary*. Studia in Veteris Testamenti Pseudepigrapha 10. Leiden.

——. 2002. "The Textual History of the *Life of Adam and Eve* in the Light of a Newly Discovered Latin Text-Form." *Journal for the Study of Judaism in the Persian, Hellenistic and Roman Period* 23: 28–41.

Turdeanu, Émile. 1974. "Dieu créa l'homme de huit éléments et tira son nom des quatre coins du monde." *Revue des études roumaines* 13/14: 163–94. Reprinted in Turdeanu, *Apocryphes slaves et roumains de l'Ancien Testament*, 404–35. Studia in Veteris Testamenti Pseudepigrapha 5. Leiden, 1981.

Tveitane, Mattias. 1966. "Irish Apocrypha in Norse Tradition? On the Sources of some Medieval Homilies." *Arv: Journal of Scandinavian Folklore* 22: 111–35.

Twomey, Michael W. forthcoming. "The *Revelationes* of Pseudo-Methodius and Scriptural Study at Salisbury in the Eleventh Century." *Source of Wisdom: Old English and Early Medieval Latin Studies in Honor of Thomas D. Hill*, ed. Charles D. Wright, Frederick M. Biggs, and Thomas N. Hall.

Ullmann, Walter. 1960. "The Significance of the *Epistola Clementis* in the Pseudo-Clementines." *Journal of Theological Studies* n.s. 11: 295–317.

Urbán, Angel. 1999. *Hermae Pastoris Concordantia*. Concordantia in Patres Apostolicos, Pars V: Alpha–Omega, Reihe A: Lexika, Indizes, Konkordanzen zur klassischen Philologie 191. Hildesheim.

VanderKam, James C. 1984. *Enoch and the Growth of an Apocalyptic Tradition*. Catholic Biblical Quarterly Monograph Series 16. Washington, D.C.

——, ed. 1989. *The Book of Jubilees: A Critical Text*. Corpus Scriptorum Christianorum Orientalium 510–11. Leuven.

——. 1997. "The Origins and Purposes of the Book of Jubilees." In *Studies in the Book of Jubilees*, ed. Matthias Albani, Jörg Frey, and Armin Lange, 3–24. Tübingen.

Verhelst, D. 1973. "La préhistoire des conceptions d'Adson concernant l'Antichrist." *Recherches de théologie ancienne et médiévale* 40: 52–103.

Verheyden, J. 1995. "Les Pseudépigraphes d'Ancien Testament: textes latins." *Ephemerides Theologicae Lovanienses* 71: 383–420.

Vezzoni, Anna. 1987. "Un testimone testuale inedito della versione Palatina del Pastore di Erma." *Studi classici et orientali* 37: 241–65.

———, ed. 1994. *Il Pastore di Erma: Versione Palatina, con testo a fronte*. Florence.

Violet, Bruno, ed. 1910. *Die Esra-Apocalypse (IV Esra), Band 1: Die Überlieferung*. GCS 18. Leipzig.

Vollmann, Benedikt. 1965. *Studien zum Priszillianismus*. St. Ottilien.

Wack, Mary F., and Charles D. Wright. 1991. "A New Latin Source for the Old English 'Three Utterances' Exemplum." *Anglo-Saxon England* 20: 187–202.

Walker, Alexander, trans. 1870. *Apocryphal Gospels, Acts, and Revelations*. Ante-Nicene Christian Library 16. Edinburgh.

Walsh, Marie Michelle. 1977. "The Baptismal Flood in the Old English 'Andreas': Liturgical and Typological Depths." *Traditio* 33: 137–58.

———. 1981. "St. Andrew in Anglo-Saxon England: The Evolution of the Apocryphal Hero." *Annuale Mediaevale* 20: 97–122.

Warner, George F., and Julius P. Gilson. 1921. *British Museum. Catalogue of Western Manuscripts in the Old Royal and King's Collections*. 4 vols. London.

Wasserschleben, F. W. H., ed. 1885. *Die irische Kanonensammlung*. 2nd ed. Leipzig. Reprinted Aalen, 1966.

Watson, Andrew G. 1987. *Medieval Libraries of Great Britain. Supplement to the Second Edition*. Royal Historical Society Guides and Handbooks 15. London.

Webber, Teresa. 1992. *Scribes and Scholars at Salisbury Cathedral c.1075–c.1125*. Oxford Historical Monographs. Oxford.

Weber, Robert, ed. 1953. *Le Psautier Romain et les autres anciens psautiers latins*. Collectanea Biblica Latina 10. Rome.

———, ed. 1975. *Biblia sacra iuxta Vulgatam versionem*. 2nd ed. Stuttgart.

Wenger, A. 1955. *L'Assomption de la Très Sainte Vierge dans la tradition byzantine du VI<sup>e</sup> au X<sup>e</sup> siècle*. Archives de l'Orient chrétien 5. Paris.

Whealey, Alice. 2002. "The Apocryphal Apocalypse of John: A Byzantine Apocalypse from the Early Islamic Period." *Journal of Theological Studies* n.s. 53: 533–40.

Whitelock, Dorothy. 1982. "Bishop Ecgred, Pehtred and Niall." In *Ireland in Early Mediaeval Europe: Studies in Memory of Kathleen Hughes*, ed. Dorothy Whitelock, Rosamond McKitterick, and David Dumville, 47–68. Cambridge.

Whittaker, Molly, ed. 1956. *Der Hirt des Hermas*. GCS 48. Berlin.

Wilhelm, Friedrich. 1907. *Deutsche Legenden und Legendare: Texte und Untersuchungen zu ihrer Geschichte im Mittelalter*. Leipzig.

Willard, Rudolph. 1935a. *Two Apocrypha in Old English Homilies*. Beiträge zur englischen Philologie 30. Leipzig.

———. 1935b. "The Address of the Soul to the Body." *PMLA* 50: 957–83.

———. 1937a. "The Testament of Mary: The Irish Account of the Death of the Virgin." *Recherches de théologie ancienne et médiévale* 9: 339–64.

———. 1937b. "The Latin Texts of *The Three Utterances of the Soul*." *Speculum* 12: 147–66.

Wilmart, André. 1933. "L'ancien récit latin de l'Assomption." *Analecta Reginensia: Extraits des manuscrits latins de la reine Christine conservés au Vatican*, 323–57. Studi e testi 59. Vatican City.

———. 1937–45. *Codices Reginenses Latini.* 2 vols. Vatican City.

Wilmart, André, and Eugène Tisserant. 1913. "Fragments grecs et latins de l'Évangile de Barthélemy." *Revue Biblique* 10: 161–90 and 321–68.

Winterbottom, Michael, ed. and trans. 1978. *Gildas: The Ruin of Britain and Other Works.* History from the Sources. London.

Woods, J. Douglas, and David A. E. Pelteret, eds. 1985. *The Anglo-Saxons: Synthesis and Achievement.* Waterloo, Ontario.

Wright, Charles D. 1987. "Apocryphal Lore and Insular Tradition in St Gall, Stiftsbibliothek MS 908." In *Irland und die Christenheit: Bibelstudien und Mission*, ed. Próinséas Ní Chatháin and Michael Richter, 124–45. Stuttgart.

———. 1989. "The Irish 'Enumerative Style' in Old English Homiletic Literature, Especially Vercelli Homily IX." *Cambridge Medieval Celtic Studies* 18: 29–74.

———. 1990a. "Hiberno Latin and Irish-Influenced Biblical Commentaries, Florilegia, and Homily Collections." In Biggs, Hill, and Szarmach 1990 pp 87–123.

———. 1990b. "The Pledge of the Soul: A Judgment Theme in Old English Homiletic Literature and Cynewulf's *Elene.*" *Neuphilologische Mitteilungen* 91: 23–30.

———. 1990c. "Some Evidence for an Irish Origin of Redaction XI of the *Visio Pauli.*" *Manuscripta* 34: 34–44.

———. 1993. *The Irish Tradition in Old English Literature.* Cambridge Studies in Anglo-Saxon Literature 6. Cambridge.

———. 2000. "Bischoff's Theory of Irish Exegesis and the Genesis Commentary in Munich clm 6302: A Critique of a Critique." *Journal of Medieval Latin* 10: 115–75.

———. 2001. "The Irish Tradition." In *A Companion to Anglo-Saxon Literature*, ed. Phillip Pulsiano and Elaine Treharne, 345–74. Oxford.

———. 2003. "*The Apocalypse of Thomas*: Some New Latin Texts and Their Significance for the Old English Versions." In Powell and Scragg 2003 pp 27–64.

———. forthcoming a. "Vercelli Homily XV and the Interpolated Version of *The Apocalypse of Thomas.*" In *New Readings on the Vercelli Book*, ed. Andy Orchard and Samantha Zacher.

———. forthcoming b. "Why Sight Holds Flowers: An Apocryphal Source for the Iconography of the Alfred Jewel and Fuller Brooch." *Text, Image, Interpretation: Studies in Anglo-Saxon Literature and Its Insular Context in Honour of Éamonn Ó Carragáin*, ed. Alastair Minnis and Jane Roberts. Turnhout.

Wright, Charles D., and Roger Wright. 2004. "Additions to the Bobbio Missal: *De dies malus* and *Joca monachorum* (fols. 6r–8v)." In *The Bobbio Missal: Liturgy and Religious Culture in Merovingian Gaul*, ed. Yitzhak Hen and Rob Meens, 79–139. Cambridge Studies in Palaeography and Codicology. Cambridge.

Zechiel-Eckes, Klaus. 2002. "Vom *armarium* in York in den Düsseldorfer Tresor: Zur Rekonstruktion einer Liudger-Handschrift aus dem mittleren 8. Jahrhundert." *Deutsches Archiv für Erforschung des Mittelalters* 58: 193–203.

———. 2003. *Katalog der frühmittelalterlichen Fragmente der Universitäts- und Landesbibliothek Düsseldorf vom beginnenden achten bis zum ausgehenden neunten Jahrhundert.* Schriften der Universitäts- und Landesbibliothek Düsseldorf 34. Wiesbaden.

Zelzer, Klaus, ed. 1977. *Die alten lateinischen Thomasakten. TU* 122. Berlin.
Zettel, Patrick H. 1979. "Ælfric's Hagiographic Sources and the Latin Legendary
    Preserved in B.L. MS Cotton Nero E. i + CCCC MS 9 and Other Manuscripts."
    D.Phil. thesis, Oxford University.
———. 1982. "Saints' Lives in Old English: Latin Manuscripts and Vernacular
    Accounts: Ælfric." *Peritia* 1: 17–37.

*Adrian and Ritheus* (*Ad*), 70, 75, 76
Adso, *De ortu et tempore Antichristi*, 19
*Advent Lyrics* (*Christ I*), 22, 31
Alcuin, 66; *In Iohannis evangelium*, 5; *Versus de sanctis Euboricensis ecclesiae*, 44
Pseudo-Alcuin, 79
Aldhelm, 1; *Aenigmata*, 29; *Carmina ecclesiastica*, 51, 54, 75; *Epistolae*, 44; *De metris*, 18; *De virginitate*, 44, 45, 48, 56, 67, 68, 70
Aldred the Provost, 5
Alfred, 13
Alfred Jewel, 5
Ambrose, 15
Ambrosiaster, 11
*Andreas*, 40, 41
*Apocalypse of Thomas* (*HomU* 6), see *Vercelli Homily* 15
*Apocalypse of Thomas*, Förster (*HomU* 12.1), 71, 72
*Apocalypse of Thomas*, Willard (*HomU* 12.2), 69–70, 71, 78
*Assmann* 14 (*HomS* 6), 69
*Assumption of the Virgin* (*LS* 20), see *Blickling Homily* 13
*Assumption of the Virgin*, Tristram (*LS* 21), 33, 34
Augustine, 56; *De civitate Dei*, 8, 17, 18; *De consensu Evangelistarum*, 57; *Enarrationes in Psalmos*, 5; *Tractatus in Evangelium Ioannis*, 5
Pseudo-Augustine, *Sermo 69 ad fratres in eremo*, 81; *Sermo* 160, 30; *Sermo* 167, 79; *Sermo* 251, 72

*Æcerbot Charm* (*MCharm* 1), 5
Ælfric, 1, 68, 84; *CHom* I, 4: 47, 48; *CHom* I, 11: 43; *CHom* I, 26: 52, 53; *CHom* I, 30: 33, 34; *CHom* I, 31: 43; *CHom* I, 37: 48; *CHom* I, 38: 42; *CHom* II, 1: 18, 46; *CHom* II, 17: 54; *CHom* II, 19: 52; *CHom* II, 22: 67; *CHom* II, 31–32: 45–46; *CHom* II, 34: 33, 34; *CHom* II, 36.2: 21; *CHom* II, 37: 49–50; *CHom* II, 38: 38, 55; *CHom* II, 39.2: 55, 56; *CHom* II, 44: 67; *HomM* 8 (*Nativity of the BVM*), 21, 24; *Let* 4 (*Letter to Sigeweard*), 18, 50, 58; *LS* (Abdon & Sennes), 57; *LS* (Auguries), 11, 52; *LS* (Mark), 48, 49; *LS* (Memory of Saints), 32; *LS* (Peter's Chair), 52; *LS* (Thomas), 55, 56

"Be heofonwarum and be helwarum" (*HomS* 5), see *Three Utterances*
Bede, 1, 16, 17; *Commentarius in Apocalypsim*, 14; *Commentarius in Genesim*, 5, 44; *Commentarius in epistolas septem catholicas*, 8; *Commentarius in Lucam*, 21, 27, 50; *Expositio Actuum Apostolorum*, 44; *Historia ecclesiastica*, 45, 68, 81; *Martyrologium*, 49; *De orthographia*, 51; *Retractatio in Actus Apostolorum*, 30, 33, 34, 37, 44, 48, 64; *De templo*, 64–65; *De temporum ratione*, 44
Pseudo-Bede, *Collectanea Bedae*, 76
*Benedictional of Archbishop Robert*, 34
*Benedictional of Æthelwold*, 33

*Beowulf,* 9, 70
*Blickling Homily* 4 (*HomS* 14), 69
*Blickling Homily* 7 (*HomS* 26), 30, 71, 72
*Blickling Homily* 13 (*LS* 20), 34, 35
*Blickling Homily* 15 (*LS* 32), 52
*Blickling Homily* 16 (*LS* 25), 69, 70, 71
*Blickling Homily* 18 (*LS* 1.2), 40, 41
*Bobbio Missal,* 79
Boniface, 8, 72; *Epistolae,* 60, 61, 68
*Bonnet Fragment,* 41
*Book of Armagh,* 58
*Book of Cerne,* 8, 30, 39, 42, 52
*Bosworth Psalter,* 16
Burghard, 72
Byrhtferth, *Enchiridion,* 5

*Cáin Domnaig,* 59, 60, 80
*Caligula Troper,* 22
*Canterbury Benedictional,* 26
Cassian, *Conlationes,* 65
*Catechesis celtica,* 60, 74
Charlemagne, *Admonitio generalis,* 58–59
Charms, 32
*Christ and Satan,* 4, 27, 31
*Christ III,* 14, 18, 31, 66, 72, 76
Chrysostom, John, 6
Clement of Alexandria, 76
Clement of Rome, 17
*Codex Amiatinus,* 16
*Codex Sinaiticus,* 76
*Collectio canonum Hibernensis,* 64
*Cotton-Corpus Legendary,* 25, 42, 43, 45, 47, 48, 49, 51, 53, 54, 55, 56
*Cura sanitatis Tiberii,* 32
Cuthbert's coffin, 8
Cynewulf, *Christ II,* 31; *Elene,* 74; *Fates of the Apostles,* 37, 39, 41, 42, 43, 46, 49, 52, 54, 55, 56, 75, 78; *Juliana,* 32
Cyprian, 15

*Damascus Document,* 11

*Descent into Hell,* 22, 31
*Durham Collectar,* 5, 8, 39
*Durham Ritual,* commonplaces gloss (C13.1), 5, 77

*Easter Day* (*HomS* 27), 31, 78, 80
*Easter Day* (*HomS* 28), 31
*Easter Day* (*NicD* and *NicE*), 31, 67
Ecgred, *Letter to Wulfsige,* 60
Ephrem the Syrian, 6
Pseudo-Ephrem, *Sermo de fine mundi,* 19
Eusebius-Rufinus, *Historia ecclesiastica,* 39, 47, 57
*Evernew Tongue,* 78

*Fifteen Signs before Judgement* (*Notes* 22), 76
*Florilegium Frisingense,* 74, 82
*Fragmentum Pragense,* 28
Fulbert of Chartres, *Sermo de nativitate Mariae,* 25
Fuller brooch, 5

Gallican Psalter, 16
*Gelasian Decree,* 7, 11, 13, 22, 24, 26, 44, 57, 71
*Gelasian Sacramentary,* 75
*Genesis A,* 9
*Genesis B,* 4, 10, 70
Gildas, *De excidio Britanniae,* 14
*Glossa in psalmos,* 24
*Gospel of Gamaliel,* 28
*Gospel of Nicodemus* (*NicA, NicB,* and *NicC*), 29, 30, 31
*Gospel of Nicodemus* (*NicD* and *NicE*), see *Easter Day*
Gregory the Great, 53; *Dialogi,* 4
Gregory of Tours, 35; *De miraculis Andreae,* 40, 41
*Guthlac A,* 4, 27, 65, 69, 81
*Guthlac B,* 31

Hadrian (see Theodore of Canterbury)

Haymo of Auxerre, *Historiae sacrae epitome*, 83

*Healey* (*HomM* 14.1 and 14.2), 69

Hexateuch (*ÆHex, Gen, Exod, Lev, Num, Deut, Josh*), 4, 9, 11, 19

Hiberno-Latin Biblical Commentaries, 1, 5, 13, 14, 24, 60, 74, 78, 79, 82

*History of Joseph the Carpenter*, 22, 24

Homiliary of Saint-Père de Chartres, 35, 39, 47, 79; *Sermon for the Nativity of the Innocents*, 23, 24

Hrabanus Maurus, 79

*Husband's Message*, 77

Hygeburg, *Vita Willibaldi*, 34

*In nomine Dei summi*, 74

*In Sabbato sancto* (*HomS* 25), 74

*Infancy Gospel of Thomas*, 23, 25

*Invention of the Cross* (*LS* 5), 77

*Ioca monachorum*, 13

Isidore, 79; *De ortu et obitu patrum*, 38, 54; *Etymologiae*, 18

Pseudo-Isidore, *De ortu et obitu patrum*, 27–28, 38

Jerome, 65; *Commentarii in Evangelium Matthaei*, 21, 26, 50; *De viris illustribus*, 64; *Epistola ad Fabiolam*, 7

John of Nikion, *Chronicle*, 15

Josephus, *De bello Judaico*, 32

Lactantius, 17

Leo I, Pope, 79

Leofric, 30, 31, 32

*Leofric Missal*, 29

*Letter of Boniface to Eadburga* (*Let* 1), 68, 69

*Liber Aethici dilatus ex cosmographia*, 19

*Liber de numeris*, 5, 74

*Liber Flavus Fergusiorum*, 78

*Liber Pontificalis*, 45

*Life of St. Margaret* (*LS* 14), 11

Liudger, 66

"Macarius Homily" (*HomU* 55), 69, 81

*Martyrologium Hieronymianum*, 78

*Marvels of the East*, 11

Milred of Worcester, 18, 74

Milton, *Paradise Lost*, 4

*Muratorian Canon*, 63

*Napier* 16 (*HomU* 58), 52

*Napier* 29 (*HomU* 26), 69, 79, 81

*Napier* 43 (*HomU* 35.1), 59, 60, 69, 79, 80

*Napier* 44 (*HomU* 35.2), 59, 60, 69, 79, 80

*Napier* 45 (*HomU* 36), 58, 59, 79

*Napier* 46 (*HomU* 37), 69, 81

*Napier* 57 (*HomU* 46), 59, 60, 79, 80

*Nativity of Mary* (*LS* 18), 23, 24

*Old English Bede*, 69

*Old English Martyrology*, 1, 24, 25, 30–31, 39, 42, 43, 46, 47, 49, 54, 55, 56

*Old English Orosius*, 11

Origen, 11, 50, 64; *De principiis*, 65; *Homiliae in Lucam*, 26, 65

*Partridge* (*Physiologus*), 17

Paschasius Radbertus, 24, 25

*Pater Noster Dialogue* (*Sol* II), 8

Paul the Deacon, *Homiliarium*, 26

Paulinus of Nola, 48

Pehtred, 59, 60

*Peter and Paul* (*LS* 32), see *Blickling Homily* 15

Peter Comestor, *Historia scholastica*, 19

Petrus de Marca, 61

*Prognostics*, 15

Prudentius, 44

*Psalterium Romanum*, 16

Quodvultdeus, *Contra Iudaeos, paganos et Arianos*, 18

Ralph d'Escures, 84
*Reference Bible*, 78
*Riddle 60*, 77
*Rogationtide* (*HomS* 32), 74
*Rogationtide* (*HomS* 33), 72
Roman Antiphonary, 14
Rufinus, 32, 37, 44, 45, 57, 65
Ruthwell Cross, 24

*Saint Andrew* (AndrewBright; *LS* 1.1), 40, 41
*Saint Andrew* (*LS* 1.2), see *Blickling Homily* 19
*Saint James the Great* (*LS* 11), 45, 46
*Saint Michael* (*LS* 24), 27
*Saint Michael* (*LS* 25), see *Blickling Homily* 17
*Saltair na Rann*, 76
Sedulius Scottus, 64
*Solomon and Saturn* (*MSol*), 8, 12–13, 27, 65, 67
*Solomon and Saturn* (*Sol* I), 4, 5, 12, 15, 24, 26, 34, 52, 70, 75
*Soul and Body I* and *II*, 69
*Stuttgart Psalter*, 29
*Sunday Letter* (*HomM* 6, KerOthoB 10), 58, 59
*Sunday Letter* (*HomU* 36), see *Napier* 45
*Sunday Letter* (*HomU* 46), see *Napier* 57
*Sunday Letter* (*HomU* 53), 60, 80
*Sunday Letter* (*HomU* 54), 58, 59

Tertullian, 15
*Textus Roffensis*, 8
Theodore of Canterbury, *Sancte Sator*, 74

Theodore of Canterbury & Hadrian, school of, 18; *Biblical Commentaries*, 6, 7, 12
*Thorpe* (*HomU* 55), see "Macarius Homily"
*Three Utterances Apocryphon* (*HomM* 5), 69, 83
*Three Utterances Apocryphon* (*HomS* 5), 69, 79, 80, 81
*Three Utterances Apocryphon* (*HomS* 31), 69, 80

*Vercelli Homily* 4 (*HomU* 9), 65, 69, 78, 81, 83
*Vercelli Homily* 6 (*HomU* 10), 23, 24
*Vercelli Homily* 9 (*HomS* 4), 14–15, 68, 69
*Vercelli Homily* 10 (*HomS* 40.3), 22
*Vercelli Homily* 15 (*HomU* 6), 67, 71, 72
*Vespasian Psalter*, 16
*Vindicta Salvatoris* (*VSal* 1–2), 31, 32
Vincent of Beauvais, *Speculum historiale*, 29
*Visio Pauli* (*HomM* 1), 67, 69
*Visio Wettini*, 65
*Vision of Adomnán*, 78
*Visions of Daniel*, 19
*Vocabularius Sancti Galli*, 28

*Warner* 43 (*HomU* 56), 83, 84
*Wednesday in Rogationtide* (*HomS* 42), 69
*Wednesday in Rogationtide* (*HomS* 44), 71, 72, 73, 74
*Willard* (*HomM* 8), 69
Wirksworth slab, 33
Wulfstan of York, *De temporibus Antichristi* (*HomU* 58), 52

Berkeley, University of California, Bancroft Library UCB 17 (*olim* Phillipps 391): 7
Berlin, Staatsbibliothek Preussischer Kulturbesitz Hamilton 553: 16
Bologna, Bibl. Universitaria 1576: 41
Boulogne-sur-Mer, Bibl. Municipale 189: 18
Brussels, Bibl. Royale II 1069: 38

Cambridge, Corpus Christi College
    41: 8, 12, 31, 34, 72
    162: 31, 78, 80
    173: 17
    198: 41
    265: 63, 64
    272: 16, 17
    288: 31
    302: 80
    303: 31
    326: 4
    391: 16, 17
    411: 16, 17
    422: 12
    448: 17
Cambridge, Gonville and Caius College 379: 8
Cambridge, Pembroke College
    24: 53, 54
    25: v, 23, 35, 39, 47, 79
Cambridge, St. John's College 35: 83
Cambridge, Trinity College B.5.2 (148): 58
Cambridge, University Library
    Ff.1.23: 16
    Ii.2.11: 30

Düsseldorf, Landes- und Stadtbibliothek K 1: B 215 + K 2: C 118 + K 15: 009 + K 19: Z 8/8 + M. Th.u. Sch.29a (Ink.) Bd. 4 (pastedowns): 64, 65, 66
Durham, Cathedral Library
    A.III.29: 25, 26
    A.IV.19: 4, 77

Einsiedeln, Stiftsbibliothek 199: 74

Florence, Biblioteca Medicea Laurenziana 1 (Amiatinus): 16

Hamburg, Bibliothek der Hansestadt, S. Petri Kirche 30b: 59
Hereford, Cathedral Library P.7.vi: 42, 48, 56

Karlsruhe, Badische Landesbibliothek
    Aug. CCLIV: 73, 74, 78
    Aug. CCLV: 79

London, British Library
    Additional 18400: 44
    Additional 37517: 16
    Additional 49598: 33
    Arundel 60: 16
    Cotton Claudius B.iv: 4, 9, 11, 19
    Cotton Faustina A.ix: 80
    Cotton Galba A.xviii: 16
    Cotton Nero A.ii: 65
    Cotton Nero E.i: 25, 43, 45, 46, 47, 48, 49, 50, 53, 54
    Cotton Tiberius A.iii: 15
    Cotton Tiberius B.v: 10, 11

Cotton Titus D.xxvi: 15
Cotton Vespasian A.1: 16
Cotton Vespasian D.xiv: 30, 46, 76, 84
Cotton Vitellius A.xv: 30
Cotton Vitellius E.xviii: 16
Harley 2904: 16
Harley 7653: 8
Oriental 6804: 28
Royal 1.E.VIII: 58
Royal 2.A.XX: 13, 57
Royal 5.E.XIII: 9, 10, 29, 30, 73, 74
Royal 5.F.XVIII: 19, 20
Royal 6.B.XIV: 44
Royal 8.C.III: 78
Royal 8.F.VI: 59
Royal 12.C.XXIII: 29
Royal 15.B.XIX: 17–18
Sloane 475: 15
London, Lambeth Palace Library
    427: 16
    487: 80

Milan, Biblioteca Ambrosiana C 73 inf.: 7, 12
Montpellier, École de Medicine 55: 23
Munich, Bayerische Staatsbibliothek
    clm 3788: 46
    clm 6433: 82
    clm 9550: 60
    clm 19410: 73, 74
    clm 28135: 80, 82, 83

New York, Pierpont Morgan Library
    M 776: 16

Orléans, Bibl. Municipale 221 (193): 64
Oxford, Bodleian Library
    Bodley 163: 20
    Bodley 343: 77
    Bodley 354: 42, 47, 55, 56
    Bodley 579: 29

Fairfax 17: 31
Hatton 114: 80
Junius 11: 9
Junius 85/86: 80, 82
Junius 121: 31
Oxford, New College fragment: 44
Oxford, St. John's College 28: 50, 51
    St. John's College 128: 20
Oxford, Trinity College 60: 44

Paris, Bibliothèque Nationale
    lat. 2628: 80
    lat. 3182: 64
    lat. 7193: 75
    lat. 10861: 45, 53
    lat. 11505: 14
    lat. 12270: 59
    Nouv.acq.lat. 1631: 67–68

Rome, Biblioteca Casanatense
    1104: 41
    1880: 27
Rome, Biblioteca Vallicelliana plut. I, tom. iii: 41
Rome, Vatican City, Biblioteca Apostolica Vaticana
    Pal.lat. 68: 24
    Pal.lat. 220: 70, 71, 72, 79, 80, 81
    Pal.lat. 235: 15, 75
    Pal.lat. 1449: 15
    Reg.lat 12: 16, 17
    Reg.lat. 49: 72
    Reg.lat. 316: 75
    Reg.lat. 1050: 27
    Vat.lat. 1274: 41
    Vat.lat. 5771: 50
Rouen, Bibl. Municipale 369: 34

St. Gall, Stiftsbibliothek
    151, pt 3: 64
    682: 79
    913: 28
Saint-Omer, Bibl. Municipale 202: 29, 30, 31, 32

Salisbury, Cathedral Library
   9: 73, 74
   11: 44
   150: 16
   165: 19, 20
   179: 25, 26
   180: 16, 17
   221: 46, 47, 48, 53, 54
   222: 42, 43, 45, 49, 50, 53, 55, 56
Sélestat, Bibl. Humaniste 1: 5

Toulouse, Bibl. Publique 208: 59

Vercelli, Bibl. Capitolare CLVIII: 51
Vienna, Österreichische Nationalbibliothek lat. 1355: 59

Worcester, Cathedral Library F.91: 40
Würzburg, Universitätsbibliothek
   M.p.th.f. 28: 71, 72
   M.p.th.f. 78: 437

Medieval Institute Publications is a program
of The Medieval Institute, College of Arts
and Sciences, Western Michigan University

Typeset in 10/13 Garamond
Designed by Linda K. Judy
Manufactured by McNaughton & Gunn, Inc.

Medieval Institute Publications
College of Arts and Sciences
Western Michigan University
1903 W. Michigan Avenue
Kalamazoo, MI 49008-5432
http://www.wmich.edu/medieval/mip

 WESTERN MICHIGAN UNIVERSITY